Gardening

in the Treasure Valley

By Margaret Lauterbach

Idaho Statesman

PUBLICATIONS

Inquiries for Margaret Lauterbach can be addressed directly to Lauterbach by writing to melauter@earthlink.net. Read Margaret Lauterbach's columns and more gardening advice at IdahoStatesman.com/Gardening.

ISBN 978-0976471868

Cover and layout design by Lindsie Bergevin. Editing and other support provided by Greg Hahn and Genie Arcano. Cover photo of Liz and Alan Percy's yard in 2009 by Darin Oswald. Back cover photo of Roger Goicoechea's yard in 2012 by Charlie Litchfield. Photo of Margaret Lauterbach by Phylis King.

This book is dedicated to my gardening grandmothers,

Grandma Shorty and Grandma 'Cutch,

who sparked a gardening fervor in me,

and to my husband, Charles Lauterbach,

who has supported my garden interests in every way.

TABLE OF CONTENTS

ACKNOWLEDGEMENTS

Over the past 40 years, I've received a lot of good garden information and advice from friends, including Debbie Cook of Boise Community Forestry; Anju Lucas, Garnette Edwards and others from Edwards Greenhouse; Kathryn Marsh and John D'hondt of Ireland; Linda Baranowski-Smith of Ohio and Karen Swaine of New Jersey; Treasure Valley residents Linda-rose Curtis-Bruce, Stella Schneider, Pat Roloff, Extension agent Susan Bell, and Sandra Ford; tomato expert Dr. Carolyn Male; soil scientist Dr. Elaine Ingham; University of Idaho pathologist Dr. Krishna Mohan; botanist Dr. Kay Klier Lancaster; Dr. Joel Gruver of Western Illinois University; Idaho Department of Agriculture entomologist Dr. Mike Cooper; and the late Dr. Charles Baker, retired Boise State University entomologist; organic garden guru Moira Ryan of New Zealand; Chloanna Bruce of Littleton, Colo.; Jaime Knoble of Pittsburgh; Dick Wilson and Ross Hadfield of the Treasure Valley. Cyber friends on Gardens, OGL, Chile-Heads, PacNWgardn, and Gardeners Corner have also been helpful over the years.

"No other human occupation opens so wide a field
for the profitable and agreeable combination of labor
with cultivated thought as agriculture. Population must
increase rapidly, more rapidly than in former times, and
ere long the most valuable of all arts will be the
art of deriving a comfortable subsistence from the
smallest area of soil. No community whose every
member possesses this art can ever be the victim of
oppression in any of its forms. Such community
will be alike independent of crowned kings,
money kings and land kings."

Abraham Lincoln, Milwaukee, Wis.; Sept. 30, 1859

PREFACE

Why should you grow a garden?

You don't have to talk in terms of botanical names such as Philadelphus lewisii to be a gardener. Gardening can be as simple as dropping a seed in a hole in the ground. Gardening has many benefits for the human who undertakes it. It:

- relieves stress.
- elevates your mood.
- gives you healthful exercise — as much or as little as you desire.
- gives you mental challenges.
- brings you close to nature and the miracles of plant growth.
- feeds you healthy food if you plant vegetables.
- heals a number of ills if you grow certain herbs.
- feeds your soul if you prefer to plant only ornamentals.

There are many reasons to plant for food. You can step out of your door and let what's ripe guide your dinner menu; eat fresh food without worrying about contamination by E. coli 0157, listeria or salmonella; or regret that your food had to be hauled hundreds of miles; try unusual vegetables without paying inflated prices for them; and get your good dose of vitamin D from sunlight.

Besides, it's fun.

We don't have much control over what affects us in these times, but you are the master of your own garden, whether it's a single five-gallon bucket or an acre of land.

You plant what you want to plant, tend it or let it go. This is a book of suggestions, and they can help you eliminate many possible mistakes.

CHAPTER 1

Getting started

What are you going to plant in your garden next year?

Herbs? Vegetables? Ornamentals? If you vow to NEVER use any systemic insecticide in your garden bed, you can blend and mix all three in the same bed. There are many ways to plan and plant a garden, and it's completely your choice. One of the reasons gardening reduces stress is that you are in charge.

There are some basics in gardening it helps to remember. Even experienced gardeners sometimes forget one or more of these fundamentals:

1. Most plants need soil in an acid range, usually expressed by a pH number.

2. Most plants need at least some sun exposure.

3. Most plants need at least some water.

4. Bare ground invites weeds.

5. Some plants are sensitive to frost, others are more resistant.

6. Most plant roots need oxygen; swamp or bog-loving plants do not.

7. Plants contain circulatory systems and hormones that may be manipulated to your advantage.

8. Most plants have a dormant period.

9. Plants protect themselves from high temperatures, and some say they protect themselves from damaging insects.

10. Plants sometimes need more food than is available in their surrounding soil.

Consider No. 4, for instance. Bare ground provides a place for weed seeds to germinate, and they will pop up unless you deprive them of soil contact, by mulching, or of sunlight, with close planting that shades the area. This is what "cottage gardens" and similar dense plantings aim to do. Weed prevention means no weeding required.

Our soil is generally quite alkaline, and if you can acidify it down to a pH of 7.0 (neutral) with organic matter, you're doing well. Most plants will grow at that alkalinity, but most prefer slightly more acid soil.

A shade-loving plant in full sun will wilt and die, and a plant needing full sun but planted in shade will fail to thrive. By the time either plant tells us a mistake has been made, it's often too late to save it.

Most plants regularly need water, not just when they're transplanted. Even drought-tolerant plants need water for the first few weeks.

If you want to grow a bog garden, bury a child's plastic swimming pool with drainage holes poked in it, and fill that with soil and water. You can keep that area wet without breaking your bank.

Some plant growth hormones are located at the top and at the ends of branches of a plant. Pruning or pinching off the top or branch tips sends those hormones lower on the plant, stimulating vegetative buds to branch out, giving you a bushier plant. Most gardeners do this with chrysanthemums and basil, but they could do the same with almost any nonbulbous plant.

Plants tell us when they need specific types of food, by the color of their leaves, overall growth and fruiting or not fruiting. Gardeners can help their plants cope with frosty weather by covering them, but plants help themselves during very hot weather by conserving moisture in their tissues and temporarily ceasing growth.

The local rules

If you're new to gardening in the Treasure Valley, here are 10 general rules to remember:

1. Unless your soil has been analyzed and found to be acidic (very few in this area are), do not put lime or fireplace ashes on your soil.

2. South of the Boise River, there's likely a hardpan, called caliche (actually calcium carbonate), that's whitish and cement-hard lying parallel to the surface of your soil, at some depth. Depths vary, depending on your location in the Valley. Before planting tap-rooted trees, dig down and break up the caliche and replace it with gravel.

3. Organic matter is gold to our soils. If your soil is sandy, organic matter will help it retain water and nutrients. If your soil is claylike, organic matter will loosen the clay and allow better drainage in time. The best way to incorporate organic matter is the lazy way. Just lay it on top of the soil and let water, earthworms, and visible and microscopic creatures move the organic matter to root zones. It will last longer in your soil if you apply it this way than if you till it in.

4. Never try to loosen clay soil with sand unless you have expert advice on the proper percentage of sand. It's very easy to turn clay soil into adobe, useful for building houses but not for a growing medium.

5. Our growing season roughly is May 10 to Oct. 10 (average dates of last and first frosts). The Valley is in different USDA growing zones, generally 7 in the low-lying areas, 6 in the Foothills. These zones refer only to the lowest expected temperature in winter, zone 7 meaning to 0 degrees, zone 6 to minus 10. It's quite possible to grow plants rated to higher zones than zone 7, if you find a place in your yard that is sheltered from frost and wind. Residents who vividly recall minus 25 degrees in 1990 remain cautious.

Sunset Magazine's "Western Garden Book" is a good gardening resource, but Sunset's zones bear no relationship to the USDA zones. Moreover, that magazine and the "Western Garden Book" are more appropriate to coastal West than inland West.

6. Since our climate is normally dry, we seldom have plant diseases common in more humid climates. If your watering system wets foliage, water early in the morning so leaves can dry before a cool evening.

7. If a little fertilizer is good for a plant, please don't think a lot of fertilizer will be better. It's usually much worse. Compost is golden for most plants, usually supplanting the need for fertilizer.

8. Organic gardeners feed the soil, so that the soil will feed the plant. Actually, the plant derives its food from mycorrhizae in the soil, but by feeding the soil, one feeds mycorrhizae, and prolongs the soil's fertility and ability to feed plants. Mycorrhizae are fungal growths in symbiotic relationships with plant roots, converting food for their uptake. Synthetic fertilizers feed the plant as they build up salts in the soil, eventually toxic to plant growth.

9. If you see insects, consider whether they're doing substantial damage. If they are, identify them accurately. Find out their life cycle, when they're most vulnerable. Can other insects control them for you? Is there a nontoxic control available? If so, does the control have to contact the insects?

10. Plan your landscape to attract beneficial insects, which will control the bad guys. Plants with umbelliferous (umbrella shaped) blossoms attract and feed beneficial insects, from bees to tiny wasps. Dill, parsley, even dandelions work.

The best way to eat local is from your own backyard

There's a new word out that describes more and more of us: We're "locavores." That is, we eat local food.

Nothing is more local than food from your own yard, whether it is grown in containers or in-ground gardens. If you are determined to reduce your food bills, you should make your garden as productive as possible.

Some ways to maximize production are:

🌿 Plant intensively, in wide beds if possible. Some soils will spread water delivered via soaker hose widely; other soils do not. The closer the planting, the less sun reaches the soil, germinating weeds, but some vegetables don't like overcrowding.

🌿 Grow upward, training or tying vines to upright trellises to use soil space for other crops. Plants such as winter squash, cucumbers, melons, climbing peas and pole beans are candidates for this treatment. You can fashion hammocks to hold heavy fruits in the trellis netting.

🌿 Plant successively. When one crop has finished producing, pull out the dying plants and plant another crop in its place.

🌿 Plant crops known to produce good-tasting food abundantly in this area. You could grow tons of zucchini in a small space, but you'd get mighty tired of that vegetable in a short time. Slenderette snap beans, Italienischer lettuce, butternut winter squash, Zephyr or Coosa (any Lebanese) summer squash, Piracicaba broccoli, Red Pontiac potatoes, Gardener's Delight cherry tomatoes, Druzba (slicers) and Opalka (paste) tomatoes have been prolific in my garden.

🌿 Grow vegetables that keep well into winter. Lettuces, carrots, Asian greens, cabbage, broccoli, parsnips, shallots, Brussels sprouts, collards and kale tolerate frost and continue growing in cool weather, but you'll have to battle the large black aphids that attack Brassicas (cole crops including broccoli, cabbage, cauliflower and kale) about that time. That's when no beneficial insects are around to help.

🌿 Plant a winter garden. Garlic and shallots grow best in winter. Plant lettuces and other greens such as spinach so they germinate and show tiny green leaves before your outdoor watering system is shut down for the winter (about the second week of October, usually). After that, seasonal precipitation takes care of watering.

🌿 Plant edible crops among your ornamentals, but you must never use systemic insecticides in a bed where you're growing edible items. Systemic insecticides are those that are taken up by roots, and flow through the plant's circulatory system to all parts of the plant. Plants that are attractive include eggplant, peppers, artichoke, cardoon, kale, sweet potatoes (a lovely ground cover) and many others. How about a border of stately blue leeks?

✿ Start saving your seeds. Most prepared foods in the grocery stores contain at least some corn or soybean products, so crop losses because of flooding or drought will keep grocery prices high. Not only will we have to grow more of our own food, but we also may have to save our own seeds. In the past, seeds have been cheap, although in recent years prices have escalated to the $3-$4 range per packet. One lettuce, Ferrari, was $7.85 a packet in a catalog I received. If it was a hybrid, that was not stated in the literature. That price will make seed savers of most of us.

Bacteria in soil may affect your mood

Do you really need an excuse to garden? Newspapers and magazines are full of the benefits of vitamin D (sunlight provides that), and there are testaments about how gardening reduces stress, contributing to mental health.

But wait, there's more!

New studies from the University of Bristol, England, indicate that "friendly soil bacteria" may alter behavior in a way similar to that of taking antidepressant drugs.

Scientists first saw the apparent mood improvements in cancer patients treated with the bacteria Mycobacterium vaccae. Then they began experimenting with the effects of the bacteria in the brains of mice.

We may not have to eat those bacteria, just touch them. Last season when I pulled out some bean plants, the aroma of fresh warm earth certainly lifted my mood.

Creating garden beds

Suppose you have a blank slate, a bare yard in which to plant. Where do you locate garden beds? First of all, consider the sun exposure. Many plants, including most vegetables and herbs for a garden, require full sun. That means at least six hours of sun each growing day. If there is shade in your yard, shaded by neighbor's trees, your house or other structures, watch to see if any sun intrudes, morning or afternoon, and for how long.

Most shady areas are not deep shade, free of any sun intrusion at all. Plants calling for part shade may be planted there. If the shade is cast by a tree, is it a deciduous tree? Its winter and early spring shade will be reduced, and more sun admitted during those times. If you're planting bulbs for early blossoms, they may grow happily in that location.

Is there a sunny area near the back door? That's an ideal location for a kitchen garden or potager. If it's a sufficiently large area, include culinary herbs in this garden. A vegetable garden is most useful when the cook can gather victuals for a meal in just a few steps. Food is fresh and at its best. A snip or two of rosemary, thyme or basil transforms an ordinary meal into a gourmet delight.

If this property is in a windy area, you may want to plant in "waffle gardens," or below the surface of the soil. Waffle gardens are easily irrigated, just letting the hose run in the depression containing your plants. Gardening in this style is not as easy on the gardener, however, as raised beds.

Raised beds warm up quickly in spring, have excellent drainage and are easily planted, weeded and harvested without straining the gardener's back. They may be treated to bar slugs with a copper strip surrounding containment boards (if boards are used) and may be higher than carrot rust flies fly. My beds are about 16 inches tall, and I don't have the carrot rust fly problems that I had with ground-level gardening. Slugs would receive an electrical jolt from copper, which some say should be 2 inches wide. Just make sure the slugs are not already inside the bed.

Raised beds lend themselves nicely to square-foot, intensive blocks or bed planting rather than rows. Plants densely crowded in blocks can produce more food than rows, spaced for gardener's paths. If your soil in the raised bed is quite sandy, drip or soaker hose-administered water won't wick sideways to any useful extent, but if your soil contains a fair amount of organic matter and/or clay, it will spread farther, enabling block planting.

You can place raised beds in problem areas such as swampy ground, where caliche or lava tubes are near the surface or even on top of old concrete patios or driveways.

If you set up a raised bed on bare ground in an area much frequented by voles or gophers, it's a good idea to cover the bottom with 1/2 inch or finer hardware cloth to prevent subterranean attacks on your plantings. We had a vole with the abilities of a Chunnel engineer make an underground approach to a beautiful dark eggplant hanging to the ground, where he/she happily ate the interior in rain or shine, unseen by human or canine. The fruit resembled a bell when I harvested it.

I don't advise planting anything except ornamentals over a septic tank drain field.

Even a raised bed can wick contaminants to root zones. Boggy or swampy areas can be largely dried by planting a willow tree in that area.

Consider microclimates on your property. Some areas may be more sheltered from desiccating winds than others, some exposed to winter arctic conditions.

The climate in this Valley is far from uniform. Eagle and Star are colder than Boise, and I know of an area south of Meridian that is colder than those communities when Boise is temperate. Stella Schneider lives in Boise's North End, where she observes Foothills frost sliding down to her area, destroying plants in spring and fall.

In addition to sun exposure, you should consider the time you'll be able to devote to your gardens. Will you be able to tend your gardens, cutting back and weeding where necessary? Or will you just give them a passing glance? If the latter, look for plants that are "low maintenance."

A Boise woman told me years ago that she loved gardening, and feared she wouldn't have opportunity to garden until she retired, but when soaker hoses and drip watering systems came on the market, she realized she could garden long before retirement. She knew that plant foliage should not enter falling temperatures while wet, but the "new" watering systems would allow her to water after work without wetting plant leaves. Cool temperatures and wet leaves are a recipe for plant diseases.

Treasure Valley residents fortunate enough to get cheap irrigation water must arrange to manage that resource on their assigned day or night. We usually don't receive much precipitation during our growing season, but the bright side of that is that we don't receive the plant diseases suffered by gardeners in moister areas. Our annual precipitation is about 12 inches, an amount some communities receive in less than a month.

We receive some snow, the amount falling in the Valley varying from year to year, but it doesn't remain for long. Areas such as the Midwest that receive snow on snow during winter see it turn gritty black and rust their cars, but it is a blanket for garden beds. It's hard to imagine, but it is warmer under the snow than it is on top of it.

It's very tempting to deposit soil under a tree and make a new bed there, but it's not a good idea. Adding soil or mulch to the area within the dripline of a tree, pulling it up to the trunk creates a "mulch volcano," inviting rodents, disease and insects to attack the crown of the tree, where roots converge with the trunk. Tree roots also need oxygen, and added soil over those roots restricts oxygen that should enter the soil, so even if you don't pull soil or mulch to the trunk, the roots may suffocate.

The Treasure Valley is clear of many diseases and insects that damage or kill plants in other parts of the country, but we have some that are not common elsewhere, too.

Before you get started, decide whether you want an organic garden or not. Organic gardens mean you'll use organic fertilizers and pesticides approved for use in organic gardens. Some folks want to be a little organic, using organic fertilizers, but still use synthetic pesticides. This isn't a good idea, for those pesticides will destroy some or much of the soil food web that nourishes your plants. Synthetic fertilizers will also damage some or many of these micro-organisms important to the health of your soil.

Here's the dirt on Valley soil

Newcomers to this area who wish to grow anything, from lawns to ornamentals or vegetables, must first cope with our soil. The river bottomland is alluvial soil, rich and black with decayed vegetation, but the first bench has been eroded by the river, the second bench by glacial outwash and possibly the river, then baked nearly white by hot sun.

The first bench has fair soil, nowhere near as rich as that on the river level, but the second bench's soil has been so tortured there's little traceable organic matter in it. Worse yet, some of that land has lava tubes or hardpan near the surface. On the Foothills side of the Treasure Valley, the hardpan is a hard clay which, when wet, acts as a greased ramp for landslides.

Across the Valley, the hardpan is caliche (pronounced KLEE-chee), a thick concrete-like layer of calcium carbonate. In my area, it's 30 inches below and parallel to the soil surface, and if we're planting a taprooted tree, we've got to hammer and/or chisel our way through the caliche, replacing it with gravel.

In some areas of the Valley, caliche or lava tubes lie just a few inches below the soil's surface. Either hardpan is impervious to liquids and nearly impossible to break up. A problem may arise when your neighbor uses a synthetic chemical as a plant drench; when it hits caliche, it can flow or wick into your yard, affecting your trees or shrubs. If the chemical is a herbicide, it may kill your trees or shrubs. If it's a fertilizer, they may be stimulated.

If you wish to garden where lava tubes or caliche are close to the surface, you'd better use raised beds, for it takes centuries for plant roots to break up such stony features.

Moreover, most of the soil in this Valley is alkaline, like most of the soils in the Inland West. Nineteenth-century farmers wagon training their way to the Willamette Valley via the Oregon Trail couldn't resist tasting the soil now and then. They'd pick up a pinch of soil, touch it with their tongue to find whether it was "sour" (acidic) or "sweet" and write about that in their journals. Throughout most of the West, the soil was sweet, or alkaline, in some cases visibly alkaline. When those emigres saw white alkali lying atop the soil, they scooped up a quantity for use as baking soda.

Those were the days before we learned about all of the microscopic critters in our soil. Even in untilled prairie soils, there's an estimated 100 million to one billion bacteria, tens to hundreds of yards of fungi, several thousand protozoa, and tens to several hundred nematodes, per teaspoon of soil, according to the "Soil Biology Primer" put out by the USDA.

These microscopic organisms make up the "soil food web," of feeding and decaying plants, and their health is crucial to the continued growth of plants and health of the soil year after year.

Most plants thrive in slightly acid soil, a pH of about 6.0 to 7.0. Soil on our benches is 7.5 to 8 (i.e., more alkaline) in their natural condition. Soil that's too alkaline or too acidic inhibits growth of most plants. A pH of 7.0 is neutral. Some plants such azaleas, Rhododendrons and blueberries prefer more acid soil. They can be planted in peat moss to avoid alkalinity in our area.

In the Treasure Valley, gardeners add large quantities of organic matter to help lower the pH to a more plant-tolerable level, and some gardeners and farmers use gypsum, a product that helps to break up clay, and, since it contains some sulfur, acidifies the soil a little.

Adding sulfur alone to acidify soil is tricky; if you overshoot your goal, you have a new set of problems.

Gardeners who move here from other areas may be tempted to put fireplace ashes on their gardens. They should not, because fireplace ashes will add to the alkalinity, which we're trying to diminish.

Some areas near the river have more acidic soil than soils higher in the Valley.

Most of Boise's North End is favored with black, rich, more acidic soil, without hardpan to cope with. This acid-alkaline balance changes in time, so you should check the pH level from time to time. Kits that measure pH in swimming pools may be sufficiently accurate for growing purposes, although generally home-testing kits for plant nutrients are not accurate.

Some gardeners hate clay soil until they've gardened in free-draining sand; then they quickly change their attitudes. Clay soil is hard to work, but it generally contains and holds nutrients that would pass quickly through sandy soil. Some of the land in the bottom of the Valley contains more sand than clay, so it's easier to work but requires more additives to hold growth nutrients.

The solution to ease working with clay soil and to get sandy soil to hold nutrients is the same: inclusion of organic matter. Organic matter tends to loosen clay so it's more friable (crumbly); organic matter also helps hold water and nutrients longer in sandy soil.

This organic matter may be fallen leaves (shred them with your mower for best results), herbicide-free grass clippings, compost, aged manure or ramial wood chips.

Ramial wood chips are chips from live tree or shrub branches that are less than about 3 inches in diameter. As they deteriorate, they do wondrous things to the texture of your soil.

This "no-till" method of adding organic matter to your soil means that you're not bringing weed seeds to light, where they may germinate, and you're not disturbing the mycorrhizal fungi or bacteria that are the agents that specifically feed your plants and ward off some disease organisms. When we "feed our plants," we're really just feeding the mycorrhizae and microscopic creatures, which then help convert our fertilizer into a form plants can use. Mycorrhizae are efficient at using nutrients, harbor bacteria that are antagonistic to plant pathogens (disease), hold water and exude glomalin, which helps soil clump.

Another way to get organic matter into the soil is to grow a "green cover crop," such as buckwheat (grows in summer, not winter hardy), annual rye, vetches, legumes, Phacelia, clovers, etc. Some are tilled in at the end of their growing season; others die out naturally. Some green manures are not winter hardy in our area, and some may be difficult to eradicate once they've finished their job.

Green manures may fix nitrogen from the air, attract pollinating insects, bring plant nutrients up from the depths to plant root zone (tap-rooted weeds do this, too), loosen heavy clay, block germination of weeds, prevent erosion, and/or add major amounts of organic matter to your soil, which, after it decays, adds nutrients future plants can use. (Nitrogen must be "fixed" into another form for plants to use it.)

Some gardeners and farmers grow forage radishes such as the large Daikon radishes, and let them decay in the ground to break up clay soils. Grazing animals may eat the greens that grow above ground while the radishes penetrate clay, thus the "forage" part of the name.

Generally we can use any organic waste such as cottonseed meal, rice hulls, straw or mint sludge or manure to add organic matter to our soils, but we must be careful of how those materials were treated prior to processing. Cottonseed meal and rice hulls may bear traces of pesticides, and mint sludge usually does contain one of the long-lasting, persistent-through-composting, herbicides. The herbicide usually used on mint and often on grain crops (parents of straw) contains Clopyralid. That substance retains its plant-killing power through at least three years of being composted, and when it passes through a grazing animal, the manure is an herbicidal solid.

Peat moss may be used, but it's costly and its water-repellent quality makes it less than ideal for general use. Some use soil aid, a partly composted sawdust, but it shouldn't be tilled in because like other semi-intact materials, it will take nitrogen from the soil until it's completely decayed, then begins to restore nitrogen. The soil aid/soil interface causes minimal disruption when it's applied to the surface of the soil.

Don't try to break up clay with sand. Unless you use the proper proportion, you could make adobe instead of lighter soil. There are commercial clay busters on the market, but some are ceramic slivers, that can harm a digging pet. Read the label.

We used to hear a lot about cultivating the garden, stirring up the soil to keep it loose, but we don't hear much about it these days, perhaps because of the popularity of raised beds. Plant roots do need oxygen, and soil that has been compacted has had the air squeezed out of it. Then one must use a cultivating tool or tiller or aerated compost tea to loosen the soil so it can permit oxygen to again reach roots. Some use a U-bar digger, rocking it back and forth to open soil.

Soil that has been walked upon, especially when wet, becomes compacted. One of the purposes of raised beds is to prevent people walking on the soil.

The late Robert Rodale wrote that soil is more valuable than gold, because when you spent the gold it was gone, but soil could provide food to infinity if well taken care of. Our soil is pretty good, not the best, but we can work with it.

It's not too hard to bring even the soil of the second bench up to nutritional adequacy with the addition of fallen leaves and grass clippings year after year. That will keep the nitrogen, phosphorus and potassium levels in good shape, but minor nutrients may be lacking. The addition of kelp meal helps provide trace minerals, as does alfalfa meal. Alfalfa meal also contains a plant growth accelerant.

Apart from that, Treasure Valley soil lacks magnesium. That deficiency is easily corrected by application of Epsom salts (magnesium sulfate). I use two tablespoons per gallon of water on newly planted tomatoes (just the one application), and if pepper plant leaves are not as green as they should be, I spray one teaspoon Epsom salts dissolved in a pint of water on the leaves. Roses also benefit from Epsom salts, one tablespoon per gallon of water once or twice per growing season.

As with all fertilizers, don't get lavish with applications. A little is good, but a lot is not. Adding too much may block absorption of other needed nutrients.

Due to the alkalinity of our soil, iron uptake by trees, shrubs and plants is restricted. Iron deficiency shows up noticeably on fruit trees and shrubs, in the form of chlorotic leaves, those with green veins and the leaf tissue between the veins yellow or pale green. You can spray new spring foliage with chelated iron to correct this problem. It may take more than one application, and remember, it's difficult to get leaves to turn green after they've yellowed. If you're using pellets in a root feeder, they should be applied very early in spring, before leaves appear.

The keys to good compost

We talk a lot about compost, what it does for plants, water retention and soil conditions, but what we really mean is that it replenishes nutrients we've taken from the soil.

We grow glorious flowering plants, and deadhead spent flowers to prevent the plant's putting energy into making seeds. Those dead flowers go into the compost to restore the soil. So do all spent plants, prunings and plant parts.

When we grow vegetable gardens, we obviously can't give those vegetables back to compost because we've eaten them. We can and do put kitchen waste, eggshells, herbicide-free lawn clippings, shredded paper and fallen leaves into the compost pile, and wherever we can find "clean" organic matter, we may add that.

When we can obtain animal manure that's free of pesticides and worm medications, we may put in a layer of that, too, to increase microbe activity in decomposition of the compost pile. It's not necessary, however.

If you have access to rabbit manure, that's very good, and should not be too "hot" even for immediate use on your plants, or it can be used in compost. Chicken manure is fine for composting, but too hot for immediate use. Hot manures are those fresh high-nitrate manures that spur microbe activity to such a level that they burn up nutrients and damage plant root tissues.

Never use cat or dog manures in compost, for they may be carrying parasite worms or eggs that will contaminate your compost. Cats may carry toxoplasmosis that can be extremely dangerous, especially for pregnant women.

Horse and llama manures should be aged at least 90 days before being added to the compost pile, I think. Both animals are regularly treated for worms, and one veterinarian I spoke with said he thought the worm medication lost its effectiveness in two to three months. I fear that fresh vermifuge would also have a killing effect on micro-organisms in a working compost pile.

One must be cautious about using any large animal manure because of the residual effect of modern herbicides. If animals have been grazing on fields sprayed with herbicides containing Clopyralid, Aminopyralid or Picloram, it passes harmlessly through animals, we're told, but these chemicals are excreted as solid herbicides. The contaminated manure keeps its broadleaf plant-killing effectiveness for more than three years of composting.

Similarly, plant material exposed to those herbicides retains that toxicity through composting for years.

For a compost pile, you're supposed to "layer" browns and greens, 25 times more browns (carbons) than greens (nitrogenous or animal wastes), then keep the pile moistened like a damp sponge, and make sure it has adequate air, top to bottom. To make sure of the latter, many people turn their compost piles regularly, or use a tool that, once thrust into the pile, extends "wings" when you start to withdraw the tool, exposing a fair amount of the pile to oxygen. Depending on the size of the pile, it may take several pokes to thoroughly aerate it.

Nitrogenous materials, or "greens," include grass clippings, alfalfa meal, blood meal, poultry and other animal manures. Browns are brown or yellow, dry, coarse and bulky organic matter.

Never use meat, bones, grease, dairy, peony clippings, walnut leaves or blight-afflicted plants in your compost.

All materials will decompose faster if they're mechanically chipped or shredded.

Lawnmowers exert sufficient vacuum power to pick up and shred fallen leaves, and that also prevents their matting and barring water when they're used as mulch. If they're used in compost, they decay faster than whole leaves.

Many folks use commercial barrel-like composters or just three or four pallets wired together. A three-pallet setup is easily accessed for turning.

Another method is sheet composting, laying your organic matter on the soil or in holes or trenches, and then tilling it in or covering it with soil.

Some compost piles heat up quickly, and may become more than uncomfortably hot. If set up next to a wooden fence, for instance, it's embarrassing and dangerous when the pile catches the fence on fire.

Compost piles set up in less than ideal layers will eventually decompose into good compost, but are regarded as "cold compost." Proper layers, moistness and air just hasten the process, creating "hot compost," but don't depend on getting "black gold" compost in 14 days. In spite of the advertising, I haven't met anyone who's succeeded to that extent with any equipment.

Compost is completed when you can no longer identify pieces in it. It can be used as mulch, or spread on garden beds or around shrubs and trees to a depth of about an inch.

It increases microbial activity in the soil food web when compost tea is thoroughly aerated and applied to soil. When I've applied it to nearly compacted soil, it turns into light, fluffy soil within days. Some folks also use compost tea as a foliar (leaf) feed to restore or maintain good health of plants.

Researchers at Laval University in Canada found that ramial wood chips worked wonders in soil conditioning when laid atop soil. The branches already had the right ratio of green (cambium layer) to brown (heartwood), and contained their own moisture.

Dead trees or shrubs lack the green layer, so they don't work as well.

Most of us build "cold compost" piles, adding a little organic matter at a time.

That works, too. Rot happens in its own time. And if we move across town, the first thing gardeners move is their compost pile. That's how valuable this black gold is.

Use your plants' health to guide your garden decisions

Another problem we have with natural soil elements is a problem everywhere: Tomato plants can only take in calcium when soil is moist, not soggy or dry. Calcium is needed for cell strength in tomatoes, and when the plant is unable to take in needed calcium, tomato fruits show up with blossom end rot. This is a condition where the bottom end of a tomato turns brown and papery, the upper part of the tomato "ripens" quickly. All that is needed, really, is a change in your watering habits, adding mulch to retain moisture or application of a commercial anti-blossom end rot spray to avoid this problem.

As long as weather was under about 95 degrees, I used to irrigate my tomatoes deeply once a week, more often in hotter weather. Using soaker hoses now, I water for an hour at a time two or three times a week, and hold the moisture in the soil with a thick mulch of our own grass clippings.

Some people advise frequent soil testing, but that can get expensive. The University of Idaho Extension Office (www.uidaho.edu/extension) charges

$35 for a soil test, reporting the NPK (nitrogen, phosphorus and potassium) content of your soil, pH and humus content. Independent laboratories in the area (listed under "Laboratories - Testing" in a telephone book) may test for those major elements plus secondary and/or trace elements, too. Call for costs and methods of sampling.

Nitrogen, a crucial element in plant vigor and growth, is easily leached by irrigation or precipitation, but phosphorus and potassium tend to stay in place. When nitrogen is lacking, plants are stunted and grow slowly, and older leaves on the plant turn yellow.

Phosphorus deficiency is indicated by slow growth, stunting, purplish coloration of leaves on some plants, delayed maturity, dark green color on leaves with brown tips on some plants, and poor fruit or seed development.

A deficiency of potassium is indicated by weak stalks, slow growth, and tips and margins of old leaves turning brown. This latter symptom may reflect a lack of water, too.

Plant problems may indicate the presence of disease. If you're watering adequately, but your plant or plants begin to wither as if they're not getting water, you might have one of the soil-borne wilts, Fusarium or Verticillium. These are fungus diseases, and gardeners are well-advised to grow resistant plants in those locations for the next three or four years.

A gardener's best course is to get positive identification of the disease, and deal with it accordingly. Sometimes one can deal with disease by means of solarization.

That means in summer, an area at least 2 feet wide should be tilled, raked smooth, deeply watered, and then covered with heavy clear plastic sheeting (such as Visqueen), and the edges weighted down. Let that area bake in the sun for about six weeks. This clears the area of soil-borne disease, but not those ubiquitous bacterial or spore-borne diseases.

This treatment may send underground mobile members of the soil food web scrambling to cooler territory, or it may kill them, but they will move back in and/or replenish their numbers quickly after the plastic is removed. If you were to use a chemical cleanser, there might be residue that would prevent that recolonization that's so important to plant and soil health.

For more on most local garden maladies, see the chapter on diseases.

If you determine your garden problem is due to nutritional deficiency, then you must make a decision whether you're going to feed the soil (and let the soil food web nourish your plants) or feed your plants directly, bypassing the soil. The first method, feeding the soil, is regarded as organic since it uses slow release organic materials, the second method non-organic because it relies on fast-acting synthetic chemical foods.

Organic sources of nitrogen include decayed leaves, chipped woody prunings, alfalfa meal, grass cuttings, manure free of Clopyralid or Aminopyralid that's well-aged (unless it's rabbit manure, which can be used immediately), blood meal, cottonseed or soybean meal, and fish meal or fish emulsion. Sources of phosphorus include bone meal, colloidal phosphate and rock phosphate. Note pets may be attracted to bone meal and blood meal and dig up plants fertilized with those sources.

Potassium sources include granite meal, greens and kelp meal.

Compost supplies all of these nutrients, but may need extra nutritional boosts at times. Coffee grounds and egg shells also boost nutritional power of garden soil.

Non-organic fertilizers must be used carefully lest they "burn" the plants you're trying to stimulate. The numbers on the package refer to N-P-K (nitrogen-phosphorus-potassium), indicating the percentage of each nutrient by weight. Thus a fertilizer labeled as 10-10-10 has 70 percent of "inert" materials, only 30 percent of nutrients.

Using organic fertilizers is easier because they're less likely to "burn" vegetation.

When you've got real problems

If your soil is horrible, one way to improve it is by using a technique called "hugelkultur," laying pruned limbs and/or rotted wood on the soil, and covering the pile with soil, wetting it down, and making sure all of the wood is still covered. After it decays, the soil will be richer and more usable and the mound diminished in size.

Rather than lose this area to an entire growing season, some users of this method place containers of plants over the mound.

To create a new garden bed, lay cardboard or at least 10 overlapping sheets of newspaper over watered, mowed weeds or grass, then top that with layers of compost, soil, leaves, grass clippings or whatever you have in abundance.

This "lasagna" treatment will smother grass and annual weeds, and give you good soil in which to plant ornamentals, herbs or vegetables.

Overtilling may do more harm than good — to your garden and to your back

I've read that the best inventors were lazy people, looking for the easiest way to do things. Some laziness may make good gardeners, too.

There's a growing movement among organic gardeners and farmers against tilling the soil. Until now, we've prized our amendment-rich garden soil tilled to soft fluff, spongy when we stepped on it.

What that tilling did that we weren't thinking about was disrupt the lives of the soil-dwelling creatures, from earthworms to bacteria. Some creatures can't make their own ways through the soil, so they have to use existing worm tunnels to move from one place to another. If we don't till the soil, these creatures have their undisturbed routes to roots.

I live on the second bench, where the soil is desert-poor. We've tilled tons and tons of organic matter into the soil, and it is a lot better than when we found it. Organic matter holds moisture in the soil and tends to break up the clay, improving drainage. That's not an oxymoron: Organic matter does both — hold moisture and improve drainage. It's especially useful in holding moisture in sandy soil.

But I don't think we need to till the way we used to. We are relocating and changing some beds, and we will do some tilling to break up clods, but we won't till the whole garden.

We have left the tomato patch free of tilling for the past few years to leave the tomato plant-friendly mycorrhizae alone.

You need not till a garden area to work in compost or other organic matter.

You can place it on the ground and let the soil-dwelling creatures, visible and invisible to the eye, move the matter down into the soil. They will do the job for you, in a surprisingly short time.

This no-tilling is especially useful if you have trees, shrubs or perennials you don't want to dig up while you add amendments or try to till around their roots. Just leave plants and shrubs in place and distribute your organic matter around them. Those who advocate fertilizing with compost usually advise a one-inch layer of compost around each plant or shrub each year.

Then you can top the compost with mulch if you want to hold moisture in the soil.

Some experts claim that organic matter worked in by soil creatures is of benefit longer than tilled-in amendments.

Gardening can still be enjoyed by those with disabilities

Do you have family members or friends who want to garden but feel they cannot because of physical disabilities? Keep in mind that each person's disability is unique to them, and what works for some may not work for your friend or family member.

Gardening gives such pleasure and such visible or scented results, it's worth a try.

Raised beds are of great value to those who find stooping or bending painful or uncomfortable. You could use containers as small "raised beds," or for a large garden, build raised beds.

If the garden area is accessible to motorized equipment, have a Bobcat or backhoe operator scrape your garden soil into ridges, then surround ridges with 2-by-8 fir or cedar, if possible. You can also use cinder blocks or stones to surround ridges, but keep in mind the width of the edging adds to the area you'll need to reach into. You can also try using raised beds without edging. As long as no one walks on the bed or there's no deluge of water, the rounded edges should hold.

If you build raised beds of more than one course, I'd advise using something like aluminum flashing inside the containment to block weeds' intrusion through the crack between courses. My raised beds are 4 feet wide, but should be no wider than 3 1/2 feet for easy reach.

Since my leg mobility is a problem, I use a Celebrity Victory brand of electric scooter for gardening. The footrest can hold a flexible tub of compost or spent plants bound for the compost or a large pot for harvesting greens, beans, broccoli, etc.

The presence of the tiller and tool basket restricts close access at the front of the scooter, but you can get closer to your beds by working from the back of the scooter.

Wear clothing that will not catch on the hand accelerator, for your scooter may take leave before you're ready, and you won't hang out in the open for long. Please don't ask me how I know.

A variety of extendable tools are available, including a trowel, three-pronged cultivator, leaf rake and regular rake. Their utility is questionable, since it doesn't take much weathering to freeze them in position, no longer expandable or contractible. My favorite weeders are a scraper with a handle about 16 inches long for seedling weeds, a cobra head weeder for grassy weeds, and a Japanese farmer's knife (Hori-hori) for firmly rooted weeds close to hand.

Special tools and even lightweight hoses are available for folks who have arthritis. Fiskars, for instance, has PowerGlide hand pruners, one handle of which rotates, and although this may require some getting used to, it's very easy on hands.

These pruners have approval of the Arthritis Foundation. Some of my readers have tried them and enthusiastically endorse them for folks with arthritis.

Other tools easy for arthritic people to use include arm support for long tools, stand-up bulb planters, weeders, extra long loppers, padded kneelers with arm supports to assist you to your feet, special gloves for arthritic hands at www.bionicgloves.com, pipes through which you can drop seeds into place, and ergonomic assists. Some of these tools will help, but some will not because individuals' needs differ.

If your friend or family member's disability is reduced eyesight, plant special beds with plants of different textured leaves, scents, heights, etc. Pebbly vs. smooth leaves, large palmate leaves vs. grassy straps, for instance can inform a sight-impaired person what they're dealing with. Mints have square stems, but most plants have round stems, for instance. It won't take long for the gardener to recognize weeds such as sowthistle or mallow by feel.

Most folks with eyesight problems see dimly at least, but if not, different approaches to garden beds are helpful. For instance, a gravel approach to a handicapped person's garden is a recognizable access, if no other bed has such an approach. Thin-soled shoes help distinguish different paths to garden beds, too.

Folks with diminished sight can feel results of pest problems, from black vine weevil notches to slug damage and aphid "honeydew."

If you live in an area with rattlesnakes, it would be a good idea to have a sighted person examine the garden bed before the person with compromised sight begins to work the plants.

The easiest gardening of all is Ruth Stout's "part the mulch and plant" system, explained in her book, "How to Have a Green Thumb without an Aching Back: A New Method of Mulch Gardening," or her "No Work Gardening Book." They were published many years ago, so used copies should be inexpensive or available through public libraries.

Mulch hides pests such as voles and slugs, but it's useful in preventing weeds and retaining moisture in the soil — a help to any gardener.

CHAPTER 2

Vegetables

AN OVERVIEW

Growing vegetables

You may start this as a lark or a hobby, but it won't take long before you begin to realize how food security is jeopardized by housing developments smothering agricultural lands, water being used for lawns instead of food production and good agricultural land being unintentionally exhausted or damaged by use of synthetic chemicals.

In other parts of America there are extensive urban agriculture movements, growing food in front yards or on commercial roofs. Neither can be as efficient as tractor-dominated agriculture, but each of us growing our own food to the extent possible enriches our individual or family food future.

When you select a site for a vegetable bed, make sure at least most of it receives at least six hours of direct sun each day. If there's some shade, that's an area for growing lettuce and other greens. You'll have to decide whether you want to grow at ground level or in raised beds.

Folks who have used raised beds refuse to go back to ground level gardening. Not only are they easier on the gardener's back for planting, weeding and harvesting, but also they warm up earlier in spring than ground-level soil and have better drainage. They're also slightly less vulnerable to frost.

Containers are equivalent to raised beds, too. Make sure containers are rated for food and have drainage holes. Drainage will be best if the holes are on the sides of the container near the bottom or if the container is raised a bit so ground or deck doesn't seal the hole shut. Container "feet" raising the bottom of the pot may be as simple as bottle caps.

Regardless of whether you'll grow in raised beds or at ground level (or in lower "waffle" gardens), you can prepare the soil by covering annual weeds or lawn with overlapping cardboard, then a layer of soil, a layer of leaves or grass clippings, a layer of compost, and so on, using whatever herbicide-free organic matter you have on hand.

It's better if you do this preparation in fall, so winter precipitation and the freeze-thaw cycles soften your layers, but if you do it in spring, you'll be able to plant in a few weeks. You're essentially building a layer cake or lasagna of soil, compost and organic matter into a productive garden bed.

For your seeds, pay close attention to varieties, and which seed company carries your selected variety. If seed racks in this area don't carry that company's seeds, you'll have to order by mail. Do it early, for companies may run out of selected seeds. If you can't find your preferred variety, use a computer search for that variety name. Seed companies drop unpopular varieties; more than 30,000 vegetable varieties disappeared last century.

If you grow OP (Open Pollinated) varieties, you may be able to save seeds for the next and subsequent years. See Suzanne Ashworth's "Seed to Seed" for cross-pollination prevention. If a seed catalog refers to a variety as hybrid or F1 hybrid, you probably won't get the same result if you save seeds. Some vegetables such as lettuce appear to not be hybridized, but beware of lettuce crossing with wild or prickly lettuce.

Remember we can grow anything that grows in a temperate zone, but can't grow many items that are tropical and require a longer growing season than we have. Our normal growing season is about five months, though we can stretch it with some tricks I mention in this chapter.

To get the most out of your garden, plan on planting one thing where another has just finished. This is called "succession planting." You can also plant some vegetables early that are resistant to frost, and plant some that will thrive long after the first autumn frost. Spinach, lettuce, Swiss chard, broccoli, Brussels sprouts, cabbage, cauliflower, bulbing fennel, corn salad (mache), arugula, cress, carrots, parsnips and beets, for instance, withstand frost.

Don't leave root crops in the ground all winter, though, for they'll split.

Start Brassicas indoors in potting soil in July for a fall crop (outdoor soil is too hot for their seeds to germinate), and start lettuce and spinach in late September for a fall harvest. Let corn salad reseed itself in June for winter greens, and plant lettuce seeds as late as November for an early spring harvest.

Learning from my experience

I started real vegetable gardening for myself in 1971, after we moved to Boise and bought property that contained a large space I could use. Prior to that time, I had never had the right sunny space, but I had helped my grandmothers garden in Colorado, and I tended to follow their leads.

Their climate is harsher than ours, and my vegetable gardening has changed quite a lot from their practice and my early one of the past four decades. In the early days, first frost slammed the door on gardening. Now I either cover or pick vulnerable vegetables such as green beans, peppers, eggplants and tomatoes and let the rest go, at least for a time.

Just before a forecast of severe cold, I harvested parsnips, scallions, kale, celery, celeriac and leeks. I could also have harvested Swiss chard, lettuce, arugula, beets, chicory and more leeks, but I didn't need them. I hoped the freezing of the soil would be temporary.

Our climate, even though a four-season climate, is sufficiently mild that we can extend our growing season for months. I do use floating row cover, not known to my grandparents as garden material, but some of these crops do not need cover for even a harsh winter.

I do have row cover over one raised bed, because year-round I shield lettuce from direct sun and wind to preserve tenderness. That bed also contains arugula, collards, mache (corn salad) and chicory.

How to lengthen the growing season

Extending the growing season is like adding sections to a blanket: We can add at the beginning of the season and/or at the end. We must be cautious about the fragility of plants at the beginning of the season, for they're not as tough as they will be after living through the hot sun and winds of summer. You can give yourself a major advantage in early-season gardening if you select a site for your garden that's sheltered from wind and has good southern exposure. In winter, our sun is low in the south, and it moves more overhead as we approach summer.

We can get a jump on growing early in spring by warming the soil with a cover of clear plastic. Clear plastic is preferable to dark plastic, because dark plastic tends to hold heat itself; clear plastic lets heat pass through to the soil. Weeds will grow under the plastic, but you can remove them later if they survive the heat.

You're trying to warm the soil to 55 degrees, a temperature favorable for root growth. Once the soil is warm in a few days or weeks, you can either cut X's in the plastic and transplant in the middle of each X, or you can remove the plastic and immediately cover the soil with a heat-retaining mulch, and then transplant into that. This treatment works best for transplants such as tomatoes or peppers, and if you intend to reuse the plastic, you'd better remove it when the plants are still small.

Not all garden plants require soil that warm. Lettuce, spinach and Brassicas, for instance, prefer cool soil. Lettuce seeds, for example, will even germinate at 32 degrees. (In summer, when we want to plant fall crops, the soil is too warm for the seeds of these crops, so we must start them indoors.)

Other ways to warm soil include laying a soil heating cable, topping it with some hardware cloth and then covering that with a few inches of soil.

This works best with direct seeding; the hardware cloth will prevent your digging into the cable for transplants. You may have to leave the cable in the soil until you've harvested all of the crop planted over it to avoid dislodging roots.

A heating cable doesn't come with an abundance of instructions, in my experience. Loop it back and forth so that it never touches itself. Some heating cables can be used to warm winter soil enough to grow lettuce throughout the winter, and some may be controlled by thermostats.

Heating cables can be used in "hotbox" versions of cold frames, but a cheaper form of hotbox growing uses fresh manure, which heats as it decays. You can use horse or cow manure to a depth of about 6 to 8 inches, mixed with some straw, and topped with a few inches of soil. Less manure will be needed if you're using chicken droppings. You may have to let it cool for a few weeks so that it won't "cook" your plants when you put them in the box.

You can also start seeds this way without using electricity for bottom heat and/or use this as a heat source to grow items like leafy vegetables in a hot box during winter weather.

Some plant a tomato in a 10-gallon can, then slide that into a pit of fresh horse manure, maintaining several inches of space between the can's drainage holes and the manure to avoid burning the tomato roots. I haven't tried this, and have heard of only one person planting like this. Several friends have planted directly in a working compost pile (warm while decomposing).

People who plant directly in compost tend to plant heavy feeders such as squash or pumpkins. They do reap a rich harvest.

Cool weather and warm-weather plants started indoors need to be "hardened off," or gradually exposed to full sun and winds. Some references advise hardening off in cold frames, but I disagree.

Cold frames shelter plants from wind, and those plants later set out in dry wind conditions will suffer and perhaps die at that exposure.

Before beginning the hardening off process, we can put frost-tender plants in a cold frame, remembering to open it during sunny days (and close it for chilly nights). Forgetting to perform either operation may destroy your young crop. (See the section on hardening off on page 46.)

Or we can shelter seedlings. English and French gardeners use glass bells (called cloches) to set over early transplants, and some folks use gallon jugs (bottom removed) or milk jugs (bottom cut 3/4 around, then the flap pulled aside and weighted with a rock).

You can increase the heat inside these jugs by placing small stones inside to soak up heat and release it slowly at night. These cloches have to be closely monitored to avoid cooking your plants. If you're using gallon jugs, removing the lids may sufficiently cool off plants. If lids are not part of the cloche you may have to set them aside for the day, but remember to replace them at night.

You can make homemade "walls of water" by gluing or duct taping two-liter plastic bottles together and cutting off the bottoms. Leave caps on the bottles and push them into the soil upside down around your transplant, then fill with water.

These glass and plastic jugs and any plastic tunnel material will conduct cold to plant leaves, so leaves must not touch plastic or glass.

We can also protect tender plants with tents or tunnels of agricultural fleece or row covers that let in light and moisture, but keep temperatures a few degrees above freezing. After edges are weighed down, you can keep the tenting elevated over plants by using beverage cans upside down over stakes. The can bottoms are smooth, so they won't tear the fabric.

To install PVC ribs to hold floating row cover or plastic sheeting above your plants, you can drive short pieces of rebar into the soil, letting them stick up a couple of inches above soil level, then arch PVC pipes over the rebar. I think dowels or stout twigs from pruned trees would work, too.

It's quite a gamble to set out tomato plants in March or April here, for instance, even with cover. Commercial Walls o' Water are very effective, even when cold temperatures freeze the water in their protective tubes, but that protection doesn't last day after day.

If you upset the diurnal rhythms of tomatoes with cold temperatures, those plants will not fully recover by the end of the season. Your harvest may be reduced because of this hazardous exposure, even though the plant hasn't been killed by freezing.

In this Valley, when snow is no longer visible on Shafer Butte, it's said to be safe to plant tender plants outdoors.

By late spring or early summer, we who dislike supermarket tomatoes and long for home-grown tomatoes want to harvest early. One solution is to transplant one plant quite early, using Walls o' Water, soil warming and any other technique to keep the plant alive. Then plant your other tomatoes out about June 1.

Our average date of last frost is about May 10. That is an average, and we often do have frosts later than that.

Ways to protect tender plants from frost damage are to make sure your plants are well watered, then cover with a tunnel of floating row cover or a large box or tented fabric falling to the ground so as to capture the earth's heat; or mist the plant with water just before the freezing temperature hits (it's usually coldest just after dawn) because the water that freezes will briefly raise the temperature a degree or two; or give a foliar spray of diluted seaweed extract 1 tablespoon to a gallon of water (according to Rodale's "Garden Problem Solver").

If you have fruit trees in bloom, and frost is forecast, stringing Christmas lights in the tree may warm it enough you'll get fruit after all. Not all Christmas lights generate heat, unfortunately. A single light bulb may keep the tree warm if it's also tented with a cloth cover.

Moving air will also prevent frost damage if the air is only marginally cold. You could set up a fan to protect your plants or tiny fruit, too.

Pushing into fall

Extending the growing season at the end is similar to that in spring: protect frost-sensitive plants by covering, sprinkling water or moving air. Most gardeners only tend to their tomatoes at this time.

After the first night's frost (perhaps two nights running), we usually have a couple of weeks of Indian summer, so it makes sense to cover tomatoes with something like an old blanket or mattress pad, anchoring it so it won't blow away.

Instead of covering, many chile lovers dig up and pot their favorite chile plants for growing indoors. Be sure to thoroughly spray upper and lower parts of leaves with Neem-based spray to guard against bringing insects indoors. The plant may drop its leaves in shock, but such plants usually refoliate rather quickly. You probably won't get much of a harvest of hot chiles grown indoors. I've had very poor luck with sweet peppers brought indoors.

Beans, tomatillos, squash, sweet potatoes, eggplants and melons are the other vegetables vulnerable to frost. Harvest before frost to protect your food-growing efforts. When temperatures are forecast to drop too low for tomato plant salvage, pick all of the green tomatoes that are about 2 inches in diameter and trusses of cherry tomatoes. Store indoors away from direct sun, but don't bother wrapping them individually in paper.

Shallow beverage boxes are ideal for storing green tomatoes because you can see ripening tomatoes in bottom layers. Periodic sorting brings ripening fruit to the top.

Instead of picking cherry tomato trusses, you can pull up the plant and hang it upside down in a frost-protected spot such as a shed or garage. The tomatoes will continue to ripen as long as there's not a hard freeze.

Brassicas such as broccoli, Piracicaba, cabbage, Brussels sprouts, etc., will attract large gray aphids, and you'll get no help from wasps. They're no longer hungry for aphids. Your outdoor hoses may already be hung up for winter, barring you from blasting aphids off plants with a jet of water, so your only recourse is to spray aphids. Soap sprays should be effective if you keep after the aphids. They multiply at an alarming rate, however.

If you're growing a standard version of Romanesco broccoli, grit your teeth and wait for freezes to kill aphids. It won't bother those plants at all.

Starting seeds

When impatience rules, I start Allium seeds first, not long after the first of the year. It doesn't show, but days are getting longer. Allium seeds are generally short-lived, being viable only for about one year.

You can plant seeds such as onions or other Alliums rather thickly in small pots, and weeks later pry seedlings apart, trim tops and bottoms with scissors for transplanting out. We plant leeks in trenches or holes made with dibbles (chopsticks work), to grow the white part of the leek to maximum size.

I start Giant Musseldorf leeks, sometimes Bleu Solaise leeks (friend Stella Schneider says they overwinter more reliably, and she's probably right), onions (storage, Cipollini and bunching) and Ambition shallots from seed. These shallots don't keep as long as shallots started in late fall from cloves, but they're quite large and less labor intensive than other varieties.

We grow garlic over winter, and if we had shallot cloves, we could grow those over winter.

When I seed indoors in moist potting soil, I keep the soil moist with chamomile tea, and move them into the greenhouse after many of the seeds have germinated.

Why tea? A hazard to newly germinated seeds is "damping off," when seedlings collapse at soil level and die. To prevent this, be sure your seedlings have adequate ventilation, and water them only with tepid chamomile tea. For the latter, use about a quart and a half of hot water, two chamomile tea bags, let steep, then cool. Watering new seedlings with cold water is quite a shock to their tiny structures, and they may die.

Plastic containers, like the six-packs you buy from your local nursery, will retain moisture better than coir (coconut husk) or fiber pots, because the latter wick moisture away from plant roots. If you've bought a soil block kit, it requires quite a bit of practice and experimentation with planting soil to get units to hold together.

Allium seeds germinate well at temperatures of about 60 degrees. Not long afterward, we begin seeding Brassicas such as cabbage, broccoli, Piracicaba, collards and kale. They, too, germinate well indoors in late January-February. Then I plant lettuce (actually sowing on top of planting mix, and then topping with glass from a picture frame to hold in moisture until seeds germinate). I plant cress and arugula the same way.

When Brassicas develop at least two true leaves, I transplant into 4-inch pots in web-bottomed flats. When those plants look dry, I can lower the flat into the tub of water on the floor of the greenhouse and soak all at once. It's preferable to watering from above because overhead watering often misses a plant or two, and the other plants don't get sufficient water to last them for a few days.

Tubs of a size that will accommodate standard 11-by-22-inch flats are available from building supply stores, where they call them cement mixing tubs. They're under $10.

In late February, I plug in the thermostat for the large rubber germination mat and let that warm overnight before planting chile seeds (including mild peppers). They need good bottom heat, nearly 80 degrees is best. I use a clear plastic cover over the flat to hold moisture. As those seedlings germinate, I move those pots to the greenhouse bench, where we water with chamomile tea when needed until seedlings develop at least two, preferably four, true leaves and I can transplant into 4-inch pots.

I then unplug the mat until mid- to late March (or later, if I'm extra patient), and start planting tomato seeds. They germinate best with bottom heat, too. After tomatoes have been moved off the heat mat, I generally germinate basil on the mat before unplugging it for the season.

There are flat black plastic "heat mats," all apparently made by the same manufacturer, on the market. Everyone sells the same thing. Vendors may hate me for this, but I strongly dislike those "heat" mats. After several hours of charging, I still could not feel heat, so I returned it for a refund. Tomato and chile seeds germinate best at 80 degrees, I've found, and those mats don't approach that heat.

Please don't use heating pads or electric blankets for heat; they're not designed for use day after day. Some people use heat mats designed for shoats (baby pigs) or for dog beds, and those should be OK and water resistant. Others use the top of the refrigerator or water heater, or a rack set above a furnace vent. The best heat mats have thermostats.

I sometimes plant squash and/or melon and cucumber seeds indoors, for transplanting out, or else I direct seed them in hills in mid-May to June 1.

Plant corn in at least four north-south rows in early May. To extend your harvest, wait until the first four rows have three leaves, and then plant four more rows of the same variety.

Early spinach is planted outdoors in September, and early lettuce about Thanksgiving, and by March both should be vigorously growing. We always planted potatoes and peas about St. Patrick's Day, and still strive for that. Planting peas for summer harvest is not a good idea, for pea weevils move in, and they devastate your crop. I tried to save seeds of snow peas a few years ago, but insects had eaten huge chunks of every pea.

Most of the Asian greens are frost-tolerant and fast-growing. If you like the taste of mustard greens, try growing Komatsuna, a large green-leafed plant that is ready to harvest about 35 days from planting. Pac Choi, Tatsoi, Chinese mustards and edible rape may be sowed as early as the garden may be worked, but the Chinese heading cabbages don't work well in our spring climate. Try them in fall.

Years ago, I tried growing bulb onions by planting in fall, but by spring when the weather warmed a bit, they acted as if they'd been in the ground for a full year, and every plant bolted to flower and seed, ruining the bulbs. Uncertain spring weather will still have that effect on onions from transplanted seedlings, as well as other touchy biennials.

You can direct seed carrots, radishes, beets, turnips, rutabagas, parsnips, bulb fennel, salsify, scorzonera, etc., prior to the last frost, but wait until almost June 1 to plant beans, chiles, peppers, tomatoes and other frost tender plants. Basil is more than frost tender, succumbing at about 38 degrees, so plant that last.

Some extra seed-starting tips

🍃 Plant in sterile potting soil, the bag of which has been closed to bar flying insects from laying eggs in it. I use six-pack cells filled with potting mix in web-bottomed flats and water from the bottom, setting flats in a concrete mixing tub of tepid water. Once all sections are soaked, then I plant seeds in the wetted mix.

🍃 It's very difficult to plant 1/8 inch deep, so I lay seeds on top and cover them with potting soil or sand sifted through my fist or don't cover them at all. Then I spritz with tepid water until the topping looks wet.

🍃 Seeds for hot chiles are often slow to germinate, but can be coaxed along by an overnight soak in one teaspoon saltpeter (potassium nitrate) dissolved in a quart of water. Then you can distribute seeds to pudding cups and pour in the saltpeter water for soaking. Later, use this solution to water seedlings, if you like.

🍃 Another way to hold moisture for germination is to cover seeded pots with clear glass or plastic wrap. Watch closely, and if mold appears, remove the cover.

🍃 You can tease apart roots of seedlings to an extent, but when faced with a thicket of emerging seedlings, you're better off to use manicure scissors to cut grooves through the thicket. Cut off the primary leaves of seedlings, and the plant dies. Some seeds, such as that for Portulaca, are as fine as soot. The seed company reports they've sold you a thousand seeds, and you see only a pinchful of very difficult to spread out seeds.

✍ Primary leaves for tomatoes and peppers (and many other plants) are opposing strap-like leaves on a small stalk. Wait for the true leaves to show before you transplant into a larger container.

✍ To develop strong seedlings, especially of tomatoes and peppers, either train a fan on them or lightly scrape across their tops every few days with an arched piece of paper. The more the seedlings move or rock back and forth, the stronger their main stalks will be.

✍ Your seedlings are plant babies, so acclimate them gradually, over a period of days, to direct sun and breezes.

Hardening off

Hardening off is the term gardeners use to indicate acclimatizing. You've sown seeds, germinated them and babied tender seedlings indoors, and now they need a gentle and gradual introduction to the out-of-doors that will be their permanent home.

Start by setting flats or pots of seedlings outdoors in dappled shade on a calm, sunny day. Leave seedlings there for about two hours, and then move them back indoors.

Gradually expand their time in dappled shade, then expose seedlings to direct morning sun or afternoon sun for an hour or so. Gradually increase this time, too. When there's no frost in the forecast, leave seedlings out overnight.

If you don't have time or ability to do this, you may be able to follow my shorter version of this. I have an old-fashioned outdoor clothesline that we tent with floating row cover, and set flats of seedlings on a shelf made of 2-by-4 studs laid over sawhorses.

The row cover protects seedlings from cool temperatures, and one side can be pulled back to expose seedlings to sun for a time each day.

After a week or two of this exposure, seedlings are pretty well hardened-off.

I've found that if the weather is drizzly and overcast, you can sometimes set out plants with briefer acclimating. Buy a slicker with a hood, and you're set for ideal transplanting.

Other pitfalls in transplanting are heat, sudden sun exposure, desiccating (drying) wind and roots touching fertilizer. Always lay a cushion of soil between fertilizer and roots (or seeds).

Some people shove a shingle into the soil on the windward side to shade and block wind. I use three-ring tomato cages over seedlings to shade only, clothes-pinning a sheet of newspaper over the top. Slanting rays hit the plant morning and late afternoon but are barred at high noon.

Someone on the Internet once asked how warm the soil had to be for planting tomatoes. Someone else answered that folklore said that if you could sit barebottomed on the garden soil for 10 minutes without discomfort, it was warm enough. An Ohio woman asked, "Is this 10 minutes in daytime or nighttime? I have to be able to face the neighbors ..."

Folklore aside, the real ground temperature should be around 70 degrees for outdoor tomato transplanting. If you transplant into colder soil, and before the last frost, you face losing the plants to frost.

You can cover with floating row cover, plastic or even blankets to ward off frost, but the soil still will be too cold for the tomatoes.

If it is too cold, the tomatoes seem to do poorly. New research by USDA scientists indicates some complicated turmoil in the early lives of cold-set plants will cause reduced yields for the rest of the life of those plants.

It's a trauma in seedlinghood that can never be overcome in hot-weather plants. When a heat-loving plant such as tomato, corn or soybean (and probably pepper) is planted too early, chilly nights disrupt the normal maturing process of the plant. Plants have circadian, or periodic, rhythms for growth, just as we have rhythms for sleep, activity and growth. Some of the plant's interior growing processes stop inappropriately when the night temperature drops to 50 degrees.

The plant's growth is in suspension until the temperature rises, then growth resumes where it left off. By that time, the circadian rhythms are dictating another function. So the delayed and the correct processes work against each other, just as a runner can't run if one foot is competing with the other.

Even photosynthesis may be damaged because of this clash of growth processes. Apparently, the plant never is able to outgrow this original setback. Our weather sometimes turns cold after tomatoes are set out, and we see reduced yields over the summer. I've heard paltry yields blamed on hybrid variety or on heirloom variety, poor soil or lacking fertilizer, but the real culprit is the cold.

Since none of us grows tomato plants 6 feet tall just to harvest one or two tomatoes, it pays to wait for the proper time to transplant tomatoes and hope the weather holds.

Using Walls o' Water may correct this problem, but if you're going to use them, set them out for a couple of days before you transplant plants inside them. That way, they'll have a chance to warm the soil.

Some recommend setting out pepper plants 10 days after tomatoes are set out. In Boise, the late Advanced Master Gardener Dick Wilson set out his peppers in June, and they took right off. I set mine out about when I set out tomatoes, but I'm going to mend my ways. Later is better.

One way you know you set out peppers too early is by a purplish streak on the skin of the fruit. It doesn't affect the flavor, but it's a rap on the knuckles of the gardener. And it may affect your yield, as the chill does.

VEGETABLES, FROM ALLIUM TO ZUCCHINI

ALLIUMS

Alliums are useful, delicious, ornamental and at times repellent, but we love them. Allium is the botanical name of onions, garlic, chives, shallots, leeks and several ornamental plants.

Most are biennial, flowering and setting seed their second year, but some set topsets (bulbils) instead of seeds, and they may set those in one year, not two. If the weather is changeable, Alliums may behave as if they've been growing for two years, even though it's only been one year. If you plant onions in fall, they'll probably all bolt to flower, ruining the bulbs for consumption in spring. Some varieties of garlic and leeks set only cloves for reproduction, their flowers (if any) apparently sterile.

Egyptian or "walking" onions produce small onion sets (bulbils) at the tops of their leaves the first year. When that leaf topples over, it lays the bulbils a leaf-length from the mother plant, where they can take root. Thus it "walks." These onions are not large bulbing onions, but are a little larger and fatter than scallions, of excellent eating quality until the top sets are produced. Then their pungency increases. They set no seeds, so are reproducible only by bulbils.

Bulbing onions are day-length sensitive. You can't properly produce bulbs of Granex, Grano or Vidalia onions here because our days are too long (really it's the night length they respond to). Walla Walla Sweets are supposedly day-neutral, but in order to have the famous sweetness, they must be grown in the soil near Walla Walla, Wash., taking up only a small proportion of sulfur contained in the soil.

None of the super sweet onions last long in storage. Bulbing onions that do last in storage tend to be thin-necked, tightly wrapped, solid bulbs with high sulfur content and pungency.

If you want a yellow, meaty tint to your chicken stock, for instance, include some of the onion's wrapper in your stock pot. For flavor, the bulb is a necessity. Bulbing onions may be yellow (wrapper is yellow), white or red. Some of the red onions are very pungent, others sweet. In either case, they don't last as long in storage as some of the yellow onions. Also bulbs may be elongated, or torpedo-shaped, rather than ball-like. Whatever the shape, it's best to grow "long-day" onions here.

These onions may be grown from seed, seedlings or bulbs. Our state has an embargo on Allium bulbs produced outside of Southwest and South-central Idaho, trying to save onion growers in western Idaho from an invasion of white rot fungus. Once that disease is in a field, Alliums may not be grown there again.

Scallions and bunching onions are also grown from seed. Some scallions are slender from top to bottom, never bulbing; others do produce small purple, red or white bulbs. Their flavor is different from that of regular bulbs, not a good substitute. An intermediate form of these onions, A. fistulosum, is short, stocky and sweet, another non-bulbing onion. Territorial Seeds, for instance, carries seeds for Shimonita variety of these leek-shaped onions.

Some of the bunching onions may be left to continue to divide at their base, but may also produce seeds. They should be divided occasionally. Some advise lifting them in cold winter climates before freezing, but I haven't, and the scallions appear healthy.

Cipollini bulbs grow wide and flat, even slightly lens-shaped. The tops of Cipollinis are concave, making removal of the stem a little difficult. These are quite sweet and tasty when cooked in stews or similar dishes. They may be white or red.

The French and people of Southeast Asia previously occupied by the French favor the use of shallots for flavoring their foods. Some say shallots melt away, leaving only the flavor, but not the crunchy texture of the cloves. Apparently that's desirable for smooth sauces. I've not seen shallots completely disappear or lose their texture in dishes I prepare, perhaps because I don't cook the right sauces.

Seeds for several varieties of shallots have come on the market in the past few years, and they grow well here, although the cloves produced from seed don't last as long as the varieties reproduced by clove.

Dutch shallots are apparently only reproducible by "cloves," although their cloves are not the pie-shaped wedges we think of as cloves. Dutch shallots are round, most about marble-sized. I haven't seen seeds for Dutch shallots available.

Potato onions are only reproducible from cloves, too, and I've never seen them available here. People who have grown them in other areas love them.

Garlic chives have strap-like leaves, with a garlicky flavor. They have white starlike blossoms, and are quite pretty, but they may quickly become thugs in your landscape. They're also known as Chinese leeks. They reproduce by underground bulbs.

Regular chives have rounded purple blossom clusters and hollow leaves like onions. Cutting off the stems stimulates regrowth of chives. Some folks also use chive blossoms in salads, when the blossoms are young and haven't yet produced hard seeds.

Shallots will rot rather than grow if their cloves are covered with soil. Cloves should be planted very shallowly, just up to their shoulders. I had shallots in the ground when the mercury plummeted to minus 25 degrees, and thought I'd lost them. When temperatures moderated, my shallots resumed growing.

Leeks are easy to grow, yet are also expensive in the grocery store. The leek is the national symbol of Wales, the only Allium with such a distinction. Bleu Solaise leeks apparently tolerate our winters better than most varieties.

If your leeks bolt to flower, feel around the base of the bulb for bulb offsets (they're flatter than bulb-shaped). They are quite flavorful, even though the flower has ruined the leek for human consumption. You may get more white bulb (the best part for eating) if you grow leeks in a trench or hill soil around the growing bulb.

Elephant garlic is really a wild Egyptian leek, marketed first by Nichols Garden Nursery in Oregon as Elephant garlic, followed by other nurseries. Cloves are much larger and milder than Silverskin, Artichoke or Rocambole garlics, for instance.

In our area, some people plant garlic very deeply, up to 12 inches deep, to avoid frost, although I'm not sure frost would harm it. For flavor, garlic is indispensable. It's usually grown from cloves, although can be grown from topsets or bulbils. Blenderized garlic may also be used to repel insects.

ASPARAGUS

If you are growing asparagus, pick only spears larger than a pencil in diameter. Leave the thinner roots to grow up to foliage (some will set seeds, too) thus feeding the roots. Be sure to give your asparagus abundant feedings of fertilizer.

BEANS

A familiar insult used to be "you don't know beans." After you read this, you will know beans about beans, guaranteed.

Beans are large plant seeds usually encased in pods, common on trees, shrubs and herbaceous plants. Some are human food, some animal food and others lethal. They're very nutritious and easy to grow.

Prior to Christopher Columbus' people taking New World beans to Europe, the main edible beans in the Old World were fava, also known as haba or horse beans. In Asia soy, mung, lablab, asparagus (yard-long), winged and adzuki beans were grown and consumed, and in the Near East, lentils and chickpeas (garbanzos) were some of the ancient crops planted and harvested by early humans.

Then came the discovery of New World beans. Phaseolus vulgaris is the botanical name for our common beans, P. lunatus the lima bean, P.coccineus the runner bean, and P. acutifoleus var. latifolius the tepary bean of the American Southwest. None of the Phaseolus species cross-pollinate with one another. They are legumes and can take nitrogen from the air and transport it to their roots, enhancing growth. That function is improved by addition of legume inoculants, available at garden centers, applied to seeds when planting.

P. vulgaris flowers are perfect (both male and female reproductive parts) and self-pollinating, so they should not cross, but a persistent bumblebee can force cross-pollination. Since that crossing shows up in seeds, you'll see cross-pollinated beans if you grow different colors or markings in your garden, this year or next year if you save seeds. Don't grow two different types of the same color or shape, if you want to save seeds.

Beans can be red, white, gray, blue, black, brown, purple, pink, yellow, green, spotted, striped, marked like an eye or a soldier, a killer whale, etc. The spot where it was attached to the pod, usually white, is known as the hilum, also known as the "eye" for some beans.

Beans are distinguished first by the way they grow, second how they're used, third by their appearance or where they come from.

Pole beans climb, and bush beans don't, or at least shouldn't. Many of the latter are "semi-runner," which means they'll lop long tendrils and take over a bed you don't want them to. Pole, bush and semi-runner beans are annuals. True runner beans also climb, and they're perennials if they survive the chill of winter.

P. vulgaris beans, even the "fall" or "October" beans grown in the South, are tender to frost. Most of those are pole beans, some with such tough pods they're only good for "shelly" beans (mature shelled beans, cooked fresh). I've had the best harvest from pole beans here by pre-germinating them indoors and transplanting out after the soil has warmed.

Bean seeds do need warm soil for germination, preferably about 70 degrees.

Another distinction is how specific beans are best used: Eat pod and beans (snap or string beans) or just fresh-hulled beans (shelly) or dry the beans before use. Beans can be used any of the three ways, but some are better as snap than dry, others better shelly than snap or dry, etc. Bean pods dehydrated on thread or string are called "leather britches" beans for their texture and toughness; it takes several hours of cooking to reconstitute them.

There are butter beans, rice beans, cranberry beans or horticultural beans, popping beans, tepary beans, soup beans, fall or October beans, string beans and stringless beans, wax beans, skinny beans (haricots) and fat beans (Romanos and some pole beans), etc.

All snap beans formerly were "string beans," but the strings of most have been selectively bred to be insignificant now. A few ancient varieties may still have stout strings.

The usual "popping bean" is the Nuna, from the Andes. That bean (P. vulgaris) only flowers and fruits on short days, wintertime for us, when frost will kill the vine. Author Carol Deppe has bred some garbanzos to serve as popping beans that we can grow.

Boston is known as "beantown" because Boston baked beans became popular there in Colonial times. Sabbath restrictions forbade all work on Sunday, so Sunday meals were cooked or prepared on Saturday night. Beans, molasses, maple syrup and salt pork put in a pot and baked at a low temperature all night made hot meals ready for Sunday.

Since the Columbian dispersal worldwide of the common beans, some are known in France as flageolets (tiny, pale green to white beans, pods inedible), haricots (also small white beans, primarily for baking), mangetout ("eat-'em-all," immature beans), beurre (yellow snap or wax beans) and pencil pod.

Italians use Borlotto dried (cranberry type of beans, mainly red-streaked), and large white cannellini beans, and pods such as Romano (broad pods, excellent as snap beans), and anellino (curved pods). Folks intending to cook broad bean pods often slice them into long thin strips, called "Frenching them." Or you could grow the slender French beans called "Haricot Verts."

"Wax" beans are just yellow-podded beans, not waxy.

Beans in the American Southeast get more complicated. Beans popular there may be identified as "cut short," "greasy," "cut short greasy," "peanut," "cornfield" or "caseknife."

"Cut short" beans are so crowded in their pods that the beans are more square than kidney-shaped. "Greasy" beans are so named because their pods lack the fine fuzz of regular snap beans, so their pods look shiny, wet or greasy. Reportedly, they have a fine flavor and are sold for premium prices.

"Peanut" beans look like Spanish peanuts, and are preferred for canning in the Southeast. They're ready for canning when the pods begin to turn pink. (Beans of this type are also referred-to as "pink beans.")

"Cornfield" or "stick" or "trellis" beans are pole beans, often grown in a "three sisters" garden. When corn is 6 inches high, plant pole beans that will climb the cornstalks, then plant winter squash seeds, the leaves of that vine shading out any weeds that dare appear.

"Caseknife" bean pods look like a pocket knife, named for the cutlery manufacturer W.R. Case Co. There are several dried "eye" beans, tiger eye, eye of the goat, etc., all with marks like eyebrows over the hilums. They're quite pretty and tasty. Calypso or yin-yang beans look like fat orcas, Appaloosas are spotted, but none are as pretty as the inedible castor beans, containing deadly ricin.

CABBAGE

Years ago, I read that the sweetest cabbages are those with conical rather than flat tops. I prefer sweet cabbage for slaws and for raw snacks, so I tried searching for the heads with the most conical tops, and they were all sweet enough for my tastes.

The flathead or drumhead cabbages often are much larger than the conical, and are used for sauerkraut, where sweetness doesn't count.

The best cabbage I've ever eaten was Emerald Cross.

One of our biggest problems was that all of the cabbages are ready to harvest at the same time. We can give several to friends and to The Idaho Foodbank warehouse, but then we have no more cabbage for ourselves for the rest of the summer. When I attended a lecture on vegetables by Ed Hume, owner of Ed Hume Seeds in Kent, Wash., I learned there's a simple solution. Hume said if you put one hand on each side of the cabbage still growing in the ground, and firmly twist the head horizontally about one quarter turn, your cabbage will sit there without splitting, waiting for you to harvest it. Splitting precedes blossoming and seed set in cabbages.

Cabbage is a cool weather crop, planted around early April or in mid-July for a fall crop in the Treasure Valley. In France and England, they plant in fall for spring harvest, but their expected low winter temperatures are significantly higher than ours.

The fall crops of any Brassica or cole crop, such as cabbage, cauliflower, broccoli, kale, collards or Brussels sprouts, have fewer insect problems than spring crops. Cool weather may bring out the black cabbage aphids, however.

As for the cabbage worms that infest or feed on the leaves or buds of all of the cole crops, they can be prevented from laying eggs by putting agricultural fleece such as Reemay or Harvest Guard over the plants, or by application of Bt. Some repellents claim effectiveness, too.

Bt is a very safe insecticide since it only affects caterpillars and caterpillar-like "worms," and is effective because it damages their digestive systems. It comes in liquid form or dust (Dipel is a popular brand). It does have to be re-applied after rains. Read the labels carefully, because some Bts are formulated to be effective against mosquito larvae and others against Colorado potato beetle larvae, instead of cabbage loopers and imported cabbage moth larvae.

All cole crops can tolerate light frosts, but hot weather speeds up their march toward flowering and going to seed, a process known as "bolting."

If you leave the root and basal leaves in the ground after cutting off your cabbage head, it will grow new small heads around the perimeter of the core. Presumably, it would not do this if you had twisted the head previously. These small heads, unfortunately, are exceptionally attractive to black cabbage aphids. If you're going to try this, I'd strongly advise using a row cover right after harvesting the main head.

Cabbage that matures in fall can be pulled and hung upside down in a cool place for later use since it can't be left in the ground without danger of damage from hard freezes.

Some seed companies such as Pinetree and Bountiful Gardens offer "cabbage mix" seed packets. If you were to plant all the seeds, you'd get early, mid-season and late, red and green, savoyed and smooth-leaved, little ones, domed ones and pointed ones.

CARDOON

Cardoon is a large gray plant, an ornamental grace in the vegetable garden, but it is edible, too. We plant seeds indoors in late winter and transplant outdoors after danger of frost has passed.

To eat this beautiful plant, tie up the leafstalks into a bunch, thus blanching the interior stalks. They can then be chopped into smaller pieces and cooked in salted water in a nonreactive pot (cuts rubbed with lemon to prevent discoloring) and served with melted butter or any other way you would serve artichokes. Cardoon leaves are said to taste like artichokes and have been a favorite on the European continent since ancient times.

In Ireland as in this country, folks growing cardoon have waited until September to tie up and blanch cardoon leaves. This is a large plant with spiny leaves, so it is daunting to consider tying it up. Most of us settle for growing it as an ornamental accent to our gardens.

My friend Kathryn Marsh, who lives near Dublin, said an Israeli gentleman laughed at her account of not using cardoon, and said in his country, folks use it young, with younger seedlings ready to replace those that have been harvested.

By last September, my cardoon had leaves that arched 4 feet, obstructing a path next to its bed. It would have taken more than two of us to have tackled that for blanching, so we didn't even try. This year, I'll try harvesting young leaves.

A cardoon perennialized in a North End garden a few years ago, although they die in winter in my more exposed garden.

CARROTS

You've probably seen the Purple Haze carrot seed on the racks. A friend has raved about their excellent flavor, so I decided to grow them myself. Purple is an original color of carrots (they're orange inside the skin, though). They were allegedly bred to be orange on the outside, too, to honor the Netherlands' House of Orange in the 16th century. Many all-orange carrots have a trace of their original purple near the stem end.

Today, carrots come in many colors. Yellow carrots have been linked with good eye health; red ones allegedly guard against heart disease and some cancers; purple carrots are powerful antioxidants. There are, of course, also orange and white carrots.

CAULIFLOWER

I've had major problems trying to grow cauliflower over the years. Usually a button would form, but the "curd," the white edible part, would not grow.

The late Ross Hadfield, an advanced master gardener, recommended planting seeds in a cold frame in February and getting an extra early start.

If the plants are started later, weather is too warm for the cauliflower to grow properly. He indicated the curd blossoms quickly, necessitating the gardener's pulling the plant's large leaves over the curd and tying them so the curd is not exposed to direct sun and to keep it white.

CELERIAC

Another unusual item you've seen in the grocery store is celeriac, or root celery. This is pretty easy to grow at home, starting seeds indoors in February or March, and then transplanting outdoors after danger of frost is past. Celeriac bulbs are gnarly in appearance, but easily peeled and diced for cooking as an unusual vegetable. Celeriac apparently requires less water than celery. Daily soaker hose watering of celery in my garden still resulted in hollow stalks, indicative of a lack of water. Celeriac roots, though, were solid, even though watered less often.

CHICORIES

Have you seen those expensive small whitish hearts of something leafy in the produce department of the grocery store?

Grocers usually call them Belgian endive, but they're really forced re-growth of chicory, a salad plant in the same family as endive. And the reason they're expensive is that they take a little extra labor to force and harvest. I planted Witloof chicory for the first time. There are other forcing chicories but this variety is common and available from several seed companies. The plants resembled large loose-leaf lettuce plants, requiring no care except regular watering after they'd been thinned to 6 inches apart. If slugs invaded, we ignored them. These leafy greens were not what we were after.

When the night temperatures dropped, we had too many other chores to handle, so we covered the chicory plants with plastic bags of leaves. A few weeks later, friends helped me dig up, pot and share several roots. We stored the pots (after watering) in our basements, topped with large upended pots to exclude light. We had cut off the greens about an inch above the tops of the roots before potting.

The purpose of regrowing without light is to obtain blanched hearts of leaves, free of the slight bitterness usually typical of chicory. The forced hearts, called chicons, were ready for harvest in about three weeks.

Roots resembled large parsnips, several already sporting a halo of emerging chicons around each root. Since the leafbag-covered plants had already started growing new tender chicons, we cut off the old foliage, and upended pots over the remaining roots in the ground, then covered pots and all with the bags of leaves. When cutting off old foliage, take care not to cut into the brown root cap or growth point at the top.

Another way of forcing chicons is to leave the roots in the ground and, after cutting off the foliage, pile garden soil over the top, using the soil to blanch the chicons as they grow.

Radicchio is just the Italian word for chicory and varieties such as Red Verona and Red Treviso may be forced, yielding lovely pale rose chicons. Red Treviso may be blanched merely by tying leaves together at the top.

These red varieties start life as green plants, turning red in fall and winter.

The botanical name for chicory is Cichorium intybus, Cichorium being derived from an Egyptian word. The European members of this family are called chicories, those that originated in Asia are called endives.

One of our prettiest and most flamboyant wildflowers in this area is another chicory, escaped from cultivation, that graces roadsides with dramatic wands of blue flowers that close up in late afternoon. Settlers planted it for salad greens, using the roasted roots as coffee substitutes. By the time the stems stretch out to flower, leaves are few and tough.

Many people develop a liking for the sharp taste of chicory or endive, and grow varieties used for leafy greens. It's a hardy type of plant, disease-free and insect-free, and can be used for "cut and come again" crops. Fertile soil and adequate moisture will allow some varieties to be harvested every two weeks.

The bitterness of chicory leaves may be eliminated or modified by washing in warm water, shredding, braising or mixing with milder greens in a salad. Chicory is a perennial but gardeners are advised to grow it as an annual for superior salads.

Nichols Garden Nursery sells a variety called Crystal Hat chicory that is a nonforcing variety. Heads are tall and erect, similar to romaine lettuce. The catalog claims washing in lukewarm water removes all traces of bitterness.

Older leaves of chicory are bitter, but you can safely add zest to your salads by planting chicory every two weeks for a continuous harvest of young leaves.

CHILES AND OTHER PEPPERS

Chiles (capsicums) for growing and eating have burgeoned in popularity over the past few years, and are continuing to whet appetites. They may be used to spice food, to be eaten by themselves as a vegetable or eaten in combination with other foods. Very hot ones can be used as an insecticide.

Species of Capsicum include C. annuum (including bell peppers and most other types of chile), although all chiles are perennials grown as annuals in cold winter areas because they're frost tender. Whoever named them C. annuum had never grown them long enough to see the stalks turn woody and perennial.

You can dig and pot them, bring them inside for winter and set them back outside after all danger of frost has passed. By spring they're alive, but usually fragile.

C. chinense is not from China, but these are some of the extra-hot chiles such as habanero, Fatalii, Scotch Bonnet and Datil. C. baccatum tends to grow on very large plants, but the chiles are usually quite small and hot (and few, in my experience). C. frutescens is the species for a few varieties, the best known the Tabasco chile.

C. pubescent, known for its "hairy" leaves, is the species that includes the black-seeded Rocoto or Manzano. Most species of chile grow in Idaho, but the Rocoto has not borne fruit in my garden despite several tries. One expert told me it needs afternoon shade.

"Chile" is the Nahuatl (Aztec) word for these fruits, which many call "peppers," because Christopher Columbus and his men thought they were in the Far East finding spicy peppers. The soup is spelled "chili." All chiles are native to the Americas, but their heat and flavor have been adopted by most cuisines of the world since the 15th century.

The British call them "chillies," many South Americans call them ajis, and many European countries call them pimentos. (Pimientos are a type of mild peppers.)

Chile growing in Idaho

Some chile lovers complain about a lack of pungency in their Idaho-grown peppers. You can increase heat or piquance of a given variety by stressing the growing plants. This can get very tricky, for if you stress the plant by withholding water, the soil dries out, the plant can't take in enough calcium, and that causes the fruits to suffer blossom end rot. Chiles should have 1 inch of water per week.

You can use a mulch of large stones to hold moisture in the plant's soil and increase heat by absorbing daytime heat and releasing it slowly over the cool of the night. Keeping the soil moist allows the plant to take up calcium and avoid blossom end rot. Or you could try a commercial spray for fighting blossom end rot.

That condition and sunscald are the two worst enemies of chiles here.

Bell peppers and European sweet peppers (which tend to be large, tapered and fairly long) have no heat at all. There is a hot bell pepper, called Mexibell, seeds for which are hard to find. The New Mexico chiles such as Big Jim, New Mex 6-4, Sandia, Espanola Improved, Joe E. Parker, etc., are moderately hot, and are all long and tapered. Big Jim is the longest, and a favorite for chiles rellenos.

The Chile Pepper Institute, affiliated with New Mexico State University, has grown chile peppers from stored old seeds from the Fort Collins, Colo., repository, and is now selling Big Jim and NewMex 6-4s as "Heritage" versions, with the heat and flavor they reportedly used to have.

These chiles are not hybrids, but open pollination over the years has modified the heat and flavor of the standard commercial seeds, according to many chile aficionados.

Eaters have been enthusiastic about the improved flavor, and even the thefts of chiles from the edges of the fields attested to the popularity of these rejuvenated chiles. When you grow them, you could save your own seeds once chiles turn red, but unless you can distance Heritage peppers by 500 feet from other peppers, cross-pollination may occur.

Higher in heat are the smaller, heavier-meated jalapenos. Jalapenos have been bred to be earlier, larger (up to about 2 inches long), and supposedly milder (the TAM jalapeno) than the original model.

Most folks roast and peel the New Mexico chiles prior to use or freezing. Those who want them milder remove the seeds, white or pink veins and placenta at the stem end, for that's where the heat (capsaicin) comes from.

Folks don't usually bother roasting and peeling jalapenos, but they may be frozen whole or chopped. Their heat may also be modified by removing the seeds, veins and placenta. Some subject red ripe jalapenos to smoking, after which they're called chipotles.

Following a general rule (of course there are exceptions), "the smaller the chile, the hotter it is." Serrano chiles are smaller and hotter than jalapenos, but they're also too heavy-meated for drying. They may be frozen. When they're smoked, they're usually known as chipotles, too, although some call them japones.

Cayenne chiles are heavy-meated and hot, much used in Indian cuisine. "Ornamental chiles" are edible, but may not be as tasty as named varieties.

Be very cautious about preserving chiles such as in salsa, for they're susceptible to botulism, a deadly disease. Some think botulism could not survive chile heat, but those people are dead wrong. Look for safe recipes for canning salsa at an Extension Office (or visit www.extension.uidaho.edu/youthfamilyhealth.asp).

Usually when folks bite into a too-hot chile, they reach for water or a cold beer. That is an ineffective modifier of heat. Milk, or better yet cream, is more effective. The key is to find an oily remedy. I don't think anything will help if you get into the hottest chiles of the world such as the Bhut Jolokia. Please don't grow them if you have small children.

Janie Lamson owns a major chile plant source in the United States, Cross Country Nursery in Rosemont, N.J. Her nursery has been praised for the vigor of its plants and the excellence of its shipping containers. She and her husband raise thousands of seedlings, planting and transplanting in three separate waves.

I think they start to germinate the first wave of plants about Feb 1. They will ship plants when temperatures are appropriate. Some plants grow too large for containers, so a couple of weeks before they ship them, they prune them back to 3 or 4 inches in height. The plants then put up a second leader and more branches before they're shipped. In doing this, she learned something about growing chiles that I didn't know either: Timely pruning of some varieties greatly increases fruiting.

She said a customer ordered many plants, two of each variety, and cut back one plant and let the other grow unpruned. He harvested nearly twice as many chiles from the plants that had been cut back as those that had not been cut back.

Now she cuts back those she grows for herself and for pod sales. Some plants such as the Vietnamese Prik y Nu and small Thai are small to begin with, so I wouldn't cut them back.

You can find all of the information about their peppers and chiles at www.chileplants.com.

How to put up peppers

If you are new to processing hot peppers, wear rubber gloves while sorting, peeling or chopping them. Most of the heat in capsicums is in their placentas, but there is some in the skin oils, too. Seeds are attached at the placenta, so they absorb some heat and can transmit it, as well.

When you get those oils on your skin and then touch a tender body part such as your eye, you'll instantly regret it.

It also helps to wear a mask to avoid inhaling capsaicin fumes.

To relieve some of the burning, wash your hands or briefly soak with some chlorine bleach in the water or with Tecnu, a poison ivy cleanser available at drugstores. Milk helps relieve the burn, too, just as it does if you've burned your mouth with a hot pepper. Gojo mechanics' hand cleaner also works for accidental exposure.

For hot peppers that are thick-meated, such as jalapenos, the easiest way to preserve them is to freeze them. If you'll want them skinless later, roast them first, cool between moist tea towels, then put into plastic bags, express air, and freeze. They'll peel easily when thawed. Or chop and then freeze them.

Thin-meated peppers may be dried in dehydrators or strung on thick threads to dry. Many varieties grown here dry to sickly pink rather than robust red.

If you're roasting peppers to be peeled, do it as soon as possible after picking. Once those glossy skins begin to wrinkle, they're very tough to peel. Also, immature peppers, those with matte finishes instead of glossy skin, are nearly impossible to peel.

If you grew jalapenos and they developed black areas on the fruits, it won't affect the flavor. Black areas are just areas of sun exposure. If you let the pepper turn red, the black vanishes. Corky areas on the jalapeno also won't affect flavor.

If you dug and brought chile plants inside for the winter, cut back on the foliage to compensate for loss of some roots, and shield from direct sun for a day or two. If the plant drops all of its leaves, water lightly until it releafs.

If you have harvested green chile peppers and strung or set them aside to dry, they will ripen to their terminal color or near that color (red, orange or brown) as they dry.

A fellow on the Chile-Heads mailing list says if you want beautiful thin-skinned dried chiles, freeze them before putting them whole in a dehydrator. The warm dry air puffs out the pods so when dry they have a "fresh pod" shape.

If you wish to save seeds, wait until the chiles have reached their ripe color before harvesting seeds. The seeds should then be identified and set aside to dry. To make sure the seeds are dry enough or stay dry, pour dry milk powder in the bottom of a jar before putting the seed packs inside.

COLLARDS

Collards are a foreign taste experience to most Northerners, and even many Southerners. But home-grown collards are far more delicious than store-bought leaves. Collards are leafy cabbage. Many cooks remove the midrib of a leaf, roll the pliable sides, then thinly slice into strips and saute in garlicky olive oil. Collard plants are large, taking up about 3 to 4 square feet of space, about the same space a cabbage plant requires.

CORN

Since the average last frost occurs about May 10, most gardeners plant corn about the first of May. You should wait until the soil temperature is warm, though, about 60 degrees. Some advise planting only seed corn treated with fungicide (colored blue or pink-purple, usually) at 60 degrees; otherwise, wait for 75 degree soil temperature.

Advanced Master Gardener Ross Hadfield always waited until the soil temperature was 80 degrees before planting corn. He did harvest bounti-ful crops, but if you wait that long, check your variety's days to maturity to determine if you'll get a harvest before Oct. 10, the average first fall frost.

Seed packets suggest prolonging your harvest by planting four rows of the same variety two weeks later, but George W. Crookham, CEO of Crookham Seeds (the Caldwell-based supplier of more than 80 percent of the world's sweet corn seed), says wait until the first planting has three leaves, then plant four more rows.

All corn is wind-pollinated, so your corn rows should be oriented north-south, and to obtain good pollination, plant at least four rows. If you're growing in a gardener-active subdivision or in a community garden, it would be a good idea to meet with others who are growing corn so you all plant the same variety. Corn may cross-pollinate easily, and instead of tender sweet corn, you may harvest tough corn that's not so sweet.

Normal sugary corn (SU) will cross with field, popcorn and sh2 sweet corns; SE (sugary enhanced) corn will cross with field, popcorn and sh2 sweet corns. For best results SE should also be isolated from the SU sweet corn. SH2 shrunken corn will cross with SU, field and popcorn, according to the Crookham website (crookham.com).

After growth starts, if there's a chilly night, corn leaves may develop a blue (anthocyanin) streak. This won't harm the stalk or the harvest.

Pollen develops on the tassel, or male "flower," that forms on top of the stalk. Pollen then is blown onto the silks of the ear, one silk connected to each developing kernel. After pollination, the silk begins to dry and turn brown. In our area, earwigs may eat silks back to the husk, but since the silks have already been pollinated, that won't affect the harvest.

There are times when we have strong winds about the time corn should be ready for harvest. If you've just irrigated or watered corn, it may "lodge," or blow over. To prevent this, some folks hill up soil around the bottom of the stalk, but that treatment is not always successful.

When your corn lodges, not all is lost. You can carefully tip stalks back upright, and if it's a whole row, thread a rope or heavy twine under the fallen stalks and pull to right them, then fasten the rope to posts at both ends of the row.

To guard against earworms getting into your corn, you can either grow a variety that has extra-tight husks or put a drop of mineral oil inside the tip of each ear after the silks have wilted. These larvae are offspring of night-flying moths, and they may grow to an inch or longer, not an appetizing sight.

How do you tell when your corn is ready for harvest? I always watched for ears that appeared cocked away from the stalk, but to make sure, feel the end of the ear. If it's rounded, the corn is ripe; if it's still sharply pointed, it is not ripe.

You can also peel back part of the husk and peek, but that gives entry to critters such as earwigs. If you do peel the husk back and the kernels appear rounded and full, stick a thumbnail into one. If it squirts a milky liquid, the corn is ripe.

CORN SMUT

There are spores of corn smut (Ustilago maydis) in this Valley. Some growers have significant infestations. They first show up as grotesquely malformed and bloated blue-silver kernels or parts of the plant. Although the fungus may show up on any part of the plant, it usually infects the kernels. If you see them like this, harvest them immediately before they turn black and emit a new spate of spores that will infect future corn plantings.

When the kernels are still blue, chop and use them as you'd use any mushroom. In Mexico this condition is known as Huitlacoche, and it's even commercially canned under the name of Maize Mushroom. You may also want to telephone some serious Mexican restaurants (not Taco Bell) and ask if they'd buy your Huitlacoche.

Only one ear in my garden was hit by this fungus, and I did see it in time to cook and taste it. I cooked it with scrambled eggs, where it tasted like a mild-flavored mushroom.

Researchers at the University of Vermont say "sugary enhanced" white corn is more resistant to smut than other varieties of sweet corn. Ohio State University researchers say dent corn (mainly used for animal feed) is more resistant than sweet corn or popcorn, and among sweet corn varieties, the larger, later-maturing varieties usually are more resistant than earlier varieties.

This fungus is also weather dependent, cool spring temperatures being unfavorable for infections. It usually appears during dry hot days, temperatures 78 to 93 degrees. Aztec growers scratched stalks at soil level with a knife, inoculating the stalks with the fungus on purpose.

CORN SALAD

My corn salad plants (aka mache, lamb's lettuce, Vit, Macholong or Verte de Cambrai) drop seeds in May. I'm a firm believer in gardening with nature, rather than trying to fight her. If that's when she wants to seed mache, so will I.

I won't see much in the way of seedlings until after I pull out the spent plants, and probably not much until late summer or fall. By winter it will be a carpet of green again. The Macholong, from Nichols Garden Nursery, has slightly larger or longer leaves than the usual corn salad, but all are delicious.

Leaves are small, but you pull the entire plant (a rosette of about seven leaves), cut off the taproot, wash the rosette and serve. It provides more green sustenance than you'd expect.

GOURDS

Most of us think of gourds as something decorative or useful, not edible. But there are edible varieties available, especially used for Italian cuisine, like the Cucuzzi and Lagenaria. The Lagenaria should be picked when it is less than 12 inches long, and used much like zucchini (as if you needed more).

Cucuzzi should be picked when 6 to 12 inches long. If left to grow, the Cucuzzi can grow to 4 to 6 feet (one source says 10 feet) long. Like decorative gourds, the skin hardens, too tough for indenting by a fingernail.

Another edible gourd, used in Oriental cooking or sometimes in the American South, is a luffa. It's also called Chinese vining okra, vegetable sponge and dishcloth gourd.

The gourd may be harvested when young and used fresh like cucumbers or cooked like okra. They grow about 12 or 15 inches long, 3 inches in diameter and are filled with a network of fiber. When they're large, they can be soaked in water and peeled. The fibrous interior can be used as a bath sponge or kitchen scrubber. These scrubbers are widely available in stores.

There are some edible gourds I have not grown yet: Chinese wax gourd or winter gourd (Benincasa hispada), edible bottle or calabash gourd (Lagenaria siceraria), bitter gourd or bitter melon, also called balsam pear (Momordica charantia).

The latter is used as a laxative at maturity, so you want to be sure of its age when you use it in cooking.

JERUSALEM ARTICHOKES

Jerusalem artichokes, or "sunchokes," are perennial root vegetables that spread, their above-ground parts growing to about 4 feet high with rayed yellow flowers. Roots are crunchy crisp and a little sweet.

JOB'S TEARS

When I received a letter from Mrs. Keith Wood of Caldwell asking about planting Coix lachryma-jobi, or Job's tears, I looked in catalogs for seeds for ornamental plants.

When I finally found seeds for Job's tears, they were not listed under ornamentals, but under grains!

I thought they would be listed under ornamentals, because I remembered when Lindarose Curtis-Bruce and I grew them in the herb garden at the Western Idaho Fair. Seeds were very hard, shaped like fat tears and used for beads.

The Abundant Life Seed Foundation catalog description said the seeds were "also good as a cereal when hulled and boiled."

It is a grassy plant, with leaves to about 2 feet long and jointed stems to about 6 feet. The grains or "tears" are borne on the tassels, and they harden to pearly white, gray or violet beads, about 1/4 inch long.

Descriptions sound like the growing requirements are nearly identical to those of corn. They require at least four rows in a block for pollination, and want warm soil, full sun and adequate water. Seeds may be planted in hills or a block, spaced about 1 foot apart.

J.L. Hudson, Seedsman, also carries these seeds, and he recommends "soaking overnight (before planting) to germinate in three to four weeks."

Abundant Life calculates it will be 105 to 120 days to maturity, and that's somewhat more than our frost-free weather usually is, so I'll start mine indoors and transplant after all danger of frost is past.

"Cornucopia, A Source Book of Edible Plants," says the hulled grains may be parched, cooked like rice or milled into flour, like other grains. In India, the grain is used to brew a beer; in Japan, the parched seeds are used as a tea.

A different variety, Coix lachryma-jobi Ma-Yue produces soft-shelled fruits that are easily threshed and are used for beverages and macrobiotic cuisine. Richters carries seeds for this variety.

Curtis-Bruce said she saw two varieties of Job's tears growing in Thailand that were different from what she'd grown. The Ma-Yuen variety probably is one that she saw.

The Abundant Life catalog reports that monks have used Job's tears for Rosary beads since the 1300s. That's not surprising, since they're hard and have a natural hole at top and bottom. These seeds will shatter and scatter if dried completely on the plant, but you can cut stalks before maturity for use in flower arrangements.

I couldn't resist ordering some black einkorn wheat seeds described on the same page in that catalog. The plant dates back about 10,000 years, and its nonshattering trait was one of the main reasons humans were able to gather and store that grain for food, settling in communities where it grew in abundance. I want to see what it looks like, this lure that prompted humans to quit their nomadic hunting-and-gathering lives.

If you're interested, Abundant Life Seed Foundation can be found at www.abundantlifeseed.org. J.L. Hudson's site is www.jlhudsonseeds.net. Richters' is www.richters.com.

KALE

Kale is easier than lettuce to grow in summer, and you can use tender kale leaves in salads for super nutrition. It lives through the heat of summer as long as it has sufficient water, but when the weather turns cool, then cold, it really thrives. Shake snow off and pick your salad. Kale is packed with vitamins and most varieties are quite pretty. It is more bitter than lettuce when eaten raw, so if you prefer, cook it. It still is full of vitamins and minerals.

Black (Tuscan, dinosaur) kale does not have a mouth-watering appearance, but it is nutritious and an important ingredient in many cooked dishes. Its color (dark gray) and pebbly surface (like dinosaur skin) are not enticing.

I had always grown Tuscan kale to full size, then pulled off the better-looking leaves for harvest. Many of the leaves had fallen prey to slugs, grasshoppers and other leaf chewers.

A better way of growing this crop appears to be growing it more like lettuce. That is, harvest it young, and replace those plants with younger Tuscan kale plants.

Kale is a biennial, flowering and setting seed its second year. A kale plant under my covered bed survived last winter, and flowered largely in every sense this spring.

You can direct-sow kale outdoors, as long as the soil is not too hot, or sow it indoors and transplant out. Transplanting removes the chore of thinning seedlings.

Kale is chewier than lettuce, but it's packed with calcium, magnesium, copper, manganese, iron, potassium, phosphorus, and vitamins B6, A, C and K. Kale contains more than the minimum daily requirement of A, C and K, the latter vital for normal blood clotting, antioxidant activity and bone health, although folks taking an anticoagulant should avoid kale because of its interference with the effect of blood thinners.

This member of the cole family is also a powerhouse when it comes to fiber, and when you cook kale, it lowers cholesterol and binds bile acids in addition to providing vitamins and minerals.

Varieties often favored in this area are Improved Siberian Dwarf, Red Russian, Ragged Jack, Tuscan and Dwarf Blue Curled Scotch. The Red Russian has a flatter leaf, so is more easily cleaned of aphids than the curled kales. The pretty ornamental kales are edible, but far from choice. They're quite bitter, and probably sprayed with pesticides.

KOHLRABI

Kohlrabi plants develop large above-ground bulbs, from which leaves sparsely sprout. Some are pale green, others purple. They have a turnip-like skin that, once removed, leaves a crunchy, crisp white vegetable that's delicious as a raw food. Kohlrabi, especially the purple variety, looks like a spaceship as it grows, so it's great for a kid's garden.

LAND CRESS

If you like the zing that watercress adds to salads, grow a land cress, sometimes called upland cress. It doesn't need the constant water that watercress does.

LETTUCE

According to the late Meridian gardener Ross Hadfield, Thanksgiving is the time to plant your first crop of lettuce seeds. Even with our mild winters, they don't germinate and spring out of the soil immediately. But he had the earliest lettuce crop on the block, and probably the earliest in the Valley.

He didn't cover the seeds, and even if it was a dry winter, he never watered them. They're on their own, mixed with sand and tamped down.

Years ago, the late Idaho Statesman columnist and Master Gardener Don Wootton gave four-inch pots of lettuce seedlings as gifts for master gardeners. Each pot had a number of seedlings of Mantilia lettuce, and I found those transplants lasted all summer. This variety was tender, delicious and slow to bolt (go to seed). Nevertheless, it seems to have disappeared from main commercial sources except for the public seed catalog of Seed Savers Exchange.

Lettuce is a cool-weather crop, and all lettuces grow nicely in cool weather. Those of us who want fresh colorful salads in summer have to watch for lettuce varieties that are said to "tolerate hot weather" or are "slow to bolt." The problem is that lettuce responds to longer days by sending up a blossom stalk. Then leaves turn bitter and are no longer palatable.

Lettuce seeds germinate most readily at temperatures between 42 and 70 degrees. Above 70, germination may fail. For that reason, you should not try to direct seed lettuce in the garden in midsummer, when the soil is warmer than 70. Neither lettuce nor cole crops will germinate in hot soil.

Washing lettuce and similar greens used to be a tedious chore, but since someone invented the lettuce spinner-washer, it's now rather easy. Most housewares departments carry these. I still do shake off each leaf or head as I pick to dislodge resident earwigs, though, before they go through the wash-and-spin cycle.

There are six kinds of lettuce, four of which are important to salad eaters in our area: crisphead, butterhead, looseleaf and cos or romaine. "Stem" lettuce or celtuce is mainly grown for the stalk. A Latin lettuce, the sixth type, is seldom available here.

Crisphead is also called "cabbage" or "iceberg" lettuce, sold in our grocery stores. They're not numerous in seed catalogs available to home gardeners, but who cares? There are so many more colorful, tender and tasty choices available in other kinds of lettuce.

Our grocery stores sell just a small fraction of the types available. Butterheads have soft floppy leaves in a loose head covering a tender creamy center. Bibb or Boston lettuces are examples of butterheads. Thomas Jefferson favored a butterhead called Tennis Ball. One commercial source for Tennis Ball seed is the Seed Savers Exchange catalog for nonmembers (www.seedsavers.org).

When you get to the cos or romaines and looseleaf lettuces, you find a broad palette of colors, patterns and leaf shapes that make salads even more interesting.

When you harvest either looseleaf or cos, you may pull off only the outer leaves for use for several harvests, the center continuing to grow and create more center leaves. Or cut plants of looseleaf lettuce about an inch above soil level. Those that are suitable for cut-and-come-again harvest will grow back, up to three times.

As the season moves closer to summer and hot weather, it's advisable to plant only those lettuces that will be slow to bolt (go to flower and seed). Keep in mind you may plant in pots, windowboxes, hanging pots or any container, as well as in the ground.

Some varieties to consider are Salad Bowl, Buttercrunch, Summertime, Slo-Bolt, Grand Rapids, Merveille Des Quatre Saisons or any lettuce identified in a catalog or on the seed packet as a "summer lettuce" or "slow to bolt." I've found the Romaine Cimarron is fairly slow to bolt.

Blanching romaine lettuce tenderizes and sweetens the outer leaves. You can do this by placing a topless and bottomless milk carton over a dry head (if it's moist, it may rot instead). Keep in mind, though, the greener it is, the more nutritious it is. Cos lettuce was discovered growing wild on a Mediterranean island named Cos. Romans loved it and took some back to Rome, from where its popularity spread. It became known as Roman lettuce, then in France, it was known as romaine, according to "The Fine Art of Salad Gardening" by E. Annie Proulx.

Some seed companies are now putting out lettuce mixtures selected and named for the season they're to be planted, such as Renee's Spring Bouquet and Summer Bouquet of lettuces.

You can easily help lettuce endure our long days and heat by providing some shade. One way is to use something like concrete blocks beside your lettuce, topped with an old screen.

Or you can cut and assemble white PVC pipe into a frame over which you can fasten cheesecloth, agricultural fleece or actual shadecloth. If you keep your framework fairly small, it's simple just to tilt it back while you harvest or weed. Most building supply centers carry shadecloth by the yard.

Some screening materials, such as black shade cloth, absorb heat and hold it. Aluminum screening tends to reflect heat, so it's preferable to shade cloth. Lightweight agricultural row cover is used by some, including me. Snow fences are used by some people who don't want to build their own lath structure. Another possibility is the lath lattice that's available from building supply houses.

Or plant lettuce among taller ornamental plants. Lettuces are beautiful and easily complement ornamentals. If you grow anything edible among ornamentals, though, be very sure to never use a systemic insecticide or a fertilizer that contains one. That type of product is taken up by the plant, and circulated to every part of the plant. If you apply it to a nearby ornamental, the toxic substance may migrate to your dinner items via water movement.

You can even grow that dependable old favorite, Black Seeded Simpson, through the summer with the help of shade. Another fine lettuce is Merlot, a rich, dark red that stands out in the green patch as well as being a focal point of a colorful salad. Forellenschuss, or Trout Back, is green with maroon speckles. One of the most popular red lettuces is Red Sails.

Bavarian lettuces withstand summer heat better than most, but there are some lettuces specifically bred to withstand hot weather. One is Jericho, bred in Israel; another is Anuenue (pronounced a-newy-newy), bred in Hawaii. I've not had good germination with Jericho and never grew it to harvest stage. I haven't yet grown Anuenue, but I intend to.

I planted Italienischer lettuce one November, and it germinated, 1/4-inch plants, then sat there in apparent dormancy until weather warmed in March before starting to grow. We started harvesting it near the end of April. As long as you cut it about an inch above the soil line, it will grow again, earning it a designation as one of the "cut-and-come-again" lettuces.

Italienischer is a lovely lettuce, with very large plants whose leaves are crisp and sweet even in summer heat. It's so slow to bolt that my November planting was from the previous summer's Italienischer seeds that ripened in fall. Territorial Seeds sells this wonderful variety, and it would be well suited to growing in containers.

Lettuce does require regular watering or it will turn bitter. Take it easy on your water meter and pocketbook by using drip or soaker hose watering. After the first watering, mulch well to retain the moisture. Use grass clippings if they haven't been treated with broadleaf herbicide.

In the garden, watch for signs of lettuce bolting. If you liked that lettuce, let one plant go to seed then cut the stalk into a large paper bag after most of the flowers have faded. The seed heads can be rubbed free of seeds. Then I'd suggest you clean the seeds as free as possible of chaff, and store them in a freezer, at least for a few weeks, to kill any residual insects.

MELONS

Late summer in the Treasure Valley is time for chins dripping sweet juices. Melons vie with peaches, pears and plums for top honors.

It's very disappointing to harvest any melon after you've coddled it for three months, only to find it isn't ripe. There are various methods to judge ripeness before you pick and cut into any melon, depending on the type.

Boiseans Chris and Mike O'Brien came up with a clever plan. They measured their watermelons around the equator or the largest girth, and kept a graph of the growth. When the growth reached a plateau, they picked the melon and cut into it. It was perfectly ripe. The next melon they tried this with was also perfectly ripe when the measurements leveled out.

The usual instructions are to look for a distinctly yellow belly where the watermelon was resting on the soil, and the tendril nearest the fruit stem in dried condition.

I thump watermelons with a knuckle. If the sound is deep and thick, it should be ripe. If the tone is high, it's probably not ripe.

One thing you could do to all of your melons to protect them from being eaten by sowbugs and/or voles is to slide a shingle or wood scrap under the melon so there's no direct contact with the ground.

Ever since a vole hollowed out an eggplant that hung to the ground, I've been wary of their eating flesh out of a melon, too. A Southern friend's father tried to raise a champion melon, picking all other melons from the vine. When he picked it, it was hollow, and there was a happy turtle inside, licking its lips.

Cantaloupes (muskmelons) are ripe when the skin under the netting is yellow or gold, and the stem parts easily from the fruit. They also smell ripe, and so do honeydews, according to some.

I look for color and texture of the skin on honeydews. They should be ivory to yellowish cream in color and have a matte finish to the skin. When the honeydew is still green, the skin is hard and shiny. When it develops the matte finish, a gentle stroke of the hand finds the skin soft and suede-like.

Charantais melons are ripe when ants invade them. They exude a wonderful aroma when ripe, but you have to get your nose close to detect it. They do not "pick themselves" like muskmelons when ripe, so keep checking.

If you ordered seeds from a seller of unusual seeds, you may have planted a Queen Anne's pocket melon, also called Plum Granny. These melons are very aromatic, and were grown to be carried by ladies in a pocket to mask body odors or set in a room to perfume the room. They were not intended to be edible, but some catalogs don't tell you that.

They are not toxic, but they are not choice edibles, either. Yuk.

Good muskmelons for our area are Charantais, Saticoy, Early Chaca and Savor F1. Burpee's Ambrosia has produced very well for us. Even when you pick any muskmelon ripe, you may get an indifferently-flavored melon. It may be weather-related, but nobody knows for sure.

OKRA

When I grew okra in this soil years ago, the plants grew into shrubs about 4 feet tall. Pods required picking every day, or they'd grow too long and get tough. Okra plants, by the way, produce lovely hibiscus-like blossoms. Tiny prickles on the pods necessitate wearing gloves while picking.

ORACH

An unusual summer green is orach (pronounced "oh-rock"). It sounds like a scary movie monster, but it's a very attractive, nutritious, easy-to-grow leafy vegetable. If you permit, it will go to seed, and you may have a lifetime of food ahead of you if you let some of the seedlings go unhoed.

A friend gave me orach seeds, and we were very impressed. Our garden was a carpet of tender green orach by March, when we tilled most of it under. Although seeds do scatter, the seedlings are easily removed.

The plant is pretty, growing to about 5 feet tall, with drooping soft leaves larger than a saucer. This variety is gray-green, giving some color contrast in the garden, as well as pleasant variance in height.

Veins are tough when the plant is large, but it's easy to tear the soft tissue from the veins when you wash the leaves. There is a spinach-like flavor in the leaves, so you may want to use this green in combination with blander greens in salads, or use it cooked, like spinach.

My friend who gave me the seeds also dries the leaves, crumbing them into hearty winter soups for added nutrition.

PARSNIPS

One of the spectacular surprises possible in a vegetable garden is the blooming of parsnips. They're biennial, so they bloom in their second year and go to seed. Plants shoot up to 5 or 6 feet tall, covered with cascading blooms and attracting all kinds of pollinating insects.

PEAS

If your soil is not well warmed, it's a good idea to presprout your peas. You can lay them out so they're not touching one another on a warm and damp paper towel. Roll up the towel, then set the roll on end in a jar. Peas may sprout in two or three days, so check them daily after two days. Make sure the towel remains damp.

Once the peas sprout, remove them and immediately drop them into pre-spaced holes in your garden. It won't make any difference if they're right-side up.

You don't have to wait for the pods to form — pea shoots are prized in Asia steamed, raw in salads and stir-fried. Use them in soups, cooked with chicken, pork or sausages. They're versatile and renewing.

Some Asians squeeze lime or lemon juice over the sprouts and eat them raw. If tendrils are old, they'll be too tough for raw food and should be cooked.

Harvest shoots at between 2 and 4 inches in length. You can grow them in a seed tray. Sprout them in the dark and then move them into sunlight for greening up and harvesting; or sow them in the ground closely together in clumps. Or you can plant them like normal garden peas, removing shoots as they appear. Removing shoots will send growth hormones down the stems and stimulate the growth of more and more side shoots.

If you have other peas whose pods you're going to harvest, remove blossoms as they form on your shoot supply peas and continue harvesting shoots. You can use either podded peas or edible podded peas (snow or sugar snaps) for the shoot harvest.

PIRACICABA

Piracicaba is probably a cross between broccoli and broccoli raab, but it shrugs off searing temperatures such as we have some summers. Broccoli and broccoli raab both surrender to hot weather, racing to blossom, set seed and die. Piracicaba seems to take no notice of heat.

It grows to about 14 inches tall, has several stalks, each topped by a small head of about 1 to 2 inches across of large dark green buds. If there are larvae among the loose buds, they'd be easily seen. You can snap off the heads when young, or cut them when older, but be careful not to cut into the area between a leaf and the stalk, because another head will form there. It has no large broccoli-like head.

This vegetable was conventionally bred by Brazilian scientists, and it was named for a river that flows in the vicinity of its development. Conventionally bred means it was not genetically manipulated as so many new plant materials are. As of now, the only seed sources in the United States appear to be Fedco, in Maine, and Nichols Garden Nursery.

POTATOES

If you intend to plant potatoes, you should plant them around the end of March. There are lots of ways to do it, and whatever works is the right way.

The way I plant potatoes is in a trench, shovel deep, with organic fertilizer spread lightly along the bottom, then topped with soil so the fertilizer doesn't touch the seed potato.

If you're growing potatoes such as Yukon Gold, you may have to use the whole potato for the "seed," since they have so few eyes (which will sprout).

Please don't make the mistake I made a few years ago, and flesh out your row with grocery store potatoes. They had been treated with a chemical to prevent sprouting, so they sat underground all season, trying to sprout but never making it.

Get your extra potatoes from the seed store.

You should have only about two eyes per chunk, attached to about 2 cubic inches of potato, to feed the sprouts and give them a good start. Some mail order places sell eyes scooped out by melon ballers, and I understand they create more disappointment than they do edible spuds.

Adding some Canadian peat moss to the planting hole or trench helps to prevent scab, according to some, but a Simplot Co. handbook blames low soil moisture at planting time for that disease.

Lindarose Curtis-Bruce, advanced master gardener and horticultural designer, says she plants beans around her potatoes, and never has Colorado potato beetle infestations.

In recent years, experts have started to say you don't need to rotate potatoes or tomatoes. A friend in Ireland, home of the potato famine (that was caused by late blight), grows his potatoes in the same field year after year. He doesn't worry about late blight (Phytophthora infestans), even though his cool, damp weather favors the disease. He doesn't spray, but instead relies on genetic diversity for disease resistance, each year growing at least some of his plants from true potato seeds.

Potato seed is free from all but one disease, that of Spindle Tuber. My friend says seed produces fresh, vigorous plants. Potato seed is borne in seed balls that resemble small cherry tomatoes, after flowering. I've seen ads from some merchandisers offering you the opportunity to grow potatoes and tomatoes from the same plant. I wouldn't advise anyone to eat these "tomatoes," but to harvest them about a month or two after they form, when they are still green and soft; cut them in half and squeeze their seeds into a small container.

Add some water and let them ferment for two or three days.

My friend just lets the seed pods sit and age in the greenhouse until he decides to harvest the tiny potato seeds. Once they're aged, they don't need fermentation to destroy germination inhibitors.

If you do ferment seeds, they should be washed in a sieve and set aside to dry. Store seeds in a cool, dry environment. The good seeds sink; the poor seeds float.

The good seeds, grown out, form small tubers which can be transplanted for the next season's crop, producing vigorous potato plants bearing tubers that may not resemble the original potato seed parent, but they should be disease-free.

PUMPKINS AND WINTER SQUASH

Pumpkins are pretty much ruined by being cut into jack-o'-lanterns and left standing out on the porch for a number of days. Candles also spoil them. But pumpkins are squash and may be used in bread, stew, soup and the ever-popular pies. In Mexico, cooks even make delicious candy out of pumpkin squares.

Keep in mind that there are many types of pumpkins, some more suitable in taste and color than others. Seed catalogs specify that some types are especially suited to pie-making.

In Argentina, cooks serve a spectacular-looking stew in a pumpkin bowl. It's called Carbonada Criolla in the "Foods of the World — Latin America" cookbook.

Not only is the flesh used, but many people also harvest the seeds for snacks. Wash seeds as clean as possible of the stringy fibers, drizzle with olive oil, sprinkle with salt and/or garlic powder if desired, put in a 300-degree oven for 30 minutes, stir and turn them over and bake another 30 minutes. They're tasty and nutritious, eaten like sunflower seeds.

Some people run unsalted baked pumpkin seeds through the food processor to combine with suet for nutritious bird treats during the winter.

If you find you like pumpkin seeds, look for the "naked" hull-less seed pumpkins. Abundant Life Seed Foundation calls this variety Lady Godiva. J.L. Hudson's catalog calls them Styrian hull-less. This may be a different variety, but it has the same type of seeds. Some people snack on these or grind them into a cracker spread, either before or after baking. The flesh is firm and usable, too.

Undamaged and unfrosted pumpkins ought to keep as well as winter squash in storage, or slices may be dried for later use. Some people bake large squares of pumpkin, peel the rind and run the squares through the food processor for freezing in pie or bread baking amounts.

Keep a close eye on your squash and pumpkins in September and early October. When their color has changed from immature shiny green or mottled to the matte color they are supposed to be when mature, try pushing your thumbnail through the skin. If you can, it will heal. If you can't, the squash/pumpkin is ripe and may be picked.

Use secateurs (pruners) to cut the stem, leaving as much stem with each squash/pumpkin as you can. If the stem is broken off, the squash/pumpkin will not keep as well as those with stem intact. Large Hubbard squashes do not need the stems left intact.

Indoors, wash off the squash/pumpkin and dry it thoroughly. Some folks use a chlorine bleach solution — one part bleach to nine parts water — to kill any disease organisms on the skin. I've used plain water and had no problems. As with other harvested foods, be gentle and avoid bruising.

Storage of pumpkins is not difficult. They do not need or survive cool conditions. Just store them in the house in an unused closet, on a shelf unit in a hobby room or your pantry.

Not all squashes or pumpkins mature at the same time.

If you're growing pumpkins for jack-o'-lanterns, don't try to use them for pies. If you want pumpkin pie, use a winter squash such as butternut in place of the pumpkin, which, after all, is closely related to squash. Some varieties of pumpkin are great for pies, but not the jack-o'-lantern varieties.

RHUBARB

Rhubarb, or pie plant, is up and ready to be fertilized with manure or compost by mid-March, generally. The plant is a greedy one, liking lots of that kind of food. Most authorities advise fertilizing in the summer or fall, but it's tough to get near roots at those times, due to the huge leaves holding you at bay, so I fertilize in spring.

It also needs water in the early spring. If you want your yummy spring "tonic" early, invert a box or a bushel basket over your rhubarb plant (water it first), to make the stems reach for the light. The color may be somewhat blanched, but stems will be tart and tender.

Bake some with sugar and a little water, then freeze it for a winter pick-me-up, if you have a large crop. Be careful not to over-pick, removing all the stalks from one part of the plant. Pick by pulling and twisting stalks from different parts of the plant and different plants. Do not cut them. Only the stalks are edible. Discard the leaves or try this: Boil them in water (1 pound of leaves to 1 quart of water) for 30 minutes; strain the water and use it as an insecticide against aphids and similar pests. As usual, use rainwater or distilled water instead of alkaline or chemically softened water. Wash utensils thoroughly for later use.

SPINACH

Many people in the Treasure Valley sow their spinach in September so it can begin growth, and when early spring begins to warm a bit, it resumes growth for an early crop to harvest. Spinach grows best in cool weather and shrugs off light frosts.

Spinach is succulent and tender in early spring, and mostly free of insects. It tastes great raw in salads and is packed with more nutrition than the cartoon character Popeye ever imagined. When summer's heat arrives, leaves grow tough and bitter. Then the plant flowers and goes to seed.

If you didn't plant your spinach in September, plant it as early as you can get into your garden, even if you have to walk on boards to avoid compacting the soil. Birds are eager to take a green break, too, and they'll nip off great chunks of leaves unless you cover the spinach with floating row cover or fencing.

Crinkled leaves are said to be "savoyed" and are typical of spinach. Some varieties have smoother leaves, though. They're easier to wash. All spinach should be harvested a leaf at a time from the outside, leaving the crown to grow.

SUMMER SQUASH

Male squash blossoms, formed on thin stalks, come out first in the season, in some varieties, and about a week later, female blossoms (those with tiny squashes just behind the flower) appear. Female blossoms open first on other varieties. It has seemed to me they can be open on different days, which definitely won't aid in pollination.

If you're as impatient as I, you can harvest those tiny squashes and sauté or grill them, blossoms and all (peek inside and make sure there isn't an insect inside first). They're so tasty you'd pay premium prices at farmers' markets for such baby squashes.

If your summer squash gets to a certain size, then rots, it's because the blossom hasn't been pollinated sufficiently to form all of the seeds.

To hand pollinate, select a male flower and a female flower the evening before they open for the first time. Use masking tape to tape them both shut so they don't open before you get there.

The next morning, remove the tape from the male flower and remove its petals. Taking care not to waste the pollen (you can hold the stem in your mouth), untape the female flower carefully. The petals will open in slow motion. Then, holding the petal-less male flower by its stem like a brush, swab it over each of the sections of the stigma of the female flower. Then tape the female flower shut again to prevent cross-pollination.

See the pumpkins entry for more details about when to harvest squash.

SWEET POTATOES

We can grow sweet potatoes in Boise; our major problem lies in the postharvest curing. They're supposed to be cured in conditions of high temperature (85 degrees) and high humidity. Since we dig sweet potatoes in October or rarely in November, our temperatures are much lower than that, and we don't have (or want) high humidity. Garnette Edwards' grandfather, founder of Edwards Greenhouse, had a special building dedicated to curing sweet potatoes he had grown in Boise, earning himself the title, the "sweet potato king" of Boise. He used wood-burning stoves and we think kettles of water on them to produce humidity.

If you grow sweet potatoes, do the best you can to emulate those hot and humid conditions.

To start, either buy sweet potatoes from a grocery store and start your own slips (sprouts) or order slips from local sources or mail order. The late Advanced Master Gardener Ross Hadfield started slips from sweet potatoes he put on his hot fireplace hearth until the slips appeared, then he moved them onto his covered porch.

He pulled slips (sometimes with roots, sometimes without) off the sweet potatoes, and planted them in potting soil, then set them out with Walls o' Water protection before the average last date of frost. Slips grow as easily as succulents, so if your slips are long, you can double your supply by cutting them in half.

You could also start them by laying the sweet potato on top of your water heater, refrigerator or other warm spot in your house, starting about February. Verify with the produce manager of your store that the sweet potatoes haven't been sprayed to prevent sprouting. Edwards Greenhouse usually sells sweet potato slips.

They grow better in sandy soil than in clay, so plan ahead, and if you have clay, work a lot of sand into the site. If you're tilling 6 inches deep, plan on adding sand to a 2-inch depth. If you use less, you risk creating adobe.

Build your soil into hills 3 or 4 inches higher than the rest of the garden, and transplant out after danger of frost has passed (or with excellent frost protection).

Side-dress with a fertilizer with readings close to 6-24-24 about two weeks after setting them out and again about a month later.

Hadfield set his sweet potatoes in the middle of X-s cut in black plastic. The plastic would be hot, but weed-free. Had he used clear plastic, it would have transmitted heat to the soil, but weeds would have grown there, too. He watered sweet potatoes with irrigation water, and the year he broke Ross Root Feeder capsules in half and let the halves dissolve in the irrigation water on two separate occasions, he harvested 175 pounds of sweet potatoes from seven hills. One weighed 23 pounds, 12 ounces.

Watch to make sure the joints of the vine don't root. If they do, it will reduce your yield.

Beware of frost in September, for in this month, sweet potatoes double their yield every two weeks from the first to the last of the month. After that, the yield increases more slowly. When frost is forecast as imminent, cover or cut the vines back to the hills and dig carefully. Unlike regular potatoes, sweet potatoes grow vertically in a clump where the main plant was situated. They're easily damaged by rough handling, so be careful.

Brush off soil and move them into a warm or hot environment. Don't be tempted to eat them right away, for they need time and curing to convert their starches to sugar.

SWISS CHARD

Swiss chard is a wonderful spinach substitute, grown in many of our gardens because it provides greens that don't turn bitter and bolt to seed in the heat of the summer. Chard is a type of beet that has been bred for its greens rather than its roots.

One import from Australia, where they call it Silverbeet chard, has green leaves but the midribs are varying strong colors, including red, pink, orange, gold and white. The vivid colors are outstanding in a vegetable garden, and they hold their color through cooking.

After I gave my pink and orange chards to a friend, we tilled under the other colors because I had transplanted seedlings of all of the colors into a raised winter garden bed.

TOMATILLOS

There is some controversy over tomatillos (Physalis ixocarpa): Some say the plant is self-fertile; others say it is self-sterile. I agree with the self-sterile faction, and recommend gardeners plant at least two plants, for planting one alone doesn't yield any fruit.

If you are growing the husk-covered green fruit used in Mexican green sauces and green chili, check the progress of the fruit by pinching the husks. When the husk begins to fill out, watch the bottom. Harvest the fruit when it changes from dark green to light green, remove the husks and rinse off the stickiness.

There isn't enough of a core to bother with. You can halve the fruits, simmer them in water until soft, then put them in a food processor and blend, if desired. I then freeze them in containers without further treatment.

If you wait for tomatillos to "ripen," they drop to the ground, are colored yellow, and the bottom is usually split and infested with dirt or earwig eggs. They're then too sweet to use in sauces.

TOMATOES

There are huge differences in varieties of tomato. Some are thick-skinned and have firm flesh, good for shipping. Others are delicate and thin-skinned. Some are prone to disease, others resistant. Some are sweet, others acidic. Some bear prolifically, others bear few fruits.

Select your variety carefully, because you can't change midsummer. I grow open-pollinated plants, many of them heirloom varieties. They don't claim to be disease-resistant, but they are, or else people wouldn't have saved the seeds over so many seasons.

Hybrid varieties have been tested by universities for disease-resistance, and the label on the tag or the seed pack will tell you what diseases that variety has resistance to. You'll see VFNT, for instance, indicating resistance to Verticillium and Fusarium wilts, nematodes and tobacco mosaic. Resistance to does not mean disease-proof.

Hybrid tomatoes, if the weather cooperates, may bear very heavily, underscoring the phenomenon known as "hybrid vigor."

Some open-pollinated tomatoes, while tasting great, have known failings. Super Sioux, one of the most popular in this area 30 years ago, usually developed concentric skin cracking around the stem end of the tomato.

Some heirloom varieties are prone to "catfacing," (fruit irregularities such as puckering) usually on the fruit's bottom. This happens when pollination occurs during cool weather. Subsequent fruits on that plant may be perfect.

Some tomato varieties are more susceptible than others to blossom end rot, a condition in which the tomato seems to be ripening quickly, but the bottom of the tomato is brown, papery and flat. This shows a calcium deficiency usually brought about by soil that's too dry or too wet to transmit sufficient calcium to the plant.

If you find this, water more often or less often to change the soil's moisture content, and, just in case, add crushed eggshell to the area of affected plants.

Dr. Carolyn Male, author of "100 Heirloom Tomatoes for the American Garden" and introducer of many heirloom varieties to American palates, maintains that early varieties of tomatoes are less flavorful than later-ripening varieties. Some early tomatoes are tasty, but generally the later tomatoes taste better to me. Taste, of course, is subjective, and what tastes delicious to one person may be repugnant to another.

Our soil is lacking in magnesium, and that deficiency can keep tomato plants from thriving and producing as they should. You can easily remedy that deficiency and may even get a larger harvest of tomatoes by watering with Epsom salts diluted in water. For tomatoes I use two tablespoons per gallon of water, and try to water with this mixture as soon as possible after transplanting. Magnesium is a minor element that is critical in the formation of chlorophyll and is useful in the absorption of phosphorus, which contributes to growth, flowering, fruit formation and disease resistance.

See the section on hardening off on page 46 to know just when and how to transplant tomatoes in the spring.

Which tomatoes work best here?

With only a couple of exceptions, I've grown only open-pollinated tomatoes for the past 20 years. They're soft when ripe and have thin, tender skins.

Tomatoes, both open-pollinated and hybrid, are distinguished by fruit size, shape, time to maturity, leaf style and plant size. Most tomatoes can be used for any purpose, large paste tomatoes for slicers, for example. Some are "plum" tomatoes (they're especially prone to blossom end rot); large oval ones are "slicers"; others are oxheart (large, roughly heart-shaped); some are paste (they have fewer seeds than slicers, may be any shape, including sausage-shaped); "stuffers" are bell pepper-shaped and mostly hollow, and some are salad tomatoes (larger than cherry tomatoes).

Oxheart tomatoes in our climate tend to develop deep cracks radiating from the stem end, and some slicers develop concentric cracks around the stem.

There also are "peach" tomatoes that have peach-like fuzz on the fruit, currant tomatoes (the size of currants), and spoon tomatoes, even smaller.

Tomatoes are self-pollinating, but it helps to jostle the plant when blossoms are open. Bees sonicate (buzz) a blossom, gently shaking pollen inside the blossom onto the style, creating a fruit.

Vines may be determinate (generally short, tomatoes supposedly all ripening at once), or indeterminate (vines grow tall, tomatoes ripen throughout the season). Patio tomatoes are small, suitable for container growth, but fruit also is small. Leaves of some tomatoes are potato leaf-like, others are regular.

Package labels specify days to harvest, counting from the date you transplant outdoors. "Early" tomatoes are usually anything under 75 days, "late" are 90 days and up. Earliest tomatoes are ready about 55 days after transplant.

Tomatoes I especially like for this area are Lollipop and Gardener's Delight for cherry tomatoes. Lollipop is a sweet yellow tomato with a slightly salty kick, available from Southern Exposure Seed Exchange. Even my late garden "helper," Tathers the terrier, picked and ate Lollipop tomatoes. Gardener's Delight, widely available, is a sweet red tomato, perfect for shish kebabs and salads.

If you have small children, a great tomato to grow is Yellow Pear. It's very productive, can be popped into the mouth whole and eaten in the garden. It's low acid and hasn't much tomato flavor, frankly.

The stuffer tomatoes look like bell peppers, and when you cut into one you find all of the seeds are clustered just below the stem, the rest of the fruit hollow (good for stuffing, then eating out of hand).

In this area I've had best productivity from Tiffen Mennonite (dark pink, slicers), Prudens Purple (dark pink, oval slicer), Santa Clara Canner (very large, perfect, red), Opalka (paste) and Druzba (tennis ball-sized, perfect, red).

The best flavored tomato I've grown is Black Krim (interior is brick red, exterior is dark brownish black). The newly popular "black" tomatoes color when they ripen, the green color remaining as red merges with the green.

Starting your own from seed is always fun, but if you can't, you can find open-pollinated tomato plants at Edwards Greenhouse and other locations.

Keep in mind, too, that some tomatoes are bred specifically for certain areas. San Francisco Fog, for example, is bred to set fruit in cool, humid conditions. Ace was bred for the inland valley of California. If you try to grow those kinds of tomatoes in a different climate, they may not produce well.

Save your tomato seeds

If you grow nonhybrid tomatoes that you like, save the seeds so you can grow the same kind next year.

The gel surrounding tomato seeds is a germination inhibitor, so for the seeds to be viable, you need to destroy the gel. The easiest way to do this is to scoop out or squeeze seeds into a container such as a cottage cheese carton, yogurt cup, etc., add a little water, and set the container aside to ferment for four or five days.

Then skim off mold, if any, and pour the fermented seeds into a sieve and rinse under the faucet. Dump the cleaned seeds onto a plastic or pottery/china plate, label with the variety name, and set to dry someplace where mice won't get at them (and where you won't accidentally discard them).

Some folks dump onto paper plates or paper towels, but wet seeds will stick to paper and you may have to plant paper with the seed.

ZUCCHINI

Pick zucchini or other summer squash when they are small, slice thinly, add a couple of thin slices of onion, and freeze in a plastic bag, air removed. You do get hungry for zucchini in late winter.

CHAPTER 3

Herbs

THE BASICS

Getting started with herbs

If you don't have a culinary herb garden, you should. It's fun to transform bland foods into taste sensations, and that's easy when you have your own herbs to snip.

Start out with basic cooking herbs, either planting them in the ground or in containers, if your space is limited. Thyme, rosemary, French tarragon, basil, mint, chives and parsley are good herbs to start with.

All of these except rosemary and basil are winter hardy here. Basil, or sweet basil, is the only one of the above list which is an annual. Thyme and parsley are hardy, and even can be harvested from beneath snow. Parsley is a biennial and will die its second year, after reseeding itself.

The two keys to maintaining a neat herb garden are:

1. Removing blossoms before seeds set.

2. Planting spreading herbs in large bottomless pots. Some gardeners sink the pots down to soil level, and remember to turn the pots once a week so invasive roots can't take hold.

Some herbs spread like crazy, invading other beds. Were I you, I would not plant lemon balm, common oregano (Origanum vulgare), marjoram or mint, unless you can definitely keep the latter two confined. Lemon balm may be impossible to confine, seeding itself promiscuously.

Culinary oregano and marjoram available to gardeners are not nearly as good as the dried versions. That plus their invasive nature argue against planting them.

To get an idea of the aroma and flavor of a culinary herb, stroke the plant lightly, then smell your hand.

Another way to familiarize yourself with the flavor of a herb is by mixing a small amount of chopped leaves in soft butter or margarine, and letting the flavor permeate for half an hour or so before tasting.

Start with small amounts and add more later. If using a recipe calling for dried herbs, double the amount for fresh herbs.

The delight of herbs

Most Treasure Valley soil is just right for growing most herbs, if it's not too sandy. Seeds fall on the soil, and the next thing you know, you have extra plants. A few herbs, such as goldenseal and ginseng, require more acid soil and are difficult to grow here.

I had seven herb beds, one exclusively devoted to culinary herbs. Grass thrust roots under a mowing strip built to exclude grass, so I have a lot of that to dig out, while protecting some overgrown thymes and my stand of caraway.

Although most caraway is a biennial, going to seed its second year, I have first-year and second-year volunteers growing side by side, so I have caraway to harvest each year. I store it in the freezer, and have fresh seeds all year.

Oriental garlic chives and sorrel both have spread in the culinary herb bed, but the golden sage plant looks bedraggled, having been overwhelmed by Calendulas. That bed is rather empty, though, awaiting sweet and lemon basils to be planted there.

My culinary sage is several feet distant, on a berm. Several people on the Internet are complaining that their culinary sage lasts only one year. Many of us replace sage every five or six years, when it becomes rangy, but to lose a culinary sage in one year means either it was planted in rich soil or it was watered too much.

Most culinary herbs grow as weeds in poor soil, watered only infrequently — and seldom, if ever, fertilized.

Thyme plants are spreading down a small slope, and soon will be cascading over the edge of a small retaining wall. That's fine with me. I love the appearance, but they should be cut back before they reach bottom.

Comfrey is another self-multiplier that's more of a problem. It has black, brittle roots, small pieces of which form whole plants. Some comfrey is great, but a lot is not.

Pruning, planting and weeding a herb garden is always an aromatic delight, more than worth the bother.

Don't shy away from exotic flavors

Do you grow herbs that flavor exotic cuisines? We can grow many of them in this area, at least through the summer.

Thai basil, for instance, has a different flavor from sweet basil, and the two are not interchangeable. Thai basil has a subtle anise flavor, but its growth requirements are identical to those of sweet basil. Harvested Asian herbs and vegetables are available in Asian markets in this area, but it is fun and convenient to grow them yourself.

Most seed companies carry seeds at least for Thai basil, Bok Choi, green mustards, Asian eggplants, Perilla or shiso, sugar peas, dill, sorrel and Chinese cabbage. Southeast Asians also love and use cilantro as much as Mexican chefs and diners do. Other cuisines use cilantro seed, called coriander.

Nichols Garden Nursery carries more than the usual line of herbs, and Baker Creek Heirloom Seeds carries even more.

Be careful with Baker Creek's seeds, though. Some of their Southeast Asian and Mexican vegetables require a longer growing season than we enjoy. I started pea eggplants (seeds from Baker Creek) one February, transplanted in mid-May, and the plants were just beginning to bloom when we had our first killing frost in October.

Incidentally, those plants evinced their ancient status with thorns on the stalks and leaves, even the undersides of the leaves. The closer to their original form eggplants are, the thornier. We call them "eggplants" because some early varieties were white, egg-sized and egg-shaped. Europeans call them Aubergines, and that's less confusing.

Three seed companies in the U.S. that specialize in Asian seeds are Evergreen Y.H. Enterprises, Kitazawa Seed Co. and New Dimension Seed. Edwards Greenhouse has a rack of New Dimension seeds, so you can buy locally.

Some gardeners may shudder, but a perennial groundcover that many think invasive and difficult to control is considered a food in Southeast Asia. That's Houttynia cordata, called "hootenanny" by some American gardeners. Many local nurseries carry the variegated Houttynia cultivar.

Andrea Nguyen, on her website, www.vietworldkitchen.com, says of H. cordata, "Some folks love [its] tangy qualities and others focus on its unusual fishiness. For this reason, it's not commonly found at the Viet table. I enjoy it with boldly flavored grilled meat."

Some of the more esoteric herbs such as Rau Ram, Rau Om, and La Lot, may be ordered from Richters in Canada. Nguyen has good information on her website on how to grow and use several seldom-seen Vietnamese herbs.

Some foods, such as lemon grass, are easily grown from starts obtained at the Asian markets if they haven't been frozen. Just cut the leaves back so the "grass" will stand upright in soil. These slightly resemble scallions, but they are tropical and not winter hardy here.

Since Southeast Asian cuisines are not heavily dependent on wheat, barley or rye, their foods are acceptable to those with celiac disease or gluten intolerances.

YOUR HERB GARDEN, BY THE SEASONS

Spring

Toward the end of April is the time of year when you regret having let blossoms go to seed in the herb bed. I have sweet cicely, anise hyssop, Calendulas and lemon balm everywhere. And oregano (Origanum vulgare) is trying to take over the world.

In May we may have to keep a weather eye open and cover frost-tender plants some nights, but we should be about free of cold weather threats for the season. This is a great time to supplement your herb garden with annual herbs.

Although most culinary herbs are perennials, many very interesting and useful ones are annuals or perennials too tender to survive our winters, so they are grown as annuals.

Herbs don't require rich soils or lavish nutrients. They do better on poor soils in super-hot weather, building up their flavorful oils in those conditions. Most of our culinary herbs, in fact, originated as weeds on wind-scoured hills in Greece, Italy and other Mediterranean countries.

Summer

The end of June means it's time to reap benefits from herb gardens. Early summer is a good time to start harvesting some herbs. Cut off French tarragon about 8 inches down each stem, pinch off a few inches of thyme, cut oregano before it flowers, snip off some leaves from lovage and culinary sage or cut several stems of parsley. You may also want to dry mint leaves (they're easier to remove if you dry the whole stem, then strip them off) for winter teas.

Harvest as much as your drying space will allow. If you have a dehydrator, it's more economical to run if it's full. If you don't, tack together some 1-by-2-inch boards into square frames, stretch some nylon net or cheesecloth across the squares, and tack it into place. Nylon net is inexpensive at fabric stores, and you may be able to find remnants.

Wash insects off, then lay cut herbs on frames and cover loosely with nylon net or cheesecloth. You can dry directly on a clean cloth, but drying will be faster with air circulation under the leaves as well as over the top. Put the frames outside on a table or bench, preferably not in direct sun.

Sun will change the color of the herbs, and our daytime humidity usually is sufficiently low to dry herbs in shade. Either take frames in overnight or put them under moisture-proof cover so evening dews don't rehydrate herbs.

Dry until herbs are crisp and leaves can be easily stripped from stems.

Some people dry large quantities of herbs like oregano by stuffing the leafy stems into pillowcases and hanging them on the clothesline. These also must be taken inside each night. You have the added benefit of wonderfully scented pillowcases.

Keep pinching back your basil, preventing it from flowering.

Chop the leaves you pinch off, and put them into ice cube trays, fill the trays with water, then put them into the freezer. Once they're frozen solid, you can pop them out and put them into a plastic bag and use the tray for other things. Whenever you fix a dish that would benefit from basil, just drop a basil ice cube into the pot.

Or you can make pesto and freeze it in usable amounts.

Harvest anise and caraway seeds when they're brown. Pound them a bit with a whisk to separate seeds from stems, and toss in the air in a light breeze to let the chaff blow away. Then put them in a plastic bag in the freezer. If there are tiny insects accompanying the seeds, they'll be killed by the low temperatures.

I leave the seeds in the freezer until I'm ready to use them and hand-sort.

Starting to harvest and preserve your herbs early will result in a larger harvest, since you'll have two or three more opportunities in a summer to harvest from regrowth of the plants you've just cut back. Package some for

Christmas gifts.

Toward the end of July is the time to make your herb gardens do double duty. Harvest flowers for ornament when you gather leaves and dry them for teas, culinary seasoning or herbal vinegars.

Herb flowers should be gathered into bunches and hung upside down to dry out of sunlight. In olden days, women hung their "yarbs" in their attics.

Most houses don't have attics anymore, so use ceiling joists in the garage, a vacant closet or cupboard, basement or an unused room shut against light.

A crawl space would work if you want to brave the spiders. If you don't want to put up "hanging nails," you could use a folding clothes drying rack.

To ward off dust, poke a hole in a large paper bag and put the string or cord tying the bunch through that, with the flowers hanging inside the bag, with the blossoms at the open end. A plastic bag might encourage mold.

Horehound, hops, yarrow and lavender provide foliar and shape interest in addition to color. They're not usual ingredients in dried bouquets, but they work. Other good candidates for drying are the Artemisias, Monardas (bee balm), Calendulas, cone flowers, feverfews, lemon verbenas, marjorams and Salvias.

Autumn

As cold weather nears, your herb garden goes indoors with ease. Just a snippet of rosemary on an otherwise bland chicken breast can wake up your taste buds. And herbs like this don't have to be limited to summer treats.

The best herbs to grow inside are rosemary, chives, basil and thyme. Rosemary usually won't survive our winters outside. Basil turns black and dead at about 38 degrees, long before other tender plants even show damage. Thyme and chives will thrive outdoors, even during very cold winters, but they're neat and compact, so easy to grow and use indoors.

Winter sunlight is not strong, so basil, with larger leaves than the other listed herbs, may struggle for life indoors. It's hard to tell when chives, thyme and rosemary are struggling. Many people also want to bring in sage and parsley. Sage plants are too large to grow indoors, and since they're hardy, grow them outdoors on the balcony, deck or patio, and go outdoors to harvest a leaf when you need one. I also harvest parsley outdoors in winter.

Winter

Indoors, pests such as spider mites latch onto dry plants and suck the juices out before you know it. They're so tiny you often can only tell you have spider mites when you see the fine webs between stem and leaf. Put a sheet of white paper under a branch and tap, then look at tiny dots moving around on the paper.

Top off your planting pots with a layer of about 3/8 inch of sand after you've potted your herbs, to prevent invasion of fungus gnats. Then mist your herb foliage each day with water to prevent spider mites from setting up shop. Remember, your home is warm and dry. Water your herbs when the soil is dry to a probing finger. That will be more often than you'd water outdoors, especially if your herbs are in a sunny window.

Winter, when you're close to your herbs without distractions of other plants, is a good time to learn to use herbs in cooking. Start out very lightly, using a tiny amount; gradually increase the amount until it's just an enhancement to the flavor of the food.

Basil traditionally is used in tomato dishes, but some people use it in combination with almost any food. Chives are flavored like onions, so they go best with baked potatoes or eggs. Rosemary is usually associated with poultry, but it may also be used with fish or eggs. And thyme is great in stuffing (with rosemary, sage and parsley) or with poached chicken breasts.

If your recipe calls for using 1/4 teaspoon of one of these herbs, note that recipes usually mean dried herbs. Drying intensifies the flavor of herbs, so if you're using fresh herbs, use double the amount called for.

The noncreeping varieties of rosemary may be pruned to resemble a Christmas tree, a lollipop or any other desired shape. These standards are costly, so if you're clever with your hands, you can make one yourself.

If you have a greenhouse window, be advised that cold air falls, and it can fall right through a double-pane window. If the forecast calls for extraordinary cold, remove your plants from that window temporarily. I've lost plants to freezing in my greenhouse window, even though it's open to a warm room.

HERBS IN THE TREASURE VALLEY

Basil

Greece gave us basil. There is some controversy about the meaning of the word; some say it comes from the Greek word for king, others from the Greek word for deadly snake.

The important fact is that there are several varieties which are delicious. Lemon, anise, cinnamon, lettuce-leaf, Piccolo, Purple Ruffles and sweet basils are delicious with tomatoes and in tomato sauces and with fish, lamb, poultry, pasta, eggs and in salads. In short, it's a widely useful herb, served raw or cooked, fresh or dried.

Basils are not hardy. They take more effort to grow, and they need to be cut back to bush out. The desirable part of basil is the foliage, and the bushier, the more useful.

The very tiny-leaved basil varieties have tender herbaceous stems, so the whole stems may be used. The varieties that have woody stems require stripping leaves before washing and using. Basil should be harvested before it blooms. You can delay blossoming by cutting it back, but the progression to flower is powerful. They survive only to about 38 degrees, long before killing frost.

There are many exotic varieties of basil available, mostly annuals, including Thai and tulsi or holy basil. Tulsi seems to be identical to Thai cooking basil (Ka Prao), but it's called tulsi in India. African Blue is a tender perennial.

Thai basil has an anise flavor, the potency of which, I'm told, diminishes to a special distinctive flavor in dishes such as pestos.

All of the basils do best with frequent cutting. Begin cutting sprigs from them before they bloom, and they will bush out, producing more and more branches and foliage.

Borage

Another wonderful annual in the herb garden is borage. The leaves are crisp, cucumber-flavored, but with fuzzy, slightly stiff hairs on the leaves. I find that easy to ignore. Some people object. They use the leaves for flavor, then remove them before eating the dish.

You have a wonderful bonus with borage, in brilliant, bright blue star-shaped flowers, which fade to pink with age. They are edible and can make a salad look truly grand.

Calendula

Yet another edible flower/herb is the Calendula, also an annual.

The seeds resemble dried worms, but they germinate very quickly (as little as two days), so they are a great choice for impatient youngsters to grow.

Calendulas are usually yellow or orange, but now some red ones are available, although there's no information whether these new ones are also edible-flowered.

The Romans named them, since they found they were in bloom on the calends (or the first) of every month. We get the word "calendar" from that word.

Blossoms are neat, cheerful and tidy when new, but as they age, they begin more and more to look like an unkempt mop of hair. This is the time to do what is technically known as "deadheading," that is, pinching off the spent blossoms. The plant will be encouraged to produce more blooms.

Catmint

Catmint usually isn't invasive, but it has snuck up on me, several plants in two beds.

It has catnip-shaped tiny leaves, blue blossoms and is a lovely ground-hugging plant. Cats are not strongly drawn to it, as they are to catnip.

Celery

A useful crop you can grow in a kitchen garden or even in a container is cutting celery, or Apium graveolens. It does not form large stalks like celery from the grocery store.

Cutting celery stalks are thin and about 4 to 6 inches high. The leaves are pleasantly flavorful, enriching soups, stews and even salads. You can freeze leaves without blanching.

I've found no appreciable difference among varieties named Afina, Zwolsche Krul and French Dinant. Richters sells seeds for Zwolsche Krul; Nichols Garden Nursery carries French Dinant; and Pinetree carries Afina. Other seed merchants carry some of these varieties, too.

Chervil

One of my spring delights is discovering a volunteer crop of chervil. Chervil, or Anthriscus cereifolium, is a wonderful flavoring herb, one of the "fines herbes" of French cooking. It resembles a fragile parsley and has a delicate parsley-like flavor, but has only a fraction of the foliage that parsley has.

Years ago, I planted it on a berm-herb bed next to my greenhouse. It grew there sparsely, but found a better place to grow: across the yard in a raised bed of compost. About the time the garden soil is ready to work in April, the self-seeded chervil is ready to be harvested.

We let parsley and chervil grow wherever they like because they can determine their prime habitats better than we. And several "beds" of parsley, along with the chervil, prove attractive to beneficial insects, especially tiny wasps.

Parsley and chervil bloom in clusters of tiny umbrella-like blossoms, but parsley blooms only the second year. Chervil, an annual, blooms the year it grows.

Harvest before the blossoms appear. If you're not using it fresh, dehydrate it. The best-flavored foliage grows in light shade. It supposedly grows to 24 inches, but in my yard the height is about 8 to 10 inches.

Its delicate flavor works best with potatoes, fish, omelets or sauces that don't overwhelm the taste. If you use it in a cooked dish, add it late in the cooking process.

It's easily grown here, doesn't take space from other plants, attracts beneficial insects and is useful in the kitchen.

Chives

In many cases there's no distinction at all between ornamentals and edibles. Many plants with edible parts are so beautiful that ornamental gardeners prize them, not realizing that the plants also are edible.

One that I enjoy is very easy to grow: It's garlic chives, also known as Chinese chives or flowering leek.

Regular chives have round hollow leaves, like straws. Garlic chives have strap-like leaves, about 1/4 inch wide. They have a mild garlic scent and flavor.

Almost all parts of the plant are edible: leaves, flower stems, flower buds and the flowers themselves. Flowers are especially pretty, lacy white umbrellas of star blossoms delicately brightening a flower bed. They sow their own successors, while the mother plant sticks around for another seven to 30 years. They overwinter here just fine.

They tolerate very high and very low temperatures and a broad range of soils. They grow best in light, fertile, well-drained soils that are at least 20 inches deep (before hitting caliche or another hardpan). Three-year-old garlic chive roots may extend that deep.

Their bright green leaves are some of the first to green up in spring. They remain fresh and crisp-looking until they flower later in the summer.

They're propagated by seed or by division of mature plants. Seeds, like those of most Alliums, are viable only a short period of time. One year is maximum for most Allium seeds unless they're pelletized.

In this area, garlic chives bloom, set seed, drop seed and germinate anew. Cold winters are no deterrent.

New garlic chive plants may seem to be slow getting settled. If they're planted in very large clumps, leaves may be narrower than usual. Once they're growing well, they don't need to be divided, like regular chives do.

If you're growing garlic chives in a location where you can avoid watering them, do let considerable time elapse between waterings. Too much water leads to surface rooting. Also, if you can, avoid harvesting leaves the first year it's planted.

The Chinese harvest leaves below the soil line to obtain the blanched succulent bases of the leaves. Others usually harvest just above the soil line, getting cleaner leaves.

I've noticed that regular chives seem to be invigorated by cutting about a half-inch above the soil line. They'll grow back rather quickly. If you're cutting the whole clump, you may cut two more times in a summer, leaving the leaves then to replenish the roots and themselves.

Most people harvest just a few leaves, enough to flavor a dish for the evening meal, so you could cut from the same plant many times each summer.

They're not usually bothered by garden insects.

You can use both types in the same ways. Chop them in whipped butter or sour cream for baked potato toppings, mince to enhance salads, or use in stir-fried meals, adding the chives when the dish is almost cooked. Overcooking makes them stringy and flavorless.

Cilantro

Some people love cilantro; others hate it. They're not just being picky — their taste buds tell them it tastes like soap. For those who love it, though ...

Cilantro is also known as green coriander, for when it goes to seed, it produces a spicy seed we call coriander. I think that seed was the center of old-fashioned jawbreaker candies, a differently flavored hot shot at the end of the sweet.

Rodale's "Encyclopedia of Herbs" says this plant, botanically known as Coriandrum sativum, was so-named after the bedbug because it emits the same unpleasant odor that bedbugs produce. I think that unpleasant odor exists while the plant is growing, and for that reason, it is not a great house or deck plant.

I don't find the odor of mature leaves unpleasant, however, and they're used often in salsas, other Mexican and South American dishes and North African and Southeast Asian cuisines. The latter seem to use the roots perhaps more than the leaves.

Growing it for the leaves is a frustrating endeavor since the plant bolts quickly to flower and seed in hot weather, and then the flavor diminishes. Some plant breeders now have cultivars on the market that don't bolt as fast as the regular old cilantro, but I grew one of those called Calypso, and I didn't use the leaves because they didn't look like regular cilantro leaves. It bolted before I realized that was supposed to be cilantro.

There are variations of cilantro, usually added at the end of cooking. They include culantro (Eryngium foetidum), a thorny version; Vietnamese coriander or rau ram (Polygonum odoratum), a water-loving perennial; and quillquina (Porophyllum ruderale). Quillquina is also called killi, papalo, papalo-quelite, tepegua, summer cilantro and Bolivian coriander.

Quillquina grows wild in Arizona, New Mexico and Texas, but residents of those states usually use cilantro instead. South Americans and Mexicans use quillquina fresh, not cooked. Pores on the leaves release an oil bearing a distinctive flavor.

Could a person to whom cilantro tastes terrible eat any of the variations without problems? I don't think so. A friend who dislikes cilantro tasted my culantro and had the same aversion.

Cilantro is one of those crops that you can grow in a container indoors if you don't find the odor offensive. To grow cilantro, you should plant the seed, and plan to plant more about every two weeks. Even though seed companies say their version is "slow to bolt," it usually does bolt to seed before you're through using the leaves. Vietnamese recipes calling for cilantro or green coriander usually specify using the roots. These plants do not have a thick root structure, so it takes quite a few plants to get to a tablespoon of roots.

Our local supermarkets also carry bunches of cilantro in the produce department.

Flat-leaved parsley looks similar to cilantro, but the flavor and aroma are quite different.

Cress

Cress is another useful "spark" for salads. There are several varieties of land cresses — upland cress, curly, wrinkled, crumpled, presto, and Persian — and of course watercress. Watercress can be grown in soil, watered frequently. Some plant it in bottomed flats — although in the wild, it is found in running water.

Land cresses grow in soil with no special water requirements. Those I've grown quickly bolt to flower and seed when the weather turns hot.

Dill

Feathery-leaved dill is an annual plant. Some varieties are favored for seed production, others for foliage ("dillweed"), although the foliage (fernleaf) dill does eventually produce seed as well.

To make dill pickles, one uses seeds, stem and leaves.

Fernleaf dill seed is widely available now, and is slow to bolt to seed.

Many people use dill for flavoring salads, lamb, pork, onions, cauliflower, green beans, eggs, cheese, poultry, carrots and many other vegetables.

Dill is very effective in attracting bees to the garden. It's easy to grow here in the Treasure Valley. We planted dill nearly 30 years ago, and when volunteers came up within a planted row we let them grow and go to seed. We used some, but not all of the crop. Even though we scraped up our garden topsoil into raised beds, there were a few dill plants growing here and there.

Epazote

Most of our culinary herbs come from the rocky soils of the Mediterranean, where prized herbs grow as weeds. But there is one culinary herb that is all American: It's epazote (eh-paw-ZOAT-eh), and it deserves wider use.

It's a native of Mexico, grows as a weed there and in the United States, although people who try to grow it from seed report some difficulty in getting it to germinate. They may be pulling it out, thinking it's a weed.

Epazote is a natural flatulence reducer, some say as good as the commercial products, but it's also delicious. Many connoisseurs insist that black beans be cooked with epazote or the dish doesn't taste right. Cooks add fresh epazote leaves half an hour before the beans are done, and sometimes add some lemon or lime juice to enhance the flavor. Three or four fresh leaves (or to taste) may be added per pound of dry pinto beans.

Those who add it to cream sauces or cheese dishes or with grilled chicken or veal say diners are unanimously enthusiastic about the flavor.

Officially, epazote is Chenopodium ambrosioides, also known as Mexican tea or wormseed. It's strongly flavored, the scent intensifying when the foliage is dried. Dried epazote is not quite as effective as an anti-flatulent herb as the fresh, however. One teaspoon of dried epazote is the recommended amount for one pound of black beans.

The plant needs good drainage, and grows to 3 or 4 feet tall in full sun, requiring no special treatment. It's an annual, tolerating a lot of hard pruning. It can be grown in a container.

Seeds are available from Nichols Garden Nursery. Better yet, buy a plant — ask at your neighborhood greenhouse.

The herb also is used to flavor corn, fish, soups, stews, chili sauces and shellfish, and it's especially fine with mushrooms and dairy dishes. Oaxacan provincial cooking specializes in epazote-enhanced quesadillas.

Epazote can be an acquired taste, but once you acquire the taste, you'll love it.

I didn't find the plant self-seeding invasively; I wouldn't consider it a pest plant. It's difficult to find in stores, so growing your own is best. Some people are allergic to the pollen, so you could prune out blossoms to prevent pollen formation and self-seeding.

Fennel

One of my favorite herbs is fennel (Foeniculum vulgare). It's very attractive, tastes good, and is the herb I use most, especially to dress up and flavor fish fillets.

I started it in an herb bed south of our house, and it re-seeded very close to the foundation. Some herb books say it grows best where the soil is slightly acid, but soil abutting concrete is likely more alkaline than that, thanks to the leaching of the concrete. Its position, though, protects it from harsh winds and winter cold, allowing this semi-hardy perennial to live on and on.

It does receive full sun, but little water.

Fine, feathery leaves are soft and have a fine anise flavor, a flavor destroyed by heat. We use fennel leaves raw, as a flavorful garnish on fish. I also snack on it occasionally when working in the yard. My plant is only about a foot in height until it goes to seed.

There are two fennels, the bulbing (Florence or Finocchio) and the non-bulbing.

In ancient Greece, it was known as a plant that would aid in losing weight, and the 17th century herbalist Culpeper wrote that all parts of the plant could be used for losing weight.

I'll attest it doesn't work for that, unless perhaps you were to eat nothing but fennel, and I think that would be a very bad idea.

The seeds are nice to munch on when working outside, too, but are irritating or even dangerous to those who are allergic to them.

Fresh leaves may be used in salads, beets, pickles, potatoes, lentils, cheese, eggs, breads, rice and similar foods. Seeds are used whole or broken in breads and other baked goods, beverages and desserts. They look much like caraway seeds when mature.

Bulbs are often cut into thin strips and used in salads or cooked as a root vegetable.

Bronze fennel is very ornamental, and is widely grown. Its leaves may be used just like those of its green cousin.

Horseradish

Americans' tastebuds require more and more stimulation. Consumers are demanding hotter peppers, more pungent mustards and other greens in our salads and sinus-clearing horseradish on our meats. You can grow all three, but do you want to? Peppers and mustards are easy, but horseradish is different.

It's easy to grow in the Treasure Valley, but not easy to grow well. If you're thinking about growing some, it's time for a "garden think-it-over." Horseradish can become an invasive weed that's very difficult to eradicate. But it's seldom bothered by insects.

The object is to grow horseradish with large, thick, straight roots that are easily peeled and grated. Too often, the roots are scrawny, stringy and end up forking into multiple thin, unusable roots. Digging one root invariably leaves root portions in the ground, and those become new plants.

As you're thinking over the prospect of planting horseradish, think about its location. If you move it later, you'll have two beds. It grows best in full sun, in deeply dug soil rich in organic matter. This is one of the crops for which double digging especially pays.

Don't bother looking for seeds, but instead use cuttings or the leafy tops attached to the growing crown of a harvested root. Some growers cut the root on a slant to indicate that's the downward side of the root. Instead of planting it straight up and down, plant it at a 45-degree angle, slant side down. The harvestable root will grow straight down. Plants are available, too, in some locations.

Some growers lift the roots when the tops are 3 to 4 inches high, careful not to disturb the tip of the cutting, and brush off the fine fibrous roots on the upper 4 inches of the root, then replant it. This is said to help produce a long, straight root.

Go easy on nitrogen fertilizer, but fertilizer with the middle and last numbers higher will contribute to the health of the plant and the size of the root. You want it to grow slowly, to concentrate flavor and pungency, so don't overwater. Underwatering is equally bad.

If you plant in the spring and harvest the following fall, you'll probably be disappointed in the size of the root and the pungency. Some growers consider it an 18-month crop. Wait until fall of the next year, and you'll get the best, most flavorful roots if you wait until after the second frost to dig.

Good horseradish sauce can be obtained from roots dug in early spring, before new growth starts.

Dig what you need, peel and grate. If you're sensitive to onions, you'll be better off if you can peel and grate outdoors. Otherwise, your sinuses may feel as if they've exploded. You can "grate" chunks in the blender or food processor, but be very wary about putting your face close to the open container and looking closely inside. Herbalist Henriette Kress of Finland says the fumes are mustard gas and can burn the corneas of your eyes. (The plant belongs to the Cruciferae family, and so does mustard.)

Grating is easier if you add liquid. Mix half water and half vinegar in a measuring cup, and add to the Horseradish chunks as needed to facilitate grating. This horseradish will be much stronger than that carried by grocery stores. Freeze jars of horseradish topped with vinegar if you're not going to use them soon. If the sauce is too strong, you can mix the refrigerated home-made sauce with some mayonnaise for immediate use.

You can also freeze extra horseradish roots whole, enjoying freshly grated "hot" sauce in midwinter. For easier digging, mulch the plants to be left in the ground. Freezing weather won't destroy them.

Lavender

Soaps, bath oils, sachets, potpourris, sleep pillows and dried bouquets all may be warmed by the sweet scent of lavender.

Gardeners have complained to me about having problems growing lavender in this area. It does thrive here, but you have to select the right varieties if you want plants to winter over outdoors.

In general, French and Spanish lavenders are not hardy here, and must be brought indoors for winter. English lavender is sturdier and should survive temperatures down to about 20 degrees below zero.

What type? How can you tell what you're buying? If the botanical name is Lavandula angustifolia, it's what is usually known as English lavender. The English lavender fortunately has a stronger aroma than French or Spanish. English cultivars Hidcote or Munstead are generally available here, and they're choice for craft projects, holding both color and aroma through drying. There are more exotic varieties, but these are the ones you're most apt to find in area nurseries.

Other English lavenders include Jean Davis, with pink blossoms, and Alba, with white. These colors do not hold through the drying process.

L. dentata and L. stoechas, the latter regarded as French lavender by some, Spanish by others, are hardy only down to about 10 degrees above zero.

During one of our mercury-plummeting zone 4 winters, not even the hardy lavenders will pull through unless they're in a favored location.

If you plant lavender outdoors, do it sufficiently early in the summer to give it time to acclimate before winter. A small purchased plant will spread somewhat and grow to a height of about 12 to 16 inches.

Lavender can be grown from seed, but generally is not (except for the variety Lady lavender) because it is slow to produce and doesn't produce true to its parents as a rule.

Lavenders are usually propagated by stem cuttings or by layering (pegging a stem to the ground) in summer. After the roots form, the plant is cut away from the parent.

This ancient herb was so commonly used to scent soap or bathwater, its name derives from the Latin word for bathing. It is also used in medicinal and culinary ways. The plant is not touchy about soil alkalinity, but it definitely prefers well-drained soil.

It grows best and flowers best if planted in full sun.

Lavender is not a very impressive plant when planted alone, but as a border, short hedge or drift, it's a lovely, scented wonder. Space plants about a foot apart.

After they're established, prune straggly plants in spring or summer, and gather flowering stems just as the flowers open. Dry on screens or hang by stems upside down.

Lemon verbena

Wait! Don't discard what looks like "dead" lemon verbena.

It is one of the most wonderfully fragrant and tasty herbs in the world.

But it's very tender to frost, so for years I've dug and brought in the plants in winter. You can do that, but you should be aware that the plant is tough.

I've sadly watched as they lost their leaves. Brown stems, no signs of life, so I tossed them onto the compost. I've discarded and bought new ones, dozens of them, over the years.

I'm not alone with this brown thumb. The editor of "The Herb Companion" has confessed to the same problem with lemon verbena.

If the plant weren't so enticing, we'd have all given up on it long ago.

Only recently I learned that leaf loss or defoliation of lemon verbena is common when its location is changed. And the leafless state often is only temporary. I have two lemon verbenas in the house. The potted one in the greenhouse did lose its leaves, then quickly began to develop new ones. The larger plant in a south window, dropped its leaves, a few at a time.

Early Spanish explorers searching for gold discovered this New World native in South America. They undoubtedly discovered its vibrant lemon fragrance when they brushed against the leaves.

It grows as a low shrub, to about 4 feet tall, with narrow 2- to 3-inch long leaves.

Leaves are dried for tea or potpourri, where they retain their sweet citrus scent for years. Leaves may be minced and used for flavoring rice or fish, poultry, salad dressings, marinades and similar dishes. In previous times, lemon verbena leaves scented the water in finger bowls at fancy dinners.

If lemon balm is used as a substitute, one must use twice as much lemon balm as the pungent lemon verbena.

It provides a wonderful scent during winter. Some experts suggest pruning the plant when you bring it in; others say wait until February. One source on the February pruning side also advises repotting at this time, resuming regular watering and full sun.

Leaf loss reduces transpiration, or water loss from the plant, so reference books all say reduce watering to avoid root rot.

You can water as much as you have in the past, but do it less frequently, or water as frequently but give less water each time. The third option is to mist with warm water.

Good luck — the payoff is worth it.

Motherwort

Wort is a very old name for a plant, and this plant has been around for centuries. It has some medicinal uses as an herb, and may be regarded as attractive for its small blossoms in the axils or joints of leaves with the main stem. Unfortunately those blossoms become prickly-coated seeds carried to other parts of the yard by pets and/or rodents, where they germinate.

Parsley

Parsley is a biennial, flowering (and setting seeds) in its second year. When it goes to seed, it stretches upward, leaving the now sparse foliage near the ground. Beneficial insects love the flowers.

Folklore has it that seed goes to the devil and back seven times before it germinates. Others say the person germinating it must be evil.

I usually buy a plant or two, and when it seeds itself, I let those plants grow where they arise, for they're difficult to transplant.

If you have trouble germinating it, buy a plant.

Flat-leafed parsley is preferred to the curly-leafed by expert cooks, but both are rich in vitamins A, B, C, calcium and iron, and both aid digestion.

Perilla

A pretty red-leafed herb, Perilla resembles Coleus and basil. The latter resemblance was fortified by its former botanic name of Ocimum frutescens; Ocimum is the botanic designation of basils. Perilla, or shiso, can spread widely by seed, and it has in some parts of the country. It's used as a culinary herb in Japanese cooking, where it's also known as beefsteak plant. It has become invasive in parts of Pennsylvania at least, where it seems to be a plant that deer avoid. A farmer in Tennessee says consuming Perilla causes ruminants (such as deer, cattle, sheep and goats) respiratory problems similar to emphysema. One way it's eaten is with raw fish, to counteract stomach parasites that may be in the fish. It may be more toxic than we realize.

Rosemary

In Shakespeare's "Hamlet," demented Ophelia has a moment of rare clarity when she says, "There's rosemary, that's for remembrance ... ."

Whether one's memory of rosemary is of ground covers or hedges, aroma or flavor, in this part of the country, remember to bring it inside before frost. Rosemary, a tender perennial, may survive a light frost, but cold usually kills it.

Rosemary Arp is said to be the hardiest variety. It was developed in Texas, and its extreme cold weather tolerances are not yet known. It has been reported to have survived winter here under a heavy mulch. Horticultural expert Lindarose Curtis-Bruce advises removing that mulch early in the spring to avoid smothering the plant.

The plant is a native of the Mediterranean area. Its botanical name "Rosmarinus officinalis," meaning "dew of the sea," reflects its shoreline growth habit.

Rosemary is easy to grow in our soil, provided it has good drainage and protection from cold winds. Plants are smaller but more fragrant on alkaline soils than on acidic.

Once rosemary is brought inside, it pays again to "remember" it. The plant has 1-inch, needle-like leaves that do not droop when the plant is dry, so it's easy to forget to water it. But too much water is fatal. Frequent mistings with water do seem to be beneficial.

Some growers advise potting rosemary in a soil mix meant for cactus to avoid root rot, to which rosemary is susceptible.

It is also extremely attractive to spider mites. You may not even know spider mites are present until you grow rosemary in the house. Fine spider webs at leaf-stem junctures signal the presence of these tiny destructive pests.

Rosemary is a widely useful culinary herb. Chopped leaves can be added judiciously to meat dishes, baked potatoes, herb butters or bread dough. As is true of many culinary herbs, however, large amounts may be toxic.

The aromatic branches are used for bridal wreaths, burned to purify air in sick wards, tossed onto coffins by funeral-goers, and burned in barbecue cookers to flavor meat. Leaves are also used for medicinal purposes, said to relieve muscle pains and headaches, and other woes.

It's also said to help the brain and improve memory.

Saffron

September usually is the month that saffron crocus bulbs are sent out. If you plant them then, you should get flowers in a year.

The Treasure Valley usually is well suited to growing saffron, because we seldom get rains between June and September.

Seed companies and nurseries usually don't mention the "no-water" requirements until they ship the bulbs with planting instructions.

When we grew saffron several years ago, we planted the bulbs in a bed that didn't get much water, but it did get some. The crocus bloomed, and it was rather exciting to harvest the stigmas, knowing how costly the spice is.

True saffron is very, very expensive, partly because each flower only has three small parts that have to be hand-harvested, then dried for use.

Twenty-five saffron bulbs may yield about 1/8 teaspoon of dried stamens. After that first year, I replanted the bulbs behind our fence, where it does not get regularly watered. I knew exactly where they were planted, so we roto-tilled weeds around that area. Then a "helpful neighbor" sprayed herbicide on the remaining weeds (and saffron) before I could hand-dig the saffron bulbs or harvest stamens. She said she hadn't known there was anything but weeds there. I lost all of my bulbs.

The botanical name for saffron crocus is crocus sativus. In some areas, apparently, the narrow grasslike leaves grow 12 to 18 inches high. Here, they were much smaller, about 8 inches long at best.

Saffron is used to flavor and color rice and fish, soups, breads and cakes. I have heard of people, objecting to the price, who stole it from supermarkets. There is a satisfactory substitute available that is far cheaper. It's called "saffron" or "azafran," and it's the dried flowers of safflower. You may have to use a teaspoonful of it to substitute for 1/4 teaspoon of saffron, but azafran is so cheap, it's not a costly flavor-color additive.

It's usually sold with Mexican spices and dried chiles, in cellophane bags. If you can't find it, ask your grocer to stock. Saffron bulbs are available from Nichols Garden Nursery.

Sage

New Westerners often ask, "Can I use sagebrush to flavor cooked foods?" The answer is "no." Emphatically.

Sagebrush is in the genus Artemisia and was correctly called an Artemisia by Oregon Trail diary-keepers. Plants belonging to this family are used for moth repellents, aromatic wreaths, and under proper expert supervision, some medical applications, but they are not safe to use for cooking.

The sage used for cooking belongs to the Salvia family, as different from Artemisias as night from day. Artemisia leaves are feathery and ghostly gray-green. Salvia leaves are broader and come in several colors.

The common sage for cooking, Salvia officinalis, grows vigorously to about 3 feet in height, and after four or five years becomes so woody it needs to be replaced. During its growth period, it benefits from frequent pruning for shape and leaf production. Leaves and twigs can be tossed on barbecue fires to smoke-flavor meats.

Culinary sage is attractive and aromatic, with spikes of handsome purplish blue blossoms in early summer.

Sage leaves should be gathered just before the plant blossoms, then dried slowly to preserve flavor, or used fresh.

Other culinary sages include pineapple, honeydew melon-flavored, fruit-flavored, and Mexican baby sage, none of which are hardy here. If you have sunny space, they're worth potting and bringing indoors for the winter. The fruity sage leaves enhance fruit salads.

Golden sage is a hardy sage, with beautifully variegated gold and pale green leaves. It has a milder flavor than common sage, but is used in the same ways. Its growth is modest, beautifying a herb bed for many years.

Purple or red-leaved sage is also hardy (though more vulnerable to low temperatures), and its strong-flavored leaves are usually used only for throat-soothing tea. The hardy Tricolor sage, with green, red and white variegated leaves is similarly used.

If you have a sheltered place in your yard where temperatures don't drop quite as low as the general area, the unusual plants may survive our winters. The fruit sages will not survive outdoors here.

You can grow common culinary sage from seed, and other varieties from cuttings. All prefer full sun and need good drainage. They grow vigorously on alkaline soil, the type prevalent in the Treasure Valley. They benefit from ordinary amounts of water.

One of my favorite herbs is the pineapple sage. It's a tender perennial that has to be quite mature to bloom. But what a bloom! It sends out slender lip-sticks of bright red blossoms, which are sweet and safely edible. A salad with borage and pineapple sage flowers is something to behold.

Sorrel

Hardy sorrel is a cool weather friend and can add refreshing lemon flavor to salads.

In the spring, tender bright green leaves poke 3 to 4 inches into the air, nearly irresistible to those of us weary of winter and store-bought greens. Garden sorrels are perennial and hardy down to Zone 4 (the coldest our weather ever gets), and early to rise.

Leaves have a lemony tang, intensifying in strength with the approach of summer. Usually they send up flower stalks in early summer that may reach to 3 or 4 feet.

Two main kinds of sorrel are used for culinary purposes: the French, and the broad-leaf or garden sorrel. Garden sorrel has long arrowhead-shaped leaves, 4 to 8 inches long; the French sorrel leaves are smaller like fatter arrowheads.

Garden sorrel, native to much of Europe and England, has been used raw in salads for centuries. The French also use it in ragouts, fricassees and soups. The flavor of French sorrel is similar, but considered superior, to that of garden sorrel.

Either grows easily here from seed. Seeds should be sown in March, the seedlings thinned when plants are 1 or 2 inches high. When seed stalks shoot up, cut them back. Roots will put out new, tender leaves. By cutting back the flower stalks at judicious times, you can ensure a long supply of the tenderest leaves for salads.

Sorrel's strong flavor would add flavor interest to a salad of lettuces and spinach, but an all-sorrel salad would overwhelm.

Sorrel has also been used medicinally, especially against scurvy.

Sweet cicely

We have a large yard, too much water-hogging grass, and our water bills are quite high in spite of our efforts to economize.

Normal water-loving plants such as ferns don't survive in my yard. Lacy leaves are an attractive complement to solid, even colorful, leaves such as Heucheras and variegated Hostas, so I keep trying to grow ferns. Some say you don't really know a plant until you've killed it three times. I've killed so many Japanese painted ferns I know the plant very well.

To make up for those failed attempts, I grow sweet cicely, an herb that looks like a fern. A friend who lives on the southern outskirts of the county once told me it was so windy there, sweet cicely was the only "fern" that would survive there.

Anise-flavored sweet cicely is as tough as old boots, but you have to watch out for the seeds, or you'll have more sweet cicely than you can handle. The seeds are about an inch long, roughly shaped like bean pods. Both leaves and seeds are anise-flavored. Seeds are green and ripen to brown.

It's difficult to transplant sweet cicely because a mature plant has a huge root. I've been told it's edible, but thigh-sized. Leaves or shredded root may be chopped over a fruit salad to enhance the flavor.

Some herb references say this herb prefers moist soil and partial shade. In my yard, it tolerates and thrives on dry soil in full shade. You can substitute chopped seeds for caraway in baking, according to one reference, but the seeds are woody and quite sharply ridged.

The usual instructions are to plant in autumn to grow from seed. It obviously seeds itself in early summer in my shady bed, however. The plant apparently lives a very long time.

Thyme

Thyme is a perennial that comes in thousands of varieties. For basic cooking, stick with mother of thyme or any other plain variety. Those with names such as oregano thyme or coconut thyme have the flavor and/or aroma of the first word in the name, so are not as good for general use.

Tarragon

French tarragon must be started from root division. It dies to the ground in winter, but re-emerges in spring, growing to a height of about 14 inches. Russian tarragon may be started from seeds, but it's not an acceptable substitute.

Wasabi

Treasure Valley residents must be developing a taste for Japanese sushi dishes, since more and more restaurants and delicatessens are offering them. One of the main condiments served with sushi is wasabi, a very pungent Japanese horseradish.

This has rather strict growing requirements, the preferred wasabi being grown in shade along flowing streams, although it can be field grown, too, as long as it's shaded and cool. Some Oregon farmers are growing it hydroponically (without soil). Until the mid-1990s, it was available only in the Far East.

Wasabi, or Eutrema wasabi, is a stubby plant, with a rosette of leaves, and a rhizome (root that sends out runners) about 1 inch in diameter and 6 inches long when it's ready to harvest. When it's ready to harvest, the plantlets attached to the rhizome are broken off and replanted. Since it takes 18 months to two years for a rhizome to grow to harvest size, it must be grown in a sheltered location, protected from frost. It would have to be grown indoors here.

The leaves and stems are edible, but the prize is the pungent grated rhizome. U.S. restaurants often serve reconstituted powdered wasabi, or wasabi paste. Many restaurants also combine freshly grated American horseradish with wasabi.

Za'atar

If you cook Middle Eastern foods, you may run into a dilemma. Israeli, Syrian and Lebanese recipes, for example, often call for za'atar or variant spellings of the same. You will find spice mixtures called za'atar that contain sumac seeds, roasted sesame seeds and powdered thyme. Some seed companies sell seeds for a za'atar herb, an oregano relative, that we can grow here.

Which za'atar is correct? It depends on where the recipe comes from. In some parts of the Middle East, they use the spice mixture; in other parts, even just the next valley, they use the herb. I don't know whether the taste is similar, but it probably is. You can get za'atar seeds for the herb from Baker Creek Heirloom Seeds or Richters. I bought a plant from Edwards Greenhouse. The spice za'atar is available in local specialty grocery stores.

CHAPTER 4

Roses

A great place for roses

Having driven hundreds of miles through Nevada and Oregon sagebrush with its muted colors, our eyes were met with an explosion of color in the form of blooming roses when we moved to Idaho in June 1971. Roses draped over low fences drew focus in cottage gardens and stood as solitary specimens in front yards in the Marsing area, a harbinger of color widespread in the Treasure Valley. Roses do grow well in this area, apparently thriving in alkaline soils, with hot summers, cold winters and sparse precipitation.

Roses come in many forms, from miniatures to climbing roses that seem to overwhelm buildings, those with single blossoms to lush cabbage-types of blossoms, some fragrant and others not. All are members of the genus Rosa in the huge Rosaceae family (which includes apples). Most are native to Asia, but some are native to western Africa, Europe and the U.S. They hybridize easily, giving us a large selection from which to choose.

Shrubs of wild roses stand in pastures along the Interstate, and here and there one sees relics of the Oregon Trail or Yellow Rose of Texas. The latter rose, a hybrid from Rosa foetida, appeared in the New York garden of George F. Harison before 1830. That it is tough is evidenced by that rose having been carried west by Oregon Trail pioneers, and planted here and there in the American West.

It and a large weeping willow were the only ornamental plants in my grandmother's farm yard in eastern Colorado. We didn't notice its presence before buying, but the house we bought in Boise had this Harison's Yellow rose in the corner of the yard. We still have it.

When buying a rose shrub, if you want a fragrant rose, ask for a shrub that has fragrant blossoms. If the label says "lightly fragrant," pass it up in favor of one that describes fragrance. Some smell like pepper to me, perhaps that is the "spicy" aroma that rose vendors specify.

Who can resist a lush, full-blossomed, fragrant rose? Not even I, even though I dug out and gave away or discarded most of my roses a few years ago, tired of pruning them. I'm ready for them again.

Some require less pruning than others, and Royal Horticulture Society experts have discovered that even the sometimes fussy hybrid teas may be sheared without regard to "outward facing buds."

When you set out to buy a rose, pay attention to what the label says about its habit (climbing, bush or groundcover), root system (grafted or own root), color, size at maturity, how many times it blooms in one season, and fragrance.

Some may also be grown in mostly shady conditions, but roses generally prefer full sun.

Anju Lucas, of Edwards Greenhouse, advises growers to use 1/2 cup of Epsom salts around the drip line when roses begin to break dormancy. She backs Rayford Reddell's fertilizing advice, published in his book "Growing Good Roses": Feed a mixture of 2 cups bonemeal, 1/2 cup bloodmeal, 1/4 to 1/2 cup Osmocote or any timed-release fertilizer in early spring and again in mid-season. She also advises spreading another 1/2 cup Epsom salts around the dripline in mid-season. This is a lot of fertilizer, but this amount is to be fed each rose twice a year. For safety, wear a dust mask when using bonemeal, bloodmeal or any dusty substance.

This is combining organic and synthetic fertilizers, a practice I'm not entirely comfortable with, since synthetic fertilizers are not taken up by soil microorganisms and are ultimately more damaging to soil than organic matter is. I would not recommend this combination for use anywhere but the rose bed, where Lucas says it works wonderfully.

If you have dogs that can access your rose bed, I'd be very cautious about using bone meal or blood meal, since canines will dig up that fertilizer (and plants, even shrubs), and eat fertilizer and soil. This combination can be fatal to pets.

All newly planted roses must be well-watered to become established, and thereafter, they should be watered deeply and less frequently to develop deep root systems. (Most are not suitable for xeriscape planting.)

If you're planting bare-root roses, unwrap the package and set the roots into a bucket of water for a few hours (no longer than 24 hours) while you dig an ample hole. Then build up a cone of soil, and set the rose on the cone to make sure it's at the proper depth (soil surface about an inch above the graft level, if grafted). When you set the bare-root plant on the cone, spread the roots down and out around the cone, and fill with the soil you removed from the hole.

After planting, mulch your roses generously with alfalfa meal or alfalfa pellets. Lucas uses two 2-pound coffee cans of alfalfa pellets around the base of each rosebush. Alfalfa contains a growth stimulant, supplementing the fertilizer.

Blossoms can be white, red, pink, yellow, orange or purple (which some call blue), and variations and combinations of those colors. Generally the white, red and pink roses are hardier than others, although there are some yellow roses that are very hardy. The purple or blue roses are touchiest about growing conditions.

There are many types, including old roses (generally those observed or introduced prior to 1867) European: alba, centifolia, damask, gallica and moss roses. These tend to bloom once in spring. Other old roses (East Asian, mainly) include: Chinas, Bourbons, damask perpetuals, hybrid perpetuals, noisettes and tea roses. These tend to bloom more than once per year.

One of the oldest known is Gallica officinalis, or the Apothecary's rose, bred before 1240. The "officinalis" in a botanical name means it has been included in a pharmacopeia (compendium of plants used medicinally). The Apothecary's rose growth habit is a number of thorny canes rising from below the soil's surface. It suckers, but is easily controlled. It was the red rose of Lancaster in the Wars of the Roses (the white emblem blossom belonged to the House of York) fought sporadically from 1455 to 1485. Their storied history is more attractive than their appearance.

In 1867, the first hybrid tea rose was introduced, opening the door for "modern" roses: hybrid teas, grandifloras, floribundas, polyanthas and miniature roses. Further distinctions include English roses, David Austin, Griffith Buck, tree roses and others. Most of these are reblooming (remontant).

General culture

Roses are best planted in full sun, a considerable distance from trees or other plants that will compete for water and nutrients, away from walls that would restrict air circulation, and in a location that has good drainage. In our area, drainage may be blocked by hardpan, which can be broken up with a pick, prybar or sledgehammer prior to planting. These site restrictions do not apply if you plant a climbing rose you intend to grow up into a tree.

If your shrub is a potted rose, plant it an inch deeper than it was in the pot, even if it's growing on its own root. Nurseries that potted it did not want to cut roots back severely so they'd be potted at a planting depth. Roses whose grafts are below soil surface will sucker, so you'll have to watch out for that, removing suckers when they appear.

After planting, mulch well to prevent water splashing onto rose foliage, but do not pull mulch tightly to rose canes. Leave a couple of inches of breathing room from the canes, to prevent crown rot.

Water deeply but let soil dry enough between waterings to permit oxygenation of the roots. If your roses are within sprinkling distance of lawn sprinklers, run those sufficiently early in the day so that the foliage can dry out before cool evening to prevent foliar disease.

Our humidity is generally so low we don't suffer from many rose diseases such as black spot, common in more humid parts of America. Occasional chilly wet springs give us that challenge.

Fertilize established roses just before spring bloom if using commercial fertilizer, then fertilize monthly until August, and then cease so the shrub can slip into dormancy.

As winter approaches, prune only long canes that can whip in the wind and damage themselves and other canes. If you must remove leaves, cut them off with pruning shears.

Remove leaves of roses that get black spot fungus and put those leaves into the garbage. Do not put them into compost, for they carry spores (a type of seeds) that will perpetuate the disease. To remove leaves, prune them; do not pull them off. Pulling off leaves creates wounds that are vulnerable to entry by bacteria, and we have a disease popularly called bacterial cane disease that afflicts roses in our area. Winter may freeze-kill some canes or parts of them, but the bacterial cane disease is more widespread. For this reason, gardeners are advised to do no severe pruning (other than removing whips) in fall. See the chapter on diseases for more on how to diagnose cane blight on your roses.

When you replace a rose, dig a large hole, and put that excavated soil somewhere else, using new soil to hold a new rose bush. Some rose growers claim there's a problem of "failure to thrive" for rose bushes planted where others have grown, but that phenomenon doesn't occur all of the time, so plant physiologists have not studied it. This "replant disease" is, however, a problem for apple orchard owners. Remember, apple trees are in the same family as roses.

Pruning your roses

In spring, when forsythia blooms, the time is right for severely cutting back rose shrubs. Why must one prune? To open the shrub to light and good air circulation, conditions that aid in preventing fungus diseases such as powdery mildew or black spot on leaves.

As a general rule for any pruning, remove the D's first: the dead, decayed and diseased branches, then remove the crossing branches that will rub through the bark, opening another cane to disease. Then remove all canes smaller in diameter than a pencil, leaving no more than six or eight strong canes the diameter of your thumb. Floribunda bushes tend to have more canes and branches, so you may want to leave more canes on that type of shrub.

Cut your canes back to 18 to 24 inches in height for many blooms (on new wood), or even lower for fewer but larger blossoms. Prune strong canes back to within 1/4-inch above an outward-facing bud, with a slanting cut made by bypass pruners. The sharper your pruners, the neater your cut. Ragged cuts are vulnerable to disease.

You may want to seal the pruning cut with carpenter's glue or a thumb-tack.

Once blossoms open, and begin to fade, remove them. If they are blooming in clusters, such as on a floribunda, remove each blossom as it begins to fade, and when all of the cluster is spent, cut the branch back to just above an outward-facing set of mature leaflets (that is, one that has five to seven leaves). If your shrub has single flowers, deadhead (remove the spent flower) by cutting back to 1/4-inch above an outward-facing leaf stalk with five to seven leaflets. As you approach winter, stop deadheading so that the shrub can form hips (seed pods) in preparation for winter dormancy.

We used to winterize roses by mounding soil over the crown and main canes to a depth of 10 to 12 inches after the ground froze, but we haven't had severely cold temperatures since 1990. Sudden drops in temperature have killed rose shrubs in recent years, however. Styrofoam-like covers are available at garden centers if you like. Folks in some climates lay climbing rose canes on the ground and cover them with soil when they fear extreme cold.

Some gardeners may mulch with leaves after the ground freezes (not tightly against the canes), and still others do nothing. If you have some freezing damage, it's likely to be minor, and will be pruned off in spring. If you pruned your rose in fall, making it vulnerable to disease, it will also be vulnerable to being frozen back farther than you'd like, and even killed.

If we have a wet cool spring, we may get powdery mildew or black spot fungus on rose shrubs. Some folks treat either with sprays of 30-50 percent skim milk to water, and control infestations. Black spot on leaves saps strength of shrubs, so prune off afflicted leaves so you don't open a leaf scar on the cane and discard leaves (do not compost them). Other folks use commercial anti-fungus sprays such as Neem. Be sure to read the label and follow those instructions.

Culture of roses is quite dependent on pruning, and that varies by type of rose.

Climbing roses should only have dead or damaged cane tips pruned off early in spring, then main pruning should occur after the main blossoming period. If your rose blooms on old wood, that just means wood formed the previous year. After the rose has lived a few years, old canes bloom more and more sparsely, and should be removed at the base. This will invigorate the plant, stimulating new flowering growth.

What's the difference between a climbing rose and a rambler? They're quite similar in their growth patterns, but the conventional distinction is that ramblers bloom once, producing masses of small flowers, and climbers produce large blossoms throughout the growing season. Some climbers have a heavy spring bloom, and fewer blossoms at a time throughout the season.

Climbing roses don't have true gripping parts such as ivy holdfasts, so they usually have to be tied to whatever they're climbing. Use a figure eight in your tie, so you don't strangle the cane, but hold it sufficiently firm that it won't chafe and rub in wind. Some that are planted to climb trees are usually wound around the tree by the gardener to a certain height, then may be "gripping" higher on the tree by means of long curved thorns into tree bark.

Old roses (those introduced before 1867) should be pruned only after they bloom, not before. Hybrid teas and other "modern" roses that produce single blossoms should be pruned 1/4-inch above a leaf stalk with five to seven leaves on the outside of the cane, using a slanting cut to repel water. Such deadheading (removing spent blossoms) should be done regularly to prevent the plant's setting seed pods (hips).

Pests on rose shrubs in our area are aphids, which may be blasted off with a hose, repelled by plantings of chives near the base of your rose bush, or controlled by sprays of soapy water or Neem, for instance. Earwigs are nuisances in blossoms, but their numbers can be reduced by laying corrugated cardboard or rolled up newspaper near your roses, and picking up those items and tapping them into a bucket of hot soapy water each morning for a few days. You can also trap earwigs in small cups of oil set just below soil surface. (Surface of the oil should be at least 1 inch below the soil surface.) Cheap cooking oil will work to kill earwigs in that kind of trap. Sluggo Plus is a new chemical control for earwigs and slugs.

Rose curculios chew on rose buds and lay eggs in the buds. These are weevils in the classic shape of Kokopelli and are black and red. Hand pick them, dropping them into a bucket of hot soapy water, but be sure to add the chewed bud to the water to destroy the eggs.

Japanese beetles first showed up in the Treasure Valley in the summer of 2012, and efforts were immediately started to eliminate that invasive creature. Handpick and drop into hot soapy water if trapping hasn't been 100 percent effective.

(For more rose maladies — including one that can infect the gardener — see the chapter on diseases.)

CHAPTER 5

Bulbs

Bulb basics

Before planting, enrich and loosen your soil by incorporating a lot of decayed organic matter (compost) in a site exposed to at least six hours of sun per day. Most spring-flowering bulbs require pure sunshine, not interrupted by shadows, even those cast briefly by power poles. Some bulbs may be planted under deciduous trees where they get dappled shade.

If you want a natural look, toss a bucket of bulbs on your garden bed and plant where they fall. Bulbs for flowers such as daffodils are easy to plant and easy to manage, since they're toxic to rodents and even deer. Tulips and some other species' bulbs are attractive to rodents, and they may eat the bulbs before you get one flower.

You can foil rodent depredation by planting bulbs in cages made of hardware cloth or you can surround them with some sharp gravel, such as turkey grit or ground oyster shells. There's also a ceramic shard grit available, but if you have dogs that might be digging in the area, the ceramic shards can shred paws and your fingers, of course.

Another layer of protection could be pegging down chicken wire fencing over the area planted in bulbs. At least rodents won't be diving in vertically.

The general rule in planting bulbs is to plant them at a depth three to four times the height of the bulb. If you're unsure about which way is "up," plant the bulb on its side. It will find its way up. Some bulbs, such as Crown Imperial fritillaries, are concave on top, and will hold water and rot unless they're planted on their sides. Bulbs such as tulips and some lilies have contractile roots and can even pull themselves deeper into soil than originally planted.

If you have a patch of one species of bulb such as daffodils or tulips that fails to bloom in spring, or blooming is sparse, the patch should be dug and divided to give individual bulbs some room, or feed the plants with a slow release 10-10-20 fertilizer.

Spring blooming bulbs are very hardy, and we have enough chill hours to satisfy their need. Even after they bloom, frost doesn't seem to take much of a toll. If the temperature drops to 15 degrees, daffodil flower stems will bend into a crook and never straighten again.

Purchase only firm, mold-free bulbs free of damage. The larger the bulb, the larger the plant it will produce, but you can also plant the small bulblets nestled against the larger bulb and they will grow, producing flowers in a year or two.

SPRING-FLOWERING

Plant bulbs in late fall, after soil temperature cools to below 60 degrees. The best selection, however, is in September in local nurseries, and even earlier by mail order. If you have a cool place to keep bulbs until late October or early November, buy bulbs when the selection is best. Otherwise, wait and buy when it's closer to planting season. Do not store them near apples, which emit ethylene gas, stimulating premature sprouting.

Most spring-flowering bulbs will multiply and live for many years, provided they're not exposed to abundant summer water or subject to rodent depredation. Some of the unusual or rare bulbs may last only one season, however.

Earliest blooming in my yard are the snowdrops, followed by winter aconite and species crocus. I don't have regular crocus, so I can't compare its earliness.

Scott Kunst of Old House Gardens advises leaving foliage at least until it's yellow. Some wait until it's browned, but unless you've planted other flowers that will hide the aging foliage, you may want to remove it when yellow or dig bulbs with foliage attached and lay them in a shaded area for the foliage to continue feeding bulbs.

SNOWDROPS

Galanthus elwesii or G. nivalis. White nodding blossoms with green inner segments, bloom in February, along with hellebores.

WINTER ACONITE

Eranthis, also called buttercup. Bright yellow blossoms in ground-hugging green rosettes of leaves erupt about two weeks later than snowdrops.

SPECIES CROCUS

Tiny bulbs planted in the lawn bring spring's promise to bleak winter grass. Yellow or purple blooms are preferable to white, because the latter looks like shipping popcorn that's blown in. They're done by lawn mowing time.

IRIS RETICULATA

They look like tall bearded iris, but they're less than 6 inches high, blooming quite early in spring.

DAFFODILS

There are early, mid- and late-season flowering, standard, mid-size and miniature daffodils, and although most are yellow, there are also white daffodils, double-flowered and daffodils with different-colored "trumpets." Some are fragrant, others not. Do not combine with other cut flowers in a bouquet. Divisions are Trumpet, Large Cup, Small Cup, Double, Triandrus (Fuschia-like blooms), Cyclamineus, Jonquilla, Tazetta, Poeticus, Bulbocodium, Split Corona, Collar, Papillon and Miniatures.

What's the difference between jonquils, Narcissus and daffodils? Narcissus is the name of the genus containing daffodils. In the South, folks refer to yellow daffodils as "jonquils," but the American Daffodil Society says jonquils are members of Division 7 of daffodils (Jonquilla), which usually — but not always — have yellow flowers, strong scent and rounded foliage.

TULIPS

Relished by rodents, and the flowers may even be consumed by humans. They were brought to Europe from their native Turkey and Silk Road environs in the 17th century. They were an instant hit, and their popularity soared when they were invaded by a virus that "broke" their color, yielding color-streaked blossoms. The so-called "Rembrandt virus" was actually killing the bulb, but collectors competed with one another to offer the most money (a year's salary) for one virus-bearing bulb. Now we call that historic hubbub "Tulipmania."

The virus is not a desirable trait, and Netherlands inspectors watch for infections, then rogue out those bulbs. Breeders have now produced blossoms that appear similar to those infected by the virus, yet the bulbs remain healthy.

Flower petals of tulips are not especially tasty, but each color tastes different, I'm told. In the Netherlands, commercial fields of tulips are beheaded about a week after they bloom to prevent their putting energy into seed development. Flower stalks are left intact because they and the foliage are feeding the bulbs so they'll bloom the following year.

Those sacrificed flower petals are fed to cattle, which eat the red petals first.

Tulip flowers come in every color except true blue, and may be single or double, early, mid- or late-season flowering, tall or ground-hugging, lily-flowered, "parrot tulips" (with curled and twisted tepals), Kaufmanniana tulips (some resemble water lilies), Greigii and Fosteriana tulips, as well as species tulips that are closer to wild progenitors.

Some reports indicate the fancier the flower, the less likely it is to return the following year.

I especially love the species tulips, short-stemmed groundlings that provide carpets of colors in early spring. The inner parts of their petals usually have a color that contrasts with the outer portions.

Tulips planted in pots should be planted with the flat side of the bulbs pointing out, toward the container rim, for a uniform display of leaves. They also root best in very cool temperatures.

OTHER SPRING BULBS

There are other bulbs that provide spring color that are hardy here, such as hyacinths, Anemones, Alliums, camas, Chionodoxa, grape hyacinths and others. We are restricted regarding Alliums, however; bulbs that come from outside our area are embargoed. That's unfortunate, because my favorite ornamental Allium is A. schubertii, whose blossom looks like a frozen rocket burst, and I don't think those bulbs are available here.

Camas requires a lot of water, although most bulbs are drought tolerant. You may see camas bloom wild in Idaho fields, but those fields are swampy.

Many spring blooming bulbs can be planted in containers. Tazetta Narcissus, popularly known as "paperwhites," are often grown on pebbles (with support), rooting them in dark cool temperatures (between 40 and 50 degrees) for two or three weeks before they start their top growth.

Special vases are available for forcing hyacinths in the refrigerator, but I don't think all hyacinth bulbs are good for forcing. Either that or I encountered some extra-stubborn bulbs.

SUMMER-BLOOMING

Plant summer-flowering bulbs in late spring, when the soil has started to warm.

LILIES

After your Easter lilies finish blooming indoors, cut off the flower (leaving the stem and leaves to feed the bulb), and keep it in a cool spot (60 to 65 degrees, preferably) in good indirect light, until all danger of frost has passed. Then plant it in a flower bed apart from other lilies, lest it transmit a disease. If winter isn't too severe, they'll come back next spring, and bloom in midsummer, their normal bloom time. They're forced into blossom for Easter by regulating heat hours. Being forced into bloom at the wrong time of year takes a lot out of a bulb, so your "Easter" lily may not bloom at all the next year, but the years after that, it will bloom in its regular time, which is midsummer.

When you plant outdoors, plant in well-drained rich soil where tops receive dappled light and roots remain shaded and cool. If you need to move them, move them in late September.

If you have Asiatic or Oriental lilies, be wary of their pollen. It stains clothing and may be difficult to remove. Florists usually snip off the pollen-bearing anthers to prevent staining clothing or tablecloths. If you do get pollen stains, put the cloth in the sun to dry. When the pollen is thoroughly dry, it will brush off without leaving a stain. You may also be able to vacuum it off, but don't try to brush it off when it's still moist.

If you don't want the lilies to put their energy into making and maturing seeds, snip the spent blossoms off the stalk so the plant's energy will go into strengthening the bulb. You could propagate new plants from the seeds, but the new plants probably would be different from the parent. After the stalks on lilies turn yellow, consider digging, dividing and/or moving them. Fall is the time to do it. Spade carefully, or if possible, feel around with your hands to pry out bulbs.

Be sure to watch for babies (bulbils, formed by Oriental lilies), and plant them in a special "nursery bed" where they can grow for two or three years until they can compete with the big guys for food and water. First prepare a new site for the mature lilies you're going to transplant.

True lily bulbs don't go dormant like tulips and others, so they shouldn't be allowed to dry out. Cannas, daylilies and rain lilies are not true lilies, by the way.

If the lily bulbs have split in two, pull them apart and plant them. If they haven't split and you want more lilies just like them, remove some scales (that is, pieces of the bulbs that pull off easily). Don't reduce the girth of the original bulb by more than one third in this scaling project.

Let the scales air dry overnight (do not wash them to clean them). Once they're dried and calloused, put them between layers of damp vermiculite in a plastic bag that's loosely folded at the top. They should remain in that condition for eight to 10 weeks, as they form bulblets.

Those should be stored in temperatures just above freezing, then planted outdoors. It will take about four years for Asiatic lilies and five years for Oriental lilies to develop to commercial size.

To transplant the original bulb, you'll need to choose a site that has good drainage, good air circulation and rich, humusy soil. Compost should give you that added organic matter.

Then plant the bulbs at least three times deeper than the bulb is tall. In other words, if the bulb is 2 inches high, plant it 6 to 8 inches deep, deeper in sandy soil, shallower in heavy clay. Do not let manure touch the bulb, and be sure to water the bulb well after planting.

Lily bulbs are not usually available in this area in the fall, but lily enthusiasts do recommend planting and transplanting Oriental lilies in fall to permit root growth during mild winter days. They won't do quite so well the first season if planted in spring.

If you did let your lilies go to seed, put seeds in a plastic bag with damp (not dripping) peat moss. Shake the bag to distribute the seeds, then put the bag in a warm place (72 to 82 degrees). Open the bag every two weeks to admit air, but don't poke around. If you don't see growth in six months, put them in the refrigerator (not the freezer) for a couple of months, then put them back in the warm place (not in direct sun). You should see signs of growth in a few weeks.

Some lilies set bulbils at the junction of the stem and each leaf. You can pluck those and plant them in a pot where you can keep them watered and watched, or let them fall to the ground and hope they will receive sufficient moisture.

GLADIOLUS AND OTHER SUMMER-FLOWERING BULBS

If you plant Gladiolus bulbs (corms, really) at least 6 inches deep, the tall flower stalk will be less likely to fall over when blossoms open. Usually in our climate, we must dig Gladiolus and Dahlia tubers after foliage has blackened by frost, but in the winter of 2011-2012, Gladiolus corms survived in the ground and sent forth foliage and flower stalks in spring in my yard. New Gladiolus corms form on top of the old ones, so they will work themselves toward the surface, and will have to be replanted. We did dig Dahlia rhizomes, cleaned and dried them, then sprayed them with Wilt-Pruf and stored them in a tub of vermiculite.

You can dig Gladiolus corms about six weeks after they bloom. Then snap off or cut the stalk as close to the corm as possible, spread corms on airy trays to dry, and about two or three weeks later, break the new corm away from the old one at bottom (a corky layer will have formed between corms). Discard the mother corm, and dust the new one with bulb fungicide and store it on a screened tray, in a mesh bag or in pantyhose, tying a knot between corms for good circulation.

You can, of course, either plant glad corms a foot deep to start with, hoping you won't have to buy new ones to replace them next summer, or dig them annually.

After frost nips foliage, dig Canna and calla lily rhizomes, Dahlia tubers and tuber-corms of tuberous Begonias. Wash Begonia and lily bulbs clean of soil, scrape off old dry layers, and after they're thoroughly dried, store them in lightly dampened vermiculite.

You can also spray them with an anti-transpirant such as Wilt-Pruf to prevent desiccation of the bulbs.

In all of the stored bulb containers, bulbs should be kept apart from one another, lest they transmit mold or moisture to another. They should never touch one another.

CHAPTER 6

Other ornamentals

AGASTACHES

Agastache foeniculum, pronounced ahg-ah-STOCK-ee and also called anise hyssop, sends up spikes covered with tiny purple blossoms, just the right size to yield nectar (food) for miniature insects, primarily beneficial insects capable of killing or parasitizing insects larger than themselves. Newer-bred Agastaches such as Black Adder, Tutti Frutti, Raspberry Summer and Summer Love have larger blossoms, attractive to butterflies and hummingbirds.

Agastaches bloom for months, a lasting haze of color. A. foeniculum is about 4 feet tall when mature, other varieties shorter. Some have fragrant blossoms, others have fragrant foliage. All produce seeds attractive to birds.

ARUM ITALICUM

A "Jack in the Pulpit" type of flower that leafs out in winter and shows early spring green. It presents a white cowl-like blossom over a yellow spadix in late spring, then produces spires of reddish-orange seed modules. These fleshy seed coverings are very irritating to human skin, so wear gloves when handling them.

"Jack in the Pulpit" is a name usually given to another member of this group, Arisaema triphyllum, which grows and flowers in late summer, prefers moist soil and is native to eastern North America. A. italicum grows well in my unimproved soil and is not demanding of copious water.

BAMBOO

If you need a tall, dense hedge in a hurry, consider bamboo. It's fast-growing, attractive and useful. It's an interesting plant, technically a grass. Some varieties are hardy down to minus 20. That's the lower range of zone 5, but when we drop to zone 4, as we used to do about every 10 years, we drop only a few degrees lower. Odds are a well-established thicket should survive.

First consider what you want it for. If you just want it to be decorative and you don't want to bother trying to contain it, buy a clumping bamboo variety. It will take more plants to fill out a hedge than if you use more invasive running bamboos that can fill in themselves. Running bamboos can be contained, but special steps should be taken for containment before planting. Since bamboo spreads by runners, a shoot may come up several feet from the original planting.

To prevent runners, dig a trench 2 to 3 feet deep, line it with an impenetrable barrier such as aluminum flashing or dense plastic set vertically, and fill in the trench without compacting the soil. Bamboo likes to grow in loose, well-aerated soil, abundant with organic matter. Another way to contain bamboo is to plant it adjacent to a water garden. Bamboo can't live where its roots are wet.

Emerging shoots of many varieties are edible and choice, if picked before they reach 12 inches high. One fellow on the West Coast admitted his running bamboo had invaded his neighbor's yard, but said the neighbor didn't know it because his dogs ate the shoots as soon as they appeared.

Clumping bamboos are Fargesia muriale and F. nitida. Both are hardy to minus 20 degrees.

The F. muriale grows to a height of 12 feet, and although it will grow in full sun, it adapts to partial shade better. This variety, a favorite food of pandas, has thin upright shoots and thin leaves.

F. nitida has dense foliage and also grows to a height of 12 feet. Canes are very strong and suitable for garden stakes. It's best if you can grow this where it will be shielded from mid-day sun.

Phyllostachys nuda produces 2-inch thick canes that shoot up to 20 to 35 feet in height. Another variety, P. aureosulcata aureocaulis, has slightly thinner canes growing 20 to 25 feet tall. If you want canes with strength such as for garden trellising, don't harvest them before they're 3 years old. Lay them on a flat surface to cure.

Fargesias nitida nymphenburg is also known as Blue Fountain bamboo because of its weeping habit. It is hardy to minus 20, and would be attractive planted alone, or as a specimen plant. Phyllostachys nigra, or black bamboo, is prized for its beauty, but it's only hardy to zero. For that reason, most people who have it grow it in containers that can be moved inside during extremely cold weather.

BAPTISIA AUSTRALIS

Also known as wild indigo, and the deep blue of its blossoms reflects that, although shrubs with other colors of blossoms have been bred. This is a native of the Southeastern U.S., but is widely adapted to soils and climate. Flowers are very hardy and very attractive, but it will spread, lupine-like, giving way to attractive seed pods. These are especially lovely paired with pink peonies, according to Anju Lucas of Edwards Greenhouse.

This plant thrives in full sun or filtered shade, and once established, it's drought-resistant. This is a difficult plant to move, since it's tap-rooted. It takes three years in ground to reach maturity, at which time it may be about 4 feet in diameter, and 3 to 4 feet tall. Prune it back by one-third after flowering to prevent floppiness.

BISHOP'S WEED

Aegopodium podagaria is a ground cover or foliage plant for pots that, singly, is attractive. The problem is that it spreads and dies to the ground in winter. The variegated version once planted next to my house has reverted to green, and is only useful to keep rainwater from splashing onto the house. Other groundcovers are more interesting, such as Lamiums.

BRUNNERA MACROPHYLLA

Siberian bugloss is an attractive shade plant with small robin's egg blue flowers in spring. It prefers light shade, and that's what it gets until the apple tree is fully leafed out here. This is one of my favorite plants, very hardy and tolerant of low water provision. In my garden, it's about 8 to 10 inches tall. It reportedly self-seeds, but may need more water for that outcome than I provide.

BUDDLEIA DAVIDII

Shrub with dense columns of tiny flowers attractive to butterflies. Also called butterfly bush. In moister climates than ours, this self-seeds to the point of invasiveness. Folks in the Treasure Valley have lost several of their mature Buddleias over the past few winters to winterkill.

Wait until spring before you prune them back. If you prune them in autumn, and we receive a sudden drop in temperature, it may damage shrub tissues beyond salvage.

Buddleia blossoms are sufficiently tiny and shallow to feed beneficial wasps as well as butterflies. B. davidii blooms on new wood, so pruning that is beneficial, but B. alternaria blooms on old wood, so don't prune unless you must.

CACTUS

Several varieties are native here. One of the most common I've seen is the Opuntia. Use a newspaper sling to move cactus plants, and be careful about the spines and glochids (tiny spines). The latter may be removed by pressing duct tape over flesh impregnated with glochids, then removing the tape. Weed around cactus with pliers.

CALIBRACHOA

Also called "Million Bells," this is a tiny version of petunias introduced in 1998 by Proven Winners. Superb in pots, it's grown as an annual. Flowers erupt so thickly that foliage is almost invisible. No deadheading is needed. In warmer climates than ours, this plant may be used as a groundcover. Fertilize in-ground plants monthly, containerized every two weeks. Prefers good drainage and full sun, but will thrive in partial shade.

CARYOPTERIS

Also known as bluebeard. Needs little care. Blooms on new wood. Should be pruned back to a low upright palm-shaped framework, then subsequently pruned back to within 1 inch of the old framework "fingers" in spring.

CASTOR BEAN (Ricinus)

Produces castor oil and the powerful poison known as ricin. Beautiful tall, rangy plant grown from elaborate bean-like seeds. Seeds are attractive to children but if ingested, one will kill a child, two will kill an adult.

In addition to being one of the most deadly poisons in nature, the seeds also contain strong allergens. If you still want to grow castor beans, start beans indoors in early March, one bean per 4-inch pot. Germination may take 14 to 21 days, but may be speeded up by bottom heat. If you have to transplant before setting them outdoors, plant in gallon pots. Plant castor beans outdoors when you set out your tomatoes. Plant in full sun, and water as much as you can spare, lightly fertilizing them every other week. Foliage is quite attractive. Some Asians say they eat the foliage, but the American Horticulture Society says all parts are "highly toxic if ingested."

CHASTE TREE

Vitex agnus-castus, an ornamental shrub that sports late summer spires of pale blue spikes covered with tiny flowers, attracting and feeding hordes of beneficial wasps and bees. I started this from seed over 20 years ago, and each spring we cut it back to about 2 feet from its mature height of about 10 feet. Leaves are described as "palmately compound with five to seven fingerlike leaflets," or very similar to illustrations of marijuana leaves.

Why is it called chaste tree? Some think seeds subdue libido, others think it does the opposite. I've never seen seeds on our shrub.

CHOCOLATE FLOWER (Berlandiera lyrata)

Could be poster flower for xeriscaping except for the fact that the flower closes when the day gets hot. It's a yellow daisy-like flower that does have a chocolate scent if you bend close. It supposedly self-sows, but must do so sparingly. The plant is coarse and rangy, but it looks OK in a spot that doesn't get watered at all. It grows to about 18 inches tall, requires full sun, and is hardy to zone 4.

CHRYSANTHEMUM

This plant blooms in response to prolonged darkness or shorter daylight hours.

In this area in late summer, nurseries sell lush pots full of budded chrysanthemums ready to bloom because they've had light-blocking cloth covers. The plants may come back the next spring or may not, if winter is harsh.

If you do have chrysanthemums in the ground in spring, fertilize them in early spring and pinch off flower buds and stem tips, continuing to pinch back until July 4.

Then you should have a bushy plant that will soon begin blooming. After blossoming begins, remove spent blossoms to prolong blooming, and when hard winter looms, cut stems back to about 4 inches. After ground has frozen, cover the plant with shredded leaves, evergreen branches or pine needles.

Dig and divide in early spring, replanting only young healthy growth to avoid a dead spot in the center of the plant.

CLEMATIS

Large blossoms in many different colors adorn this hardy, long-lived vine that thrives in this area. To plant it, first enrich your soil with compost, then plant it 2 to 4 inches deeper than it was in its pot, protect it from being accidentally stepped on, water it well and give it something to climb on. Keep roots cool with mulch. A vine accidentally stepped on or otherwise bent just stops growing, according to Anju Lucas of Edwards Greenhouse.

Select a variety hardy to at least zone 5; zone 4 is better. Pinch off blooms the first year to encourage root development. Fertilizing with potassium or tomato fertilizer also encourages root development. Keep track of the variety you've planted, for different varieties must be pruned differently.

Sometimes an apparently vigorous vine appears to collapse and die. This Clematis wilt usually attacks very young vines, less than three years old. The vine is not dead; just cut out the "dead" material, even to soil line if necessary. It may take a year to send up new shoots, but it will. Some Clematis cultivars grow vines up to 20 feet or longer, others manage only about 5 feet.

A simplistic and not entirely thorough pruning recommendation is if the plant blooms in early spring, prune after blooming. If it blooms later in the spring and a light flush of blossoms in September, lightly prune in late February or March. The third group blooms only on new growth, and blooms from early summer to fall. If you don't prune it back, it will continue to grow, blooming only on the far end. For these Clematis vines, prune to two or three buds about March.

CUT FLOWERS

These include many annuals such as zinnia, Gaillardia, cosmos, Gladiolus, marigolds, daisies, Rudbeckias and sunflowers.

DAHLIAS

About a week after a killing frost, dig Dahlia tubers by starting to dig about a foot away from the stalk that you've trimmed to a few inches above soil line. Wash off soil, leave a bit of stem on the tubers or else they won't grow next summer, and let them dry upside down in a frost-free area for a day or two, dust with sulfur to prevent fungi, and spray with anti-transpirant and store in vermiculite.

In spring, if they're still plump and firm, you can divide Dahlia tubers, leaving at least one eye or bud per section. These tubers are living plant tissue, so must be protected from mold and dehydration, especially when they're dormant.

Local hobbyists display blossoms and photos of Dahlias at the Western Idaho Fair each summer. Boisean Tim Garland, a hobby hybridizer of Dahlias, had his white anemone type of Dahlia accepted as a "new variety" by the American Dahlia Society in 2009.

DAYLILIES

Look closely at a diamond-dusted daylily flower, and you'll be enraptured. If it's aromatic too, you'll fall in love with the genus, one that is mostly trouble-free. Diamond dusting means the petals show white sparkling bits among the colors of the flower. Daylilies (Hemerocallis) are not true lilies. They're fleshy-rooted perennials that don't grow from bulbs as lilies do. Flowers last for just a day, hence the name. As long as you meet some minimum requirements, they're as tough as old boots. They survive spray from salted winter roads, being uprooted and not immediately replanted, being chewed on by deer, and exposed to drought.

They need a well-drained soil, preferably rich with organic matter, fertilizer topdressing on the soil surface when spring growth is emerging, mulching with 3 or 4 inches of material to protect in winter, and dividing every three to five years.

For most varieties, the more sun exposure the better. Only a few tolerate some shade, and they will bloom less than those in full sun. All require plentiful water when first planted and through their first year, but are tolerant of some drought after they're established. They can be planted at any time the ground is not frozen hard. They're good at holding soil on a slope, too.

Some folks plant them under maple trees, giving them extra water to compensate for the thirst of tree roots. Some daylilies that grow in a half-day of shade may have clearer colors — especially those with red or purple blossoms — than the same cultivars grown in full sun.

There are 30,000 to 40,000 different varieties of Hemerocallis on the market and so many professional and amateur hybridizers at work that there's an almost constant replacement of varieties. If you want an old variety, you'd better find someone who's growing it and bargain for a root.

Hemerocallis includes about 15 species, and they include nocturnal flower opening or diurnal; single, double or spider (narrow-petaled) flowers; ruffled or smooth flowers; evergreen or dormant plants; aromatic or non-aromatic; diploid, triploid and tetraploid chromosomes; miniatures or standards; re-bloomers; those with diamond-dusted flowers; blossoms in nearly every color except blue; and early, mid-season, and late-blooming.

Dormant varieties are recommended for Northern gardeners, evergreen varieties for the hottest areas of the country. Chromosome numbers are mainly important to breeders. The old H. fulva, the orange "ditch" daylily, is a sterile triploid, propagating from roots and often seen as a relic of an abandoned farmstead.

Deadheading, or removing flowers just below the bump (ovary) prevents seed. If you want to grow daylilies from seed, be advised that it will take about three years before they bloom in our climate. Seed-grown daylilies often are disappointing.

When blooming is no longer profuse, your daylilies may need to be divided. Dig up the whole clump, hose off soil, then separate roots by teasing them, putting spading forks back-to-back in the clump and prying, or using a sharp meat cleaver or ax to cut the roots apart. Discard damaged roots; these are vulnerable to rot and disease.

When your daylily has finished blooming and the scapes (stalks) begin to brown, look at the stalks for proliferations, or tiny new daylilies forming on the scapes. These clones may be harvested (cut an inch above and an inch below the proliferation) and treated as green cuttings. They should be protected from freezing, etc., until spring, then planted out.

Daylily buds and flowers are edible. Some savor them with sorbets or fruity sherbets, others steam or saute them.

DELPHINIUMS

One of the most dazzling displays you can make at the back of your flower bed is to plant Delphiniums there. They grow tall, stately and with long-lasting spikes of flowers that blossom from the bottom up. They are perennials, and will be back next year, too, if given minimal care. They seem to like our alkaline soil and are not greedy for water, although they should be well mulched. They should not be allowed to dry out, nor should they have constantly wet soil. Delphiniums prefer full sun, but can be grown in dappled shade.

A welcome introduction in the middle or front of the flower bed is the small Delphinium known as Blue Butterfly. It grows to about 14 inches and blossoms for quite a long time.

All of these flowers are very hardy, tolerant of frosts. Mulched for winter, they can survive zone 4 winters (below minus 20 degrees). They grow best with rich food such as sheep manure, and mulch helps to keep the roots cool and moist. (Be careful that the sheep haven't grazed on persistent herbicides.) Delphiniums' main enemies in our area are slugs and powdery mildew. You can use the same treatments for powdery mildew prevention and slugs that you do for roses.

Delphiniums do best with about one plant per 18-inch square, and many require staking against winds. If you plant them against a wall for support, however, the winds will beat them against the wall, ruining the plant. If you cut the tall Delphiniums back to about 6 inches after their first flowering, they often flower again in the same season.

Each little blossom on the flower stalk has a center portion of reproductive parts, the anthers, stigma, style and ovary, collectively known as the eye, or the "bee." It does look like a bee in the flower, especially if the eye or bee is yellow. Usually the bee is a different color than the flower, so when Delphinium growers are talking about color, they talk of the color of the flower and the color of the bee.

Delphiniums used to be blue, white or purple, but some have been bred to red and pink flowers, too. English Delphiniums tend to be stockier and stronger, not requiring staking. The Pacific hybrid series, the Round Table Delphiniums, are beautiful, but definitely need to be supported.

For many years, we were unable to get English Delphiniums here, but that has changed. Edwards Greenhouse has been carrying English Delphiniums and some bred in New Zealand that have English Delphinium ancestry. Anju Lucas of Edwards Greenhouse said she planted some of the New Zealand plants one July at her home near Star, and they grew to 6 feet and were fully in bloom at Thanksgiving. She did not stake them, in spite of the Star area's reputation for winds, and the plants weathered the winds quite well.

When you're ready to plant, call garden centers for information on variety availability.

DOGWOOD (Red Twigged or Red Osier)

Cut this shrub to within 2 inches of the ground its second year, and cut back to two buds of previous year's growth thereafter. A yellow barked variety is also available, both attacked by cankers and scale at times. Hard pruning forces new colorful growth of stems that add winter interest. The shrub will grow tall, wide and rangy unless pruned annually.

ECHINACEA

Echinacea purpurea became a focus of plant breeders in the 1980s, and when the variety E. purpurea Magnus was awarded Perennial Plant of the Year in 1998, its popularity with gardeners skyrocketed. Not only is it said to be one of the finest perennials in the U.S., it's also the source for the most widely sold and used herbal supplement in the nation. Native Americans used it to cure many ills, but most people today use it to stimulate the immune system and to ameliorate cold symptoms.

Breeders of this wonderful Native.American plant have developed an amazing palette of blossom colors, double blossoms and scent. The plants are quite hardy, bloom over a long period, are showy in wildflower settings or in more formal ornamental gardens and long-lasting as cut flowers. They're long-lived perennials, and should be divided about every four years.

There are nine Echinacea (eh-kin-AY-sha) species native to the Eastern and Midwestern U.S. They thrive in meadows, rocky open woods, roadsides, wherever the soil has an abundance of calcium and magnesium, and generally any place they don't have competition from other plants. That lets us out for native growth, since our soil is lacking plentiful magnesium.

Yet we certainly can and do grow Echinacea in ornamental and herb gardens.

This is a plant that loves full sun, fair soil and tolerates some drought.

In 1997, a fellow in the Netherlands found a double-flowered seedling in his cut-flower fields, and gave it to a friend who marketed it as Razzmatazz in 2003. Others began trying to breed for double blossomed plants and succeeded in producing some acceptable doubles (and some ugly flowers, too).

Dan Heims of Terra Nova wholesale nursery has done considerable breeding of Echinaceas using yellow-blooming E. paradoxa in the parentage, increasing the flowers' color range. He advises customers to debud these Echinaceas their first year so that instead of flowering, they'll put their energy into developing side roots in addition to their first-year tap roots.

He specifies those with E. paradoxa in their lineage be so treated, but some plantsmen advise treating all Echinaceas that way. Echinaceas can reseed themselves, so watch for that and prevent seedlings' flowering their first year. You can improve the soil for them by watering a time or two with a tablespoon of Epsom salts in a gallon of water.

Flowers are borne atop a stiff stalk. The composite flowers of rayed florets are arranged in a cone, long-lasting in the garden bed or in cut flower arrangements. The flowers attract and feed many nectar drinkers such as bees, wasps and butterflies, and the seeds are valuable for feeding several small bird species.

Although two new cultivars, one named Mac 'n' Cheese, the other Tomato Soup, are enjoying wide popularity, Anju Lucas of Edwards Greenhouse, says they're not best for our area because their colors fade out quickly in our bright sunlight. Instead, she prefers Flame Thrower, an orangish-yellow single flower, and Hot Papaya, a red-orange double flower, both descended from the yellow E. paradoxa, native to Missouri, Arkansas, Oklahoma and Texas.

"E. purpurea" implies all flowers are purple, but they're not, even in their wild state. Nevertheless, that is the proper botanical name for this coneflower. Some are naturally white, the E. paradoxa is yellow, and E. purpurea tennesseensis mauve.

E. purpurea grows naturally in most of the Eastern states (except New England), the Midwest and west to Colorado. It doesn't grow wild in the northern tier of states from Minnesota west. Range fires and heavy grazing open up vegetative growth, making way for Echinacea. Echinacea does its own part preparing a place to grow by emitting a substance from its roots that inhibits the growth of nearby plants.

This allelopathy (toxicity) should have an effect on where we place it in an ornamental garden. E. purpurea usually grows to 2 and a half to 3 feet tall, although the white-flowering variety is shorter. The flowers of E. purpurea tennesseensis tend to turn toward the sun and follow its path.

ELM

Tree owners can be considerate of neighbors having to remove elm seed-lings from garden beds by reducing the showers of elm seeds that fall and blow from every living elm tree in the Valley. Timing is crucial for chemical control with Florel Fruit Eliminator, spraying the tree at mid- to full-bloom stage, prior to fruit/seed set. It may also be used on trees such as cottonwood, maple, oak, sweet gum, crabapple and horse chestnut.

Elms have been under attack by Dutch elm disease, elm leaf beetles and now elm seed bugs. The latter infestation is a nuisance in homes, where the bugs intrude to overwinter in warm surroundings.

EQUISETUM (Horsetail, Scouring Rush or Snake Grass)

An ancient plant that you should grow only in containers. For more, see the chapter on weeds.

ERYNGIUM GIGANTEUM

Gardening's connection with Halloween usually is thought of as restricted to pumpkins for jack-o'-lanterns or Baby Boo (or Lumina) white pumpkins. But gardening does have its ghosts.

Gardening's ghost is not a wispy wraith, but rather a handsome, bristly plant. Ellen Ann Willmott, gardener and writer, apparently thought the large, pale sea holly, Eryngium giganteum, was not sufficiently appreciated, so whenever she visited others' gardens, she managed to drop some seeds for E. giganteum in proper places. Her hosts didn't see her do it, but when the plant germinated, they knew it was "Miss Willmott's ghost." Folks seldom noticed it until it was large and inescapable, then the comment arose, "Ah, Miss Willmott was here."

One reference says this "Kilroy was here" plant may have been pseudo-named for her in recognition of her prickly temperament. She gardened in England, France and Italy from 1905 until the 1920s, and was awarded the Victoria Medal of Honor by the Royal Horticultural Society. She was quite fond of other plants as well, but even here in the Treasure Valley, we know that E. giganteum is Miss Willmott's Ghost. And it is sold by local nurseries.

The short-lived perennial resembles a large thistle with steel-blue flowers. It contrasts quite nicely with green leafy foliage. It obviously also produces viable seeds, and reseeds itself. So grow your own "ghost" and enjoy the plant while you get a chuckle out of the nickname.

EUONYMOUS ALATA

Also called burning bush, this ornamental is very susceptible to root rot from overwatering and collar rot from mulch being pulled tight against stems or trunk. Do not plant in lawn if you're watering every other day.

EUPHORBIA LATHYRIS

Gopher purge, or gopher spurge, is an interesting plant but can be invasive. It has milky latex sap that can be very irritating to ungloved hands. In spite of its common name, it does not repel gophers.

EVERGREENS

Water your needled and scale-leafed evergreens deeply before winter, and tie the limbs if shape is important to your landscape. After plant moisture has descended to roots, you could use an anti-transpirant spray such as Wilt-Pruf.

Use that spray on broadleafed evergreens, too. Broadleafed evergreens may change their color for winter (Mahonias, e.g.), and others curl their leaves in response to cold.

FLAX

I love sky-blue flowers, especially in spring and early summer. One of the prettiest blue flowers is borne by a simple little plant grown by humans for over 5,000 years. Linen flax has been used for food, medicine, linseed oil, linoleum and linen. It was linen from flax that was used for Biblical clothing, from swaddling clothes to shrouds. Egyptians wrapped mummies in layers of linen. Flax seeds are used for food or are pressed to remove oils. Stems are treated to be spun and woven into linen, a lengthy and fairly complex process.

My blue-flowered flax blooms at the same time as the orange and pink Oriental poppies; it's a self-seeding annual. There are different flaxes, some annuals and one perennial. My flax is fiber flax, Linum usitatissimum Regina. The Linum genus includes some 200 species of plants found in northern temperate regions, some with different-colored blossoms.

Plants are upright, about 10 inches to 3 feet tall, with very narrow leaves alternating along the stalk. The blossoms are five-petaled, about 1 inch across. When blossoming is done, round seed heads at the tops of the stalks hold seeds for next year or for other use. Herb seed sources such as Richters have species known for seed production or long and strong stems for linen production.

Flax doesn't grow readily in heavy clay or sand, but it will grow in any other type of soil. Give it at least six hours of sun per day. Blossoming occurs about 60 days after sowing and blossoms are quickly followed by round seed heads.

If you're growing it for fabric, make sure the soil is evenly moist from germination through blooming. Hand-pull weeds. Fibers are at their strongest 90 days after seeding. Harvest at this time is strongly recommended. Pull plants, knock the dirt off the roots and hang to dry with root ends together. When it's dry, draw stem straw through a toothed instrument called a "ripple" to gather seeds. Then you're ready to "ret" the stems. This is a kind of rotting off of the non-essential parts of the stems.

You can either lay them out on the ground, weighing them down so winds won't move them, for "dew retting." That takes eight to 10 weeks of tending and turning. Or you can "water ret" them in a pond or a tank. Time involved depends on the temperatures, but it's a matter of days, not weeks. Then you're ready for "breaking" and "scutching" to remove pith and bark, then "hackling" to make the flax ready for spinning. All of these steps involve drawing the stems through toothed instruments or over edges to dispose of non-essential parts of the stem.

It's far easier and more enjoyable just to plant flax for the beauty of their blossoms.

FORSYTHIA

It takes as many heat hours for forsythia to bloom its shock of yellow flowers as it takes for crabgrass seeds to germinate. So we time our application of crabgrass pre-emergent treatment to when forsythia blooms. This is also a convenient marker for spring weather that has developed sufficiently that we can prune roses severely without danger of a hard freeze.

Forsythia blooms on mature wood, but not wood older than one year. It should be pruned immediately after blooming. Renew old shrubs by removing one-third of the stems at ground level each year for three years. This is a very resilient shrub. I've even cut the entire shrub to the ground, and it regrew. F. suspensa is more of an arching shrub than vase-shaped and is spectacular on an elevation, branches cascading down a slope or steps.

GAILLARDIA

Blanket flower blooms even in extreme heat and will bloom all summer. It has a daisy-like flower, usually yellow petals with a red center, but other cultivars are red-bronze. It self-seeds and if not persistently thinned will take over a flower bed.

GERANIUMS

The indoor-outdoor plant, botanically Pelargonium, is tender to frost, so gardeners either buy new ones each spring or overwinter them in paper sacks in the garage or take cuttings and root and grow them over winter.

True Geraniums, members of the Geraniaceae family, are also known as cranesbills for the shape of their seedheads. They are hardy here and bloom all summer.

Some are upright, others trailing and used as groundcover. Flowers are rose, blue, purple, pink or white. They grow in a slowly expanding clump in my yard.

GRASSES, ORNAMENTAL

Large and small, green, red, black or variegated relieve the monotony of winter landscapes. Even tall dormant grasses swaying in the breeze or carving patterns in infrequent snows are interesting to look upon. Folks who have moved here from warmer regions may look for Pampas grass, but that's not hardy here. The large grass that is hardy here is Miscanthus, nearly the size of Pampas grass.

Miscanthus needs to be divided from time to time, and gardeners faced with that chore usually cut the clump short, dig it, then use a chain saw to divide it, and replant the divisions.

Grasses spread by seed or runners, and are usually identified as clumping or creeping, tufting, mounding, arching or upright, and cool-season or warm-season. Cool-season grasses grow most in early spring and late fall, and are dormant during summer's heat. Warm-season grasses thrive during the heat of summer, then die to the ground in fall. Clumping grasses expand slowly, creeping grasses expand quickly by stolons (horizontal underground runners) or rhizomes.

HELLEBORES

Usually known by this close version of the botanical name (Helleborus) or Christmas or Lenten rose, depending on when it blooms. This wonderful shade-loving perennial may bloom in December (a Christmas rose) or April (Lenten rose). It thrives in our winters, but fails to bloom in the coldest weather. When temperatures moderate, it opens blossoms. By year's end, foliage looks ragged, begging to be removed. Cut it off near soil line, so the winter sun can give enough warmth for new leaves and buds of hellebores to erupt. They need excellent drainage, and prefer some moisture, but are far from water hogs.

These plants idle between cold spells, then a bit of warmth renews their growth cycle. Their blossoms tend to nod and may be hard to see if foliage grows too lush.

They set seeds and will seed themselves if conditions are right (moisture and bare ground), and three years later they're ready to bloom. Some say they're a long-lived perennial, others say they have short lives. It's a good thing they seed themselves. They grow to 18 inches tall (about 12 inches in my shade bed).

The December bloomer produces 2-inch blossoms, white to greenish white, fading to purple with age. The later-blooming hellebore's blossoms are white, greenish white, purple or rose. They often don't survive attempts to move them.

The flowers resemble the single blossoms of wild roses. A tradition among many in England is to float the flowers of the Christmas rose in centerpieces or finger bowls at Christmas dinners.

HEUCHERA

Many of us fall in love with Heucheras, their beautiful round, lightly lobed leaves varying in color from predominantly white to plummy purple. They bear bell-like blossoms on wiry stems towering over compact clumps of foliage. They bloom in many colors, some known as coral bells, but the foliage is the main attraction.

Most of these species, about 55 in number, are hardy and withstand shade, although their leaf color may be affected by how much sunlight they receive. In northern climes, many species thrive in full sun. In hotter areas, those species grow better with at least some shade. Sun exposure varies from species to species, so heed label directions. If you have a purple-leaved variety, be sure it gets some direct sun or else you'll find the purple fading to green.

They're easily grown in our area, tolerating our soil. Heucheras prefer damp but well-drained soil, and you can retain moistness with mulch. Standing water will rot them, so don't plant them in a depression, where melting snow will drown them.

Heucheras are more than just a pretty face, though. For one thing, they're named after an 18th century German medical professor-botanist who specialized in medicinal plants. His name was Johann Heinrich von Heucher. Most of us in America pronounce it "Hugh-kera." Heuchera is a medicinal herb. It's also known as alumroot for its strongly astringent root and was used by Northwest native tribes to aid in digestion, stanch bleeding, reduce inflammation and shrink swollen tissues.

Heucheras are native to North America, from mountain highlands in the Pacific Northwest to arid canyons in the Southwest, and the villosa species are native from West Virginia to Alabama and Indiana. They may be propagated by division of clumps, seeds or leaf cuttings (provided a heel from the stem is included). They don't breed true from seed, according to some amateur growers, who found all of the seedlings attractive. Seeds germinate in three weeks at 65 to 75 degrees.

Most Heucheras are evergreen through winters, but by spring they need some judicious pruning to correct their "tatty" appearance. Every three to five years they should be divided. They tend to grow long "necks," sticking out of the soil. When they do that, dig them up and replant, planting the "necks" below surface level.

Some of the most significant varieties have been bred in the United States by Dan Heims of Terra Nova nursery in Oregon and Charles and Martha Oliver of Primrose Path nursery in Pennsylvania. Both breeders have written books on Heucheras. Heucheras apparently cross easily with tiarellas; the crosses are termed Heucherellas.

HIBISCUS SYRIACUS (Rose of Sharon or Shrub Althea)

Large summer-flowering shrub that thrives in our area. It's tolerant of our alkaline soil, and once established, drought-tolerant. It has grown in this country since about 1790, as old as our government. Flowers form on new growth. You can prune in March, cutting back to leave three or four buds on each shoot. If you want larger flowers, prune back to two or three buds. They benefit from a dressing of good compost but are not tolerant of synthetic fertilizers. Rose of Sharon may sow itself and become a nuisance plant.

HOLLY

I always loved the green prickly leaves and red berries of holly, so I tried to grow a holly here before I knew much about that shrub. You need a male and a female shrub to get berries, but the shrub I planted was supposed to be self-fertile. These shrubs can grow very large and are vulnerable to quite a list of insects and diseases, including scale, whitefly, holly leaf miner, bud moth, leaf spots, cankers, bacterial blight, twig dieback, spot anthracnose, leaf rot, leaf drop, powdery mildew and leaf scorch, for instance. I was spared those woes by the shrub's early death, as it was not at all tolerant of drought conditions in my yard. If you have access to irrigation water, you might be able to keep such a shrub properly watered, but it's not an easy one to maintain if you use metered city water.

HONEY LOCUST

Honey locust trees were my dad's favorite tree because you didn't have to rake the leaves.

We used to have honey locust trees (Gleditsia triacanthos) in our back yard here in Boise. They were lovely trees, but when their leaflets fell off the leaf stalks (petioles), they stayed on the lawn until the dogs' fur captured them for a trip inside. These little stalks are very difficult to rake, inconveniently turning so the rake tines glide right past them.

On the other hand, honey locust trees cast delightful dappled shade. We had to have our trees removed to make room for a house addition, and I especially miss them when I'm hardening off spring seedlings. Their shade was perfect.

Honey locusts are quite hardy, surviving down to minus 40 degrees, but do not thrive in areas of the country with high heat and humidity. They tolerate our sparse water and our alkaline soils. These are fairly fast-growing trees, stretching about 2 feet per year. Black locust trees look similar, but they're usually loaded with nasty thorns. Black locusts are a different species, Robinia.

Both species are subject to the locust borers that we have in abundance in the Treasure Valley, but honey locusts are far more resistant than the black locusts.

Our honey locust trees blossomed with fragrant "shy" greenish-yellow blossoms much loved by hummingbirds, bees and loud yellow warblers. Black locusts have white, extremely fragrant blossoms.

Incidentally, some chile growers in the Treasure Valley set their pepper seedlings out in the garden when the black locusts blossom. Large flat pods filled with bean-like seeds follow the blossoms, and if you don't want added trees, pick up the pods before they drop the seeds. Squirrels may beat you to them. Some cultivars of honey locusts produce few, if any, pods.

Indicative of the trees' attractiveness is the fact that some cultivars are named Elegantissima, Majestic, Perfection, Shademaster and Imperial.

Another cultivar, Sunburst, is very popular in this area. New leaves erupt as golden, eventually turning to green. I suspect these golden leaves on the Sunburst honey locusts contributed to one man's insistence that there was widespread disease of trees in the Valley. He used to show up occasionally at the Extension Office, insisting there was a "cover-up."

A canker attacks some honey locust trees, Sunburst being most susceptible of the cultivars. When elm trees began disappearing in large numbers due to Dutch elm disease, they were too often replaced with honey locusts. Then honey locusts existed in such numbers insects and diseases caught up with them, and tree experts are now advising more diversity in urban tree planting.

Honey locusts are subject to witches' broom, powdery mildew, rust, midge pod gall, webworm and spider mites, and of course the locust borers, the adults of which resemble wasps or yellow jackets with thick straight bodies, no waists.

Leaflets turn gold in autumn, and the whole petiole (slender stem) falls with the leaflets.

Branches are generally very pliable, but they cannot withstand heavy snows when fully leafed. An early Colorado snow peeled my dad's honey locusts like bananas, limbs on the ground, the trunk still standing. One heavy rain in the Boise area bent our honey locust branches to the ground, giving our 12-inch-tall Cairn terrier the opportunity to mark his territory on a branch that usually waved 12 feet off the ground.

HOPS

A fast-growing decorative vine, not usually included among ornamentals, but since it will quickly hide an eyesore, I'll include it here. The vines have straight vertical rows of thorns about 1/8 inch apart, so wear gloves when working with hops vines. Plant root starts in spring, and to obtain flowers, you'll need a male and a female. Nichols Garden Nursery carries hops vine roots for gardeners. The cone-like flowers, called strobiles, are used in brewing beer.

The flowers are mildly sleep-inducing, so some herbcrafters use them in "sleep pillows." Leaves and vine cuttings are also used in teas for medicinal purposes. Flowers should be picked when yellow-green, before they've dried out. Hops vines are deciduous and should be cut back when leaves drop. Roots multiply.

HOSTAS

Hostas are great for groundcover in dappled shade or even deeper shade. White or yellow Hosta leaves really "pop" into view, lighting dark shade in the ornamental garden. The size, shape and colors of the leaves are quite diverse, ranging from 2 inches to several feet wide. You may treasure a particular Hosta variety and encourage it to fill in a specific area, or you may prefer to grow different specimens in that area, heightening visual interest. Hosta leaves may be blue, light green, dark green or mostly yellow, with variegations in the center or at the margins of the leaves. Variegations may be white, yellow or light green, all depending on the variety.

If you have a bed you'd like to plant with Hostas for the first time, till to a depth of about 12 inches, and fill with half as much organic matter as you have soil. Organic matter may be leaf mold, compost, Canadian peat moss or Milorganite. Adding this much organic matter will raise the surface of the bed a few inches, adding to drainage capability. To plant a Hosta, dig a hole 12 inches deep, and as wide as the Hosta is expected to be at maturity. Untangle roots, cut tangles if they're stubborn, and plant the Hosta as deep as it had been in the container. I'd wait a week or two before fertilizing.

Appropriate Hosta fertilizers may be liquid, granular, extended release granular or compost. Avoid placing granular fertilizer on top of new growth, eyes or leaves of Hostas. Instead, if you're using this type of fertilizer, apply it to the edge of the bed. Do not apply any fertilizer to Hostas after July, because they need to start shutting down growth, preparing for winter dormancy. Good times to fertilize are early in spring, six weeks later, and early to mid-July. If using compost or a slow-release fertilizer, you may have to fertilize only once or twice.

Hostas need 1 inch of water each week, or else leaf tips will droop, then show brown margins. Hostas do blossom, although most Hosta blossoms are insignificant compared to the voluptuous foliage. Blossoms, of course, turn into seeds, and you may experiment with breeding your own Hostas. Be advised, though, that Hostas don't necessarily come true from seed unless they're H. ventricosa.

Mature Hosta seeds are dark brown or black, thicker at one end than the other. They may be planted indoors in late fall or early winter. Barely cover seeds with planting medium, keeping them well watered in good light for the two to three weeks it takes for germination to occur. Then keep them well-lighted while leaves develop. It may take five years to mature in pots, according to expert Linda Baranowski-Smith, so put them outdoors in summer and then winter in an unheated garage.

When no shoots are growing from the middle of an established clump, it's time to divide. Lift the entire clump, wash soil from the roots, and cut with a sharp knife to divide. Spring is easiest time to divide, but divide only the fast-growing Hostas at that time. Do not divide Sieboldianas or Tokudamas in spring, but wait until August, at least. You can also divide these in fall or winter.

Slugs are the worst pests of Hostas in our area. Fresh coffee grounds are sometimes effective against slugs, but more effective is the solution I call "Captain Midnight" magic. You don't have to tie a towel around your neck as little boys do, but go out after dark armed with a flashlight and a spray bottle of 50 percent household ammonia, 50 percent water. Spray every slug you find. The solution dissolves slugs but does no harm to plants.

Advanced Master Gardener Stella Schneider sets her spray bottle to mist, then sprays back and forth on bare soil and on adjacent grass. White spots appear, then vanish as the formerly unnoticed slugs die. This spray must touch slugs to be effective; there's no residual effect.

HYDRANGEAS

Hydrangea is a combination of two Greek words meaning water vessel.

That should tell you something right away about the growing needs of this beautiful shrub. It is not a bog plant needing its roots in standing water, but it thrives in moist soil. The soil may occasionally be wetter than moist for a brief time but should not be dryer. It should be well-drained and rich in organic matter.

So if you want to plant a Hydrangea in your yard, locate it near other water-loving plants or on the same watering circuit. If you plant it near dry-loving plants, they'll die from too much moisture or if you attend to their needs, it will be too dry for the Hydrangea, and you'll have toasted foliage.

Of the main species of shrub Hydrangea, three grow well in this area and are generally hardy: H. paniculata, H. quercifolia and H. arborescens. The oak-leaf Hydrangea (quercifolia) is hardy to minus 20, so if we have a zone 4 winter (colder than that) it may be winter-killed. The other two are hardier. All produce huge clusters of blossoms in summer to late summer if they've survived two threats: incorrect pruning and late frosts. They also have attractive fall foliage.

You often can avoid the damage from late frosts by planting your shrub on the north side of your house. There, it will recover from dormancy more slowly and set buds later than if it were on the south side, usually a warmer location.

The oak-leaf Hydrangea blooms on old wood, so any pruning should really be limited to pruning out dead wood (make sure it's dead before cutting). You can determine death of limbs or shrubs or trees by scratching the bark with your fingernail. If it's brown beneath the soft exterior, it's dead. If it's green, it's still alive.

H. arborescens and H. paniculata bloom on new wood and may be pruned hard or to the ground in late winter or early spring. Some people prune H. paniculata grandiflora (nicknamed "PeeGee" Hydrangea) as a small tree rather than a shrub. All tolerate light shade, but bloom best if they have four hours of direct sun each day. Most gardeners prefer to locate them so they'll get morning sun, but afternoon sun is OK, too.

One problem with growing Hydrangeas in the Treasure Valley is most of our soil is a bit too alkaline for them. If yours appears to be struggling or growth has stopped, wait for a cool spell and give it some acid fertilizer such as Miracid or ammonium or aluminum sulfate.

Hydrangeas tend to be floppy, but early in the season, you can place stakes and twine to hold up weak branches. Growth will be lush and conceal the supports early in the summer. Pruning the paniculata or arborescens back to two lateral buds helps strengthen branches.

Some perennial experts are enthusiastic about a Hydrangea called Annabelle. It has white snowball blossoms that may reach 12 inches across under the right conditions, and is seldom bothered by insects. The shrub is fast-growing, to 3 to 5 feet in height and width. Some varieties of Hydrangea bloom pink. This color can be changed by the addition of aluminum sulfate, but be careful with that. This fertilizer reportedly is harmful to some plants, such as Siberian iris.

The color of the blossom is dependent upon the soil's pH, or alkalinity. An alkaline soil produces pink blossoms, and acid soil produces blue. Shades in between pop up, too, depending on the soil's ability to take up iron and aluminum. Acidity regulates how much a plant may use of either mineral. I've been told a good dose of iron filings from a machine shop planted around a Hydrangea produces rich purple blossoms, but this would make the soil hazardous to hands.

Snowball-shaped and voluptuous conical Hydrangea flowers are useful and easily dried.

Climbing Hydrangeas are hardy here, and there are spectacular specimens in Boise. H. anomala, the climbing Hydrangea, is deciduous and fastens itself to its support by means of "holdfasts" (aerial roots). If it isn't supported in time, it sprawls. By "in time," I mean the climbing Hydrangea doesn't grow, stretch out, blossom or do anything vine-like for its first three years. Then it takes off.

Some folks caution against letting plants with holdfasts climb stucco or brick because those aerial roots hold moisture and can cause rot. They're certainly a nuisance if you must pull a vine away from the structure so you can paint it.

Many people plant climbing Hydrangeas to grow up established trees. This works because climbing Hydrangeas will bloom in sun or shade. One may grow up to 50 feet, with proper support. They aren't particular about soil, but they do like lots of water.

Fragrant blossoms resemble those of the lacecap Hydrangeas, flat blossoms with opened flowers principally around the circumference. They may have a diameter up to 5 inches. After leaf fall, the vine's bark exfoliates to some extent, giving winter interest if it's visible against its supporting background.

IRIS (Tall Bearded and Siberian)

If you're growing bearded iris, those with a "furry" growth on the droopy petals ("falls"), use a Sharpie pen to mark on the leaves of each non-blooming iris so you'll know which ones must be dug and separated. If it's been years since you've divided them, divide them in the summer after blooming. They usually need to be divided about every three years.

It's easier to handle iris if you snip off long fan leaves into an inverted V, so the leaves stand up without flopping. Dig, then discard any spongy rhizomes at the center of the stand, dig or rake in good compost in the bed where you plan to re-plant them, then lay them in so the top of the rhizome is at or slightly above the soil's surface. Plant so the fans of leaves are pointing outward.

It's best to divide them before September, if you expect blossoms the next spring. September divisions sometimes bloom in spring, sometimes not.

Newly replanted iris will need regular water until they're settled. Once established, these iris are very drought tolerant. They don't thrive if fertilized with a heavy dose of nitrogen, and they won't bloom and may even rot if planted too deeply or mulched. That rhizome needs sun exposure.

I expressed doubt that a reblooming iris would bloom a second time in our climate, since rebloomers hadn't blossomed a second time for me. Boisean Mary Mangum set me right — they do rebloom in our area if treated right. Mangum's father, the late Keith Chadwick, hybridized many remontant (reblooming) irises in his gardens in Sand Hollow, north of Caldwell. He recommended early spring fertilizing (February to March) with a fertilizer fairly low in nitrogen, higher in phosphorus and potassium.

A 6-12-12 mixture would be good on these irises. The exact number is not as important as the lower nitrogen figure contrasted with the higher P and K numbers.

Mangum said she fertilized her reblooming irises as late as June, and they blossomed a second time, but she's having trouble finding fertilizer with a lower N number. Another iris expert tells me that alfalfa (meal or pellets) is good for irises, but manure is instant death for them.

Although the spring-blooming tall bearded irises seem quite drought-tolerant, Chadwick's instructions for encouraging a second bloom included watering them through the summer to prevent them from entering dormancy. Mangum said she watered hers twice a week.

Remontant irises may bloom more than twice in a season. The beautiful iris listed as a 2009 favorite, Oasis Amy, at the Sandhollow website indicated it was hybridized by Chadwick (and named and introduced in 2004), reblossoms in July, and blooms over and over again until frost. Sand Hollow iris gardens are located at 14000 Oasis Road; many of Chadwick's hybridized irises bear Oasis as part of their names. Another of Chadwick's daughters, Cathy White, began tending his iris gardens north of Caldwell after he passed. She sells rhizomes of irises he hybridized, as well as heritage and historic irises.

Mangum said she has about 40 varieties of her dad's hybridized iris in her yard in Boise, and she's been hybridizing irises herself, but hasn't yet gotten any of her seedlings to bloom. It takes at least two years for iris seedlings to blossom, so you have to be patient to see what you'll get after daubing pollen from one remontant anther onto the stamen of another iris, remontant or not.

Are they as lightly fragrant as the first iris blossoms of spring? Perhaps not. Mangum said she hadn't noticed aroma when she worked around them. But they are as lush and showy as their first blossoms of the year.

Siberian is an elegant version of iris blossoms, smaller, more slender and graceful than tall bearded iris. It grows in a clump. When the center of clump begins to die out, it's time to divide.

Divide carefully, Siberian iris may sulk for a year before resuming blooming. Flowers can be white, gold, violet or purple.

IVY

One of the biggest curves gardening can throw is embodied in evergreen ivy (Helix). Leaves from the same variety, grown in different circumstances, may bear little resemblance to one another. Leaves on the same branch may look different from each other. It does not come true from seed, either.

Ivy is a vine, climbing trees and buildings with "holdfasts," right? That's true only when it's young. Juvenile ivy is a vine; mature ivy is a shrub. If that doesn't throw garden design out of kilter, nothing will. It may take decades to outgrow that vining juvenile stage, however, giving a landscaper some breathing room.

The holdfasts dig into brick, mortar and siding, leaving permanent scarring. They can cause structural damage, too. English ivy is a nuisance plant in many areas because it grows so abundantly in deep shade it crowds out native plants, and can even kill trees by climbing, its weight breaking limbs.

About the only way to get rid of it is by cutting off vines and pulling the plant.

LAMB'S EARS

If you're new to this area from a hot, humid climate, you'll be pleasantly surprised at how easy it is to grow lamb's ears or Stachys byzantina (also known as Woolly Betony) in the Treasure Valley. The soft, white, hairy leaves hold moisture that produces rot in humid conditions, but not in our dry climate. This is one of those accent plants that invite petting, and the leaves are shaped like lamb's ears.

It's ground-hugging, except for the vertical shafts of blossoms. Those blossoms set seeds that may be transported by wind or insects, so a new planting of lamb's ears may crop up in an unexpected location.

It's not a thuggishly invasive plant, and when it reappears in a new location, it's easily seen and removed. To prevent self-seeding, remove flower stalks when the flowers are still in evidence. They often are used in dried bouquets or wreaths, and one close relative, S. grandiflora or big betony, is grown for its decorative flower spikes. While the plant is in bloom, the foliage tends to deteriorate, but removal of the flower stalks will keep the plant concentrated on foliage production.

One very good location for lamb's ears is in a child's garden. Children love the soft, furry feel of the leaves. They were soothing wraps on wounds when they were used for that purpose in the Middle Ages. That usage led to still another name for the plant: woundwort.

Lamb's ears is a hardy perennial (to Zone 3 — that is, 40 degrees below zero) that will grow in shade, but prefers full sun in our climate. Each plant will spread, and later can be divided. At a certain point, there'll be some dieback in the center of the planting, and new divisions can replace the old dead area.

This is a good candidate for the front of the flower border, usually growing no more than about 4 inches tall. The bloom stalks rise to about 14 inches. In our area, the foliage usually is attractive from spring until autumn if bloom stalks are removed. These plants supposedly prefer moist soils, but they don't get it in my yard, and they thrive anyway.

Water early in the day so that water on leaves evaporates before nightfall. Divide in spring every four or five years to maintain plant vigor. Since this is one of those plants that doesn't do well with wet foliage, do not divide or cut back just before winter. Snows can rot foliage and roots.

By the way, the variety Helene von Stein has unusually large leaves, but the foliage seems to hold up well. Silver Carpet, another variety, does not flower, so you're saved from the task of deadheading.

Another white, hairy plant for the ornamental garden is Salvia argentea, or silver clary sage. It is a biennial and glorious its first year with huge oval leaves covered with silvery down.

The second year, when it's about to go to seed, the foliage loses its silvery down, changes color to gray-green, and looks tattered. Either woolly plant is a stunning eyecatcher in an ornamental garden.

LILACS

Some lilacs produce suckers in abundance; others don't. My lilacs don't sucker, but the next-door neighbor's lilacs sucker into our yard. We've dug them and supplied many families in Boise with lilac shrubs.

I think they produce plain lavender blossoms, and that's OK because they also produce that wonderful lilac fragrance. Breeders have developed many colors of lilac blossoms and even a few that bloom twice a year. Some lilacs are bred to be dwarfs, but if left unpruned, will grow to 12 feet or so.

Prune lilacs after their spring bloom is finished. If you don't prune them, they just grow taller and bloom anyway. They're quite forgiving of neglect.

A good resource is the Firefly book, "Lilacs for the Garden" by Jennifer Bennett. None of the lilacs are native to America, but some come from central Asia and China, others from eastern Europe. Botanically, lilacs are known as Syringa vulgaris.

A complication is the fact that the Idaho state flower is the syringa (that's the common name), or Philadelphus lewisii (the botanical name). Our state flower is NOT related to the lilac. The confusion of names is unfortunate.

Lilacs grow nearly anywhere if drainage is good, and they get at least four hours daily of sun, and they don't object to drought conditions. Some do develop powdery mildew, but it doesn't seem to be fatal because it usually occurs in mid- to late-summer, after the leaves have fed the roots. There are other fungal diseases, too, such as Pseudomonas syringae, that affect lilacs.

These diseases favor hot humid weather, so our low humidity usually protects lilacs, roses, tomatoes and other plants from those blights and diseases.

New lilacs sometimes wait years before they bloom. Then some bloom heavily one year and lightly the next. Other reasons for not blooming include insufficient sun (they need four hours daily), pruning in the summer and removing next year's buds, or overfertilization.

If your shrub is old and large, you can rejuvenate it by removing one third of the shoots each year for three years, starting with the oldest (largest). Cut them near the soil line. Bennett says if the shrub is in poor condition, cut the entire shrub to within 2 inches of the ground at one time. You will lose blossoms for two years if you cut it completely down and wait for new growth.

You can grow lilacs as a hedge, alone or interplanted with other shrubs. Plant them at least 18 inches apart, in a single row. After planting, cut them back so that you'll have bushiness at the bottom of your hedge. If you wait a year or longer, you'll never get them to develop that low thick growth that makes a good hedge. As the bushes grow, prune them in an inverted V shape, squaring off the top, so that the sides are exposed to sunlight all the way to the ground. Do all of your lilac pruning immediately after the flowering ceases.

Some lilacs have good fall leaf color, too. S. oblata and Cheyenne turn bronze to dark purple; and S. meyeri, hyacinthiflora and pubescens, subspecies Panda, turn burgundy.

Not all lilacs have green, heart-shaped leaves, either. Some have variegated gold and green foliage, and those should be grown in full sun. Others have variegated green and white foliage, and those should have part shade. One even has fernlike foliage (S. protolaciniata).

Dwarf varieties grow only half as tall as regular lilacs, up to 6 feet, but if left unpruned, may grow taller. Those cultivars include lilacs named Miss Kim, Palibin and Prairie Petite. Those that may bloom a second time, in the fall, are S. meyeri and S. pubescens subspecies microphylla.

LINDEN

These are some of the most beautifully shaped trees in the Valley. May be responsible for allergic reactions when they bloom in June and July.

LONICERA FRAGRANTISSIMA (Winter honeysuckle)

Some call this shrub "first breath of spring," but its botanical name is Lonicera fragrantissima. Woody plant expert Michael Dirr says it is deciduous, but this shrub's leaves hold on late and reappear early. I may have missed the deciduous habit in previous colder years in my back yard. I thought it was evergreen.

It grows as a shrub, not a vine as many honeysuckles do. It's about 10 feet high, spreading about 10 feet at the apex.

I've never seen berries on this honeysuckle, but some folks in other parts of the country claim birds plant this shrub from seed-bearing berries so easily it's invasive. Other people deny it's invasive. I haven't found volunteers of this shrub, so like butterfly bushes (Buddleias), they are not invasive in our area. Birds do pick and nibble on the flowers, perhaps savoring the sweet nectar near the base of the flowers, and this year it was first to bloom, feeding early honeybees and butterflies.

LUPINES

One of my favorite flowers is the lupine, with stately columns of perfect flowers. Lupinus polyphyllus is one of the garden versions, L. perennis the wild flower. This flower is commonly known as Quaker-bonnets, Bluebonnets, or just lupines.

Why "lupine," derived from the Latin for wolf? It was thought that lupine "wolfed" all of the soil nutrients for itself, since it thrived where other plants did not. Actually, just the opposite was true: It was feeding nitrogen to poor soil. It is a legume, taking nitrogen out of the air and passing it through its roots into the soil. It's said to be a "short-lived" perennial, with a perhaps two- to three-year lifespan. A lupine I had in an exposed flower bed did die after two years.

But I've had a large pink lupine on the east side of my garden toolshed for about six or seven years. I know it's not reseeding because I removed the bloom stalks before the seed pods mature or open. It's just happy in that sheltered location.

One year it was attacked by the largest aphids I've ever seen. They were about the size of the lady beetles that are supposed to eat them. Those aphids would make hungry lady beetles "open wide." I handpicked the aphids and haven't seen them back. Like other lupines, though, mine is attacked by powdery mildew after blooming.

Powdery mildew is a fungus. Fungicides (that is, they kill funguses) are available at garden stores.

Lupines may be grown from seed, but there are some tricks to know. Seeds planted in fall, in sandy, sunny soil, often produce blooming plants by spring. Left alone, they will self-sow freely. They develop tap roots while young, so they don't transplant easily. Grow them where you can leave them. It may help to nick or scarify the seeds. Lupines combine especially well with young pine trees, but will get too shaded to survive when pine trees approach maturity.

The Russell hybrid lupines, with two-toned bright colored blossoms of red, pink, indigo and purples, may be too bold for some garden plans, but they're a highlight in others. Russell lupines usually take about a year from seeding to produce a blossoming plant.

By the way, the wild blue lupines (L. texensis) are commonly known as

Texas bluebonnets. The perfect, sweet pea-like blossoms attract bees and other beneficial insects with "banner" petals. The insect climbs into the space between the banner and two lower petals that form a keel-like structure, pushing down the keel and revealing the reproductive parts. Their pollen then transfers to the insect, assuring reproduction with the next lupine blossom it visits. Lupine honey is rare but exquisitely flavored.

The leaves are "palmate," that is, like a hand with seven to 11 outstretched fingers. Lupines are toxic to livestock, at least cattle and sheep, at some point in their lives. Consumption of lupines by pregnant cows can cause skeletal birth defects in calves.

MAHONIA (Oregon grape)

Native shrub, from British Columbia to northern California. Erect, with broad evergreen leaves, turning to bronze in winter. In our area, birds plant Mahonia here and there. I tried to transplant those "free" shrubs several times without success, but birds finally planted a Mahonia where I wanted it.

It takes any sun exposure, but it's in part shade in my yard. Large clusters of flowers in late spring give way to edible blue-black fruit. I've been told it makes wonderful jelly. Since it's a native, it's hardy, of course, as well as drought-tolerant. Nurseries in this area sell potted Mahonia that survives transplanting quite well.

MONARDA (Bee balm)

This wonderful plant for humans, insects and hummingbirds is an herb and a lovely ornamental. It is said to be invasively spreading, but in my yard it grows in poor soil and a minimum of water, and it behaves itself. I'd welcome some spreading.

Red is the usual color of the blossoms, but they also may be pink, salmon or lavender. They look like a fireworks display and hummingbirds love them.

Monarda is native to the eastern and Midwestern United States. Native Americans in the vicinity of Oswego, N.Y., brewed tea from the leaves for medicine and pleasure. Shakers and other settlers who began copying that practice, called it Oswego tea, and it became popular throughout the colonies.

During the time of the Boston Tea Party, when colonists were boycotting

British-imported black tea, they drank Oswego tea instead.

Monarda may be annual, biennial or perennial and can be propagated by seeds. Stems are square like their cousins, the mints. They grow to be about 3 feet here, and may look rangy. But they can be tamed, according to "The Well-Tended Perennial Garden" by Traci diSabato-Aust.

She advises cutting them by about a third in early May, then cutting back by a third a second time if they get spindly. This will delay the flowering a few weeks.

Flowering can be increased by deadheading spent flowers on young plants, but it won't do much for old plants. After blooming, the foliage often gets powdery mildew and looks ratty. It can be cut safely down to the new, clean foliage at the base of the plant.

Monarda takes full sun or shade, and it is hardy to zone 4. You probably should divide clumps of Monarda about every three or four years. You can use minced leaves on fruit salads, in yogurt or in iced teas. Or dry the leaves for three days or less and use for tea.

Since the common name is bee balm, that means it was originally used as a medicine. If it were bee mint, it would point to culinary origins. Medicinally the plant has been used for coughs, sore throats, flatulence and nausea. Does it work? Who knows? But at least the "medicine" is pleasant.

OSTEOSPERMUM

A fairly new African daisy has taken the gardening world by storm. They're not winter hardy here, but most of us grow them as annuals and buy new ones in spring.

It's hard to resist those dazzling white petals surrounding an electric blue center or those eye-catching spoon-shaped petals. I bought one of the latter, then watched it revert into regular daisy-like blooms during some very hot weather. Specialists said it would recover, and sport the spoon-shaped blossoms with the next flush of flowers, if weather permitted.

All Osteospermums stop blooming in the heat of summer and close overnight.

Regular deadheading will prolong the blooming period. They should be well-watered, especially their first two weeks in the ground. They are tender perennials, so if you like your present plant bring it indoors over winter or take cuttings to overwinter.

PEONY

Each April is time for the red tips of peonies to poke through the soil. Before these very long-lived perennials get full leaves, you can support them against toppling by using an expensive frame, by using bolt cutters on a three-ring tomato cage or by laying a square of chicken wire loosely on the ground, over the red tips. The adaptation of the tomato frame requires cutting just above each circle, giving you three supports. Only the largest would be suitable for peonies. The chicken wire ought to be a flat square larger than the diameter of the peony plant. The peony will lift the chicken wire into place as leaves develop. Watch it in case there's some adjustment necessary.

Either way, there's a brief but critical time in which to support peonies. If you miss that deadline, you might as well forget it until next year.

When you plant peonies, the eyes on the roots should not be planted more than 2 inches deep. If you plant them deeper, the peonies will not bloom. They need good sun, good drainage and good sanitation. Established peonies will also benefit from some 5-10-5 or similar formulation fertilizer (don't use nitrogen heavily or else you'll get foliage and no blooms).

Once regular peonies begin blooming, cut some blossoms before the outer petals begin curving backward, strip off the foliage, bundle them and hang them upside down in a dark closet, leaving them to dry. It may only take a week or so to have gorgeous dry flowers suitable for enduring bouquets.

Botanist Kay Lancaster suggests another way to preserve buds. That is to cut stems of about 6 inches in length when the buds are just beginning to show color, strip off leaves and store them in a tightly closed plastic container lined with a single thickness of wet paper towel. Store in the vegetable drawer of the refrigerator.

When you want a flower, remove one from the container, pick off the green sepals (thick leaves) around the bud, and remove most of the stem. Float the bud in a low bowl of warm water, and within 24 hours, it should be in full bloom. This should give you an extra month of blossoms.

Ants often are seen on peony buds. Peony buds have specialized tissues that secrete nectar, attracting ants that in turn protect the peonies from attack by other insects. So don't use insecticide or a spray of water to remove them.

Peonies are tough plants, but they are subject to some diseases. Thanks to our dry climate, we seldom see blights, but if you do see any blackening foliage, pull it off and put it in the trash.

Peonies also are notorious for succumbing to Botrytis blight. Three conditions are necessary for the formation of Botrytis, according to Dr. Krishna Mohan, professor of plant pathology at the University of Idaho Research and Extension Center in Parma: high humidity, succulent tissues and lack of sanitation in the vicinity. Botrytis spores live on dead organic matter, especially petals and spent blossoms. Spores are easily dispersed by wind, so if they're in the right place when the humidity is high (even from sprinkling), they can infest your peony. Injury to the plant increases the risk of invading disease. For this reason, people are usually advised to cut out peony foliage and stems in fall and dispose of them. Do not compost them.

PHILADELPHUS (Mock orange)

The scent is that of orange blossoms. Late-spring bloomer, needs to be cut back after blooming or it will get leggy and sparse. It's tolerant of our alkaline soils and sparse watering. The P. lewisii variety is popularly known as syringa, and is the state flower of Idaho. (See more under Syringa.)

PLUME POPPY

One of the celebrated "tough plants for tough places," plume poppy grows to 8 feet in height, sporting deeply lobed gray-green leaves with white downy backs and flowers with many stamens and no petals. Even slight breezes evoke its attractive colors. It spreads, but can be kept in check with occasional root pruning. Needs full sun or light shade, not much water. Apparently quite tolerant of alkaline soil.

POPPY (Oriental and annual)

Perennial Oriental poppies grow in large clumps, enter dormancy in midsummer, then resume growth in autumn. They have large hairy leaves and voluptuous flowers in shades of orange, pink, red or purple.

When the large, showy Oriental poppies (Papaver orientale) have definitely finished blooming, cut back the foliage. You may leave the seed heads for dried bouquets if you like, but the foliage is beginning to look tattered and will continue to deteriorate the rest of the summer if you don't cut it back.

New foliage will appear in later summer to last through winter, sort of a living mulch. The Oriental poppy is a perennial, reappearing each year. Oriental poppy blossom stalks rise from a base rosette of leaves.

If your poppy has leaves on the bloom stem, it isn't an Oriental poppy. It's P. somniferum, or opium poppy. This annual poppy also is known as the peony-flowered poppy. It is not illegal to sell seeds for the opium poppy (some call it breadseed poppy), and it is for sale through several seed companies. But it's illegal to grow it in the United States.

If you're going to divide an Oriental poppy or take a root cutting, do it during the plant's dormant period, either mid-summer or in winter, but remember these poppies don't like to have their roots disturbed.

Poppies may not reproduce true to seed. If you wish to increase your supply or to share with a friend, you're better off starting from a root cutting. Poppies grow well in our soil and have modest water requirements. We haven't had any insect problems with our poppies.

The Oriental poppy is a lovely flower, and so is the annual Shirley poppy.

I'm growing the latter in the back yard, where they'll self-seed. Shirley poppies are P. rhoeas, and they're also known as corn poppies, field poppies or Flanders poppies. The dazzlingly beautiful silken blooms last for only a day.

The almost magical appearance of the red poppies on battlefields after World War I was the inspiration for the American Legion's Memorial Day paper poppies we buy and wear on lapels. The flower grows only on disturbed soil, and World War I disturbed a lot of land.

Apparently the seeds lie dormant in the soil until it's disturbed and the seeds are exposed to light. Removing seed heads and blossoms, or deadheading, prolongs the blossoming period of Shirley poppies. All poppies' seeds are held in handy little pods, like pepper shakers.

Shirley poppies are a strain of wild cornflower poppies, selected by the vicar of Shirley and grown by him to develop a range of pastel colors with white edging on the petals called a picotee. They will revert to the wild solid-colored petals unless you continue to select only those with picotee edging for seeding.

Bees love them and lie on their sides to gather pollen. Other perennial poppies include P. burseri or alpinum, a small rock-garden type of poppy, and P.

nudicale or Iceland poppy. The California poppy is an Eschscholzia. The blue poppy that thrives in maritime conditions is a Meconopsis.

PRIMROSES

Primroses in the grocery stores are so pretty and enticing each spring. I often buy some, plant them and prepare to say goodbye to them, expecting that I won't see them next spring.

Several very good gardeners also report that primroses (Primulas), supposed to be perennial, don't last here. I think the trouble is lack of water rather than cold weather. They're supposed to be hardy to zone 4 (below minus 20 degrees).

An expert organic gardener in New Zealand, Moira Ryan, acknowledged the plant's hardiness. The wild primrose (P. vulgaris) is "found from Norway as far south as the Mediterranean in the Balkans, in Asia Minor and even in North Africa," she wrote, "but I think that in all the hotter places you would find it at a high altitude (cooler) and most commonly in woodland where the summer would not be very hot. Even in the mild climate of Britain, they rarely in nature grow out in the open, but usually in woodland or hedgerows, picking places with deciduous cover so they have plenty of sunshine at flowering time."

Aha! Our Boise summers are too hot for their survival. I had suspected their requirement for moist soil was the determining life or death factor. These are essentially woodland plants, growing in shade, roots set in moist soil enriched with humus. Most of us in this Valley don't water abundantly or as often as primroses would like. Summer heat and drought destroy them.

Ryan said wild Primulas were pale yellow and a light bluish pink; other colors were bred commercially.

"As often happens, a strong constitution is often sacrificed to obtain unusual colors and large size," she added.

I'm told P. sieboldii are "easy to grow, " but I also know that the fellow who says that grows them in a sunken child's wading pool filled with peat and sand (and of course, water).

If you're starting from seeds, sow in a moist soil-less medium and keep at room temperature for three weeks, then move them into the refrigerator for five weeks. Some may germinate before five weeks is up, so move those out into space that's warmer, but below 70 degrees.

The colorful plants are not costly, so if they brighten your days and beckon to spring, treat them as an annual and enjoy. Some people put them in pots on the windowsill, others brighten dull flower beds with their cheerful blossoms. And they'll rejuvenate a patio, planted thickly in tall planters.

Outdoors, they need filtered shade, slightly acidic soil and moistness. Our soil is quite alkaline, so it would be helpful to add humus and peat or coffee grounds to lower the alkalinity. If they're still surviving in fall, mulch them with shredded leaves and top with evergreen branches. Leaves left whole will mat and kill what you're trying to protect.

If we insist on growing them as perennials in our climate, Ryan suggested planting them out in the open for spring flowering then transplanting them to shade and mulching heavily to keep roots cool for the summer, returning them to open space in autumn to await spring flowering.

PYRACANTHA

Also known as firethorn. Inch-long spines inflict more pain than you'd expect from the puncture of the thorn, but the shrub is evergreen with colorful orange berries following white clusters of flowers. It is one of my favorite shrubs.

It grows easily in the Treasure Valley and provides ornamental berries relished by birds, as well as providing good protection from predators. Cats chasing birds skid to a stop, rather than trying to follow the birds into a dense Pyracantha. Raptors can't get in either, because they're too big. If they worked their way into a Pyracantha, avoiding thorns, their prey would be gone.

We have two huge Pyracanthas at the front of our yard. They have stood through the minus 23-degree years, attesting to their hardiness. The center of the bushes probably is dead material, but hundreds of quail take night and afternoon refuge there. Winter afternoons, after their naps, quail begin hopping out of the bushes, one by one, shaking and rearranging feathers. It's like clowns climbing out of a Volkswagen beetle at the circus. You're always amazed at how many are in there.

Other birds also take refuge in those bushes, winter and summer. Some days, we pass one of the bushes to get to the mailbox, and the joyous birdsong suddenly hushes as we approach, the hush reminding us how loud the song was. Pyracantha grows as a standalone shrub, a hedge or an espaliered shrub.

If you're espaliering, pay attention to the weight of the branches. A Pyracantha growing against a friend's garage in the North End toppled away from the garage, obstructing a walkway.

A cluster of townhouse-type homes on the north side of Emerald, east of Cole, has an unclimbable fence along Emerald, unclimbability reinforced by Pyracantha bushes along the fence. An effective people deterrent, but kind to wildlife.

If you want to plant a Pyracantha, look for one that is disease-resistant. Pyracanthas are susceptible to fire blight, scab and powdery mildew. Locate the shrub where it will have good drainage. Pyracanthas don't tolerate "wet feet." It can grow in some shade, but does best in full sun.

A Pyracantha may spread to 15 feet or more and grow to 20 feet tall. The leaves are evergreen, setting off the beauty of the orange berries. A flock of Bohemian or cedar waxwings or other berry-loving birds will strip the berries in short order, especially if other food is scarce that winter.

QUERCUS

Oak trees are numerous in this Valley. In mast years — those years when forest trees produce seeds (nuts) most heavily — acorns are produced in abundance, while other years harvest may be light.

QUINCE

Flowering quince (Chaenomeles) provides brilliant sparks of color in spring all over the Valley. If fruit sets, it is edible in jams and jellies.

REDBUD

Redbud (Cercis) trees are pretty, blossoming pink or white (not red as you'd expect from the name) in spring. These trees, members of the Leguminosae family, are small with pretty heart-shaped leaves much loved by leaf cutter bees. Those bees cut dime-sized circles from leaf margins inward, to line their nest cells. Redbud trees may live to 90 years, but they're susceptible to canker and Verticillium wilt (see chapter on diseases).

RHODODENDRONS

Everybody loves Rhododendrons. Everybody except me.

Some are attractive in other people's yards, but I don't want one in my yard. For one thing, they're not happy in our Valley. The soil is too alkaline, water is parceled out in small, affordable amounts, and the air is too dry for them. They love acid soil and moistness, such as a heavy fog or humidity nearly intolerable to humans.

My dislike of them is from experience. In the 1960s, we lived in Ellensburg, Wash., in a rented house. There were white Rhododendrons planted along the rear of the lot. The blossoms looked like dirty facial tissue, from their emergence to their demise. I spent hours pulling off the brown-tinged whitish petals, resenting the chore every moment.

West of the Cascades, Rhododendrons grow to be gigantic; east of the Cascades the soil and climate are similar to ours, but that area is colder and windier.

However, I have learned more about Rhododendrons than I really wanted to know.

They demand good drainage, prompting people in some areas to "plant" them on top of the ground, surrounding the roots with a soil-humus mixture. If your soil drains well, you could plant a rhody in the hole, but amend the soil with peat moss and/or sulfur to make it more acidic. Its preferred acidity is 5.5 to 6.0 pH. We're lucky here if we can get our pH down to 7.0. Aluminum sulfate is a no-no, since the aluminum will damage the shrub.

Be sure you plant the shrub at least 1 or 2 inches shallower than it had been planted. Rhododendron roots are near the surface, so you'll have to pull rather than hoe weeds that germinate beneath the shrub. You can prevent weeds' germination and retain moisture by spreading a good mulch under the shrub, but don't mulch right up to the trunk. Do not plant near a foundation or concrete wall or sidewalk, since concrete leaches a little alkalinity when wet. Morning sun and afternoon shade or dappled light is best.

When the rhody is young and small, encourage branching by pinching the leaf buds at the tips of branches. Deadheading will encourage more flowering, but be careful when you remove the spent blossoms, for other flower buds are directly behind the spent flower.

Rhododendron roots are fine and slow-growing, so give the shrub a good start by soaking the rootball in water before planting, and water regularly thereafter. If leaves droop in the cool of the morning, the shrub needs water. Fertilize with an acidic fertilizer such as Mir-acid or a Rhododendron food. Do not fertilize with a nitrogenous fertilizer after June.

Yellowing leaves indicate a fertilizer need. If the yellowing leaves are the old leaves, the shrub probably lacks magnesium. Fertilize with Epsom salts. If the new leaves are yellowing, the shrub is deficient in iron. That deficiency is usually based on soil pH, so test that first and then spray leaves with chelated iron or add ferrous sulfate to the soil.

An admission: Since first writing the preceding critical comments in 1999, I've succumbed to temptation and have planted two Rhododendrons, both red-flowering.

SEVEN SONS

Grows as a shrub or can be pruned to a single trunk (tree). Botanically it's Heptacodium miconoides. Fairly new introduction from China that blooms white in autumn — clusters of seven small fragrant blossoms — that are then followed by red calyxes (calyces) that adorn the shrub or tree until November. Its exfoliating bark is also attractive.

STAR OF BETHLEHEM

Some regard this as an ornamental, and the bulbs are sold by some vendors for ornamental use, but they're garden thugs, spreading by bulb and seed. Blooms six-petaled white flowers in May, then grassy foliage indicates its enduring presence.

SUMAC

When fall colors began to appear in the Valley, one of the earliest to blaze red is the sumac, or Rhus. These hardy shrubs or small trees are native to North America, and adaptable to different soils and conditions, so long as they're not standing in wet, boggy soil. They grow fine in full sun or some shade, too. They probably would not thrive in deep shade.

They're not suitable for specimen trees, foundation plants or for container planting because they tend to sucker freely. This habit makes them ideal for some landscaping situations, where a mass planting is needed to obscure cuts, fills or banks. Buy and plant one tree, and you get three or four in a year or two.

The staghorn sumac, so-named because of the arrangement of its branches and their resemblance to the antlers of a deer, grows to 20 or 25 feet in height in a cultivated situation. It can grow much taller in the wild. The spread is usually equal to or greater than the height. The staghorn (R. typhina) blooms greenish yellow in late June to early July, then sets fruit, a large hairy "drupe," narrowly pyramidal in shape.

Seeds from this drupe are one means of propagation, but they need scarification (nicking) and stratification (freezing and thawing). Removing suckers and transplanting is probably the easiest method of propagation.

Rhus is subject to aphids, scales, mites, rusts and leaf spots, but nothing seems to be very serious. The staghorn is especially susceptible to Verticillium wilt, a disease that plugs the tree's circulation system and may result in death.

Other sumacs available include finely cut-leafed varieties of the staghorn sumac, R. trilobata or skunkbush sumac (not a contender for an aroma prize) and R. aromatica, or fragrant sumac, which grows to only 6 feet in height, suckering in a mound-like appearance. There are many others in this genus, some 200 species, mainly grown for their dazzling fall colors.

The genus also includes poison oak and even poison ivy. Yet another toxic cousin, poison sumac, is found east of the Mississippi. Poison ivy has been used as an ornamental shrub for wreaths, in England and Japan, undoubtedly a short-lived decoration.

SUNFLOWERS

Cut flowers, human snacks or wildlife food come from mood-lifting sunflowers. What sight could be more joyous than a yellow sunflower against a clear blue sky? When mammoth sunflower heads point toward the ground, squirrels pause to study them and birds lick their beaks. If you want to eat the seeds yourself, you'll have to be wary and quick.

The heads are ready to be harvested when the backs of the seed heads are brown rather than green and the seeds are plump and fully formed. You can harvest them with about a foot of the trunk attached and hang them in a critter-free setting to continue to dry. Mice can find a thousand ways to get to them, so beware.

One year I grew them for the squirrels and birds, but I wanted to parcel them out. The squirrels had a different idea and wanted to gorge themselves all at once. To do so, they ate a squirrel-sized hole in the lid of a heavy plastic garbage can and left only sunflower hulls in the can. Maybe the seeds would have been safe in a garbage can with a locking metal lid, but I wouldn't guarantee it.

When the seeds and heads are good and dry, and the seeds are easily removed, harvest them wearing heavy gloves, pushing seeds back and forth until they pop loose. It's best to have a tarp or an old sheet to catch the flying seeds.

If you like salty sunflower seeds, make a brine of water and enough salt so that when you dip your finger in, it tastes salty. Soak the seeds in this brine for five or six hours, then spread the seeds out to dry. When they're dry, bake them in a single layer on a cookie sheet in a 350 degree oven for about 10 minutes. Let them cool before eating. An alternative way of roasting them is in a hot wok, cooking and turning them quickly, or in a hot skillet, shaking it to prevent burning, then pouring seeds out to cool.

SWEET PEAS

Sweet pea fragrance can sweeten a home or the whole yard.

Old garden wisdom calls for planting them on Presidents Day, but some people advise starting them indoors and transplanting them outside when other gardeners transplant theirs or a reliable garden center says the time is right.

Sweet pea seeds germinate when the soil temperature gets to 55 to 60 degrees, but I don't believe Treasure Valley soils are that warm by Presidents Day. Start them indoors on that day, and transplant them outdoors in late March or early April. That should do it.

Some say they don't transplant easily, but botanist Kay Lancaster says sweet peas grown in pots that are 2 inches square and 4 inches deep develop a fine root structure that transplants beautifully. The main reason they should be planted out early is that they may completely stop flowering in our hot summer weather. They love cool weather such as that common in England.

It may be a good idea to start working the bed the summer before you plant. Select a site that's sheltered from the wind but gets plenty of sunshine, and where the sweet pea roots will not have to compete with tree or shrub roots for moisture or nutrients. Many gardeners dig a trench a foot deep or deeper and fill it with compost, then plant seeds in that compost. The compost feeds the plants and holds moisture, just the way sweet peas like it.

If the seed packet instructs you to "chip" the seeds for germination, remove a tiny part of the seed coat opposite the "eye" of the seed. Some people use a triangular file, sandpaper or a toenail clipper for this, but be careful not to damage the white tissue inside the seed coat.

Be sure to harden off your tender seedlings before planting them outdoors. Outdoor acclimatization for a lengthening period of time over the course of about a week should get them ready for the elements.

As for fertilizer, these are legumes and can fix nitrogen from the air for themselves. Too much added nitrogen means fewer blossoms and more leafy growth. As it is, sweet peas can easily grow to 8 or 10 feet, so they'll need something to climb. And they'll need help staying up, so you'll have to tie them now and then. Look for a fertilizer that's heavier on the last two numbers than the first.

Once sweet peas begin blooming, keep them picked to prolong the blossoming period.

SWEET POTATO VINES

Even the vines of culinary sweet potatoes are attractive, yet breeders have introduced black and chartreuse ornamental sweet potato vines, too. Trained among clumps of flowers in a flower bed, their leaves shade the soil, prevent weeds from germinating and retain moisture.

SYRINGA

Syringa is the common name of the Idaho state flower, whose botanical name is Philadelphus lewisii. (Yes, named for its discoverer, Meriwether Lewis, who gathered a sample May 6, 1806, near Potlatch.) Syringa is the botanical name for lilacs, mentioned earlier.

Our state flower also is known as mock-orange (for its lovely scent), Lewis syringa, Indian arrowwood and pipe tree. Native Americans used syringa for arrows and the Nez Perce even used that wood for bows.

Why are the lilac and P. lewisii both named syringa? One source says it's because both have hollow (pithy, really) stems used for shepherd's pipes. Both are spring-flowering shrubs, but the flowers are not at all alike. Lilacs are clusters of tiny, trumpet-shaped flowers; the wild syringa (P. lewisii) has white flowers 1 to 2 inches across with bright yellow centers. Even their aromas are quite dissimilar.

The Idaho syringa is technically a wildflower; the lilacs we're familiar with are not.

The wild syringa is not usually browsed by deer, and the extent to which it has been browsed is an indication of the severity of the winter, the condition of the winter range and, of course, the hunger of the deer. Wild syringas in bloom can look like a snowbank from a distance if the cluster is tight and large.

TREE OF HEAVEN (Ailanthus)

One of the most misnamed plants in the world. See the chapter on weeds.

TREES General care

Fertilize in spring, up until June 15, then stop to let tree prepare for winter dormancy. Water deeply through heat of summer and before winter. Do not succumb to temptation and build a raised bed inside the tree's canopy and against the tree's trunk (see "crown rot" in the chapter on diseases).

If you don't want mutilated trees, carefully select trees you plant under electric, telephone or cable wires. The Boise Community Forester's office (in the blue pages, under Parks & Recreation) has tree suggestions for homeowners. They recommend trees that, at maturity, will not be tall enough to interfere with those wires. If you're planning on planting a tree near the street, it's a good idea to check with the Community Forester's office anyway, because that space may be under its control.

When planting a tree, it's a good idea to break up the caliche layer with a maul or prybar, even if the tree you're going to plant isn't a taprooted specimen. The deeper a tree's roots grow, the more drought tolerant it will be and the less vulnerable to strong winds.

Do not permit helpers to operate weed whackers where the string may damage the bark, and do not permit folks mowing the lawn to bang into trees with mowers. They call the latter "lawnmower blight," and it can severely damage trees. Some bark is thinner than other bark, and the tree's circulatory system lies just beneath the bark. That is where borers go to feed, and if they meander completely around the trunk, they can kill the tree. Now, because of improvements in technology, we can also have "weedwhacker blight."

To an extent, a piece of damaged bark doesn't seem to be life threatening to a tree. The tree somehow works around it — enough cells still working to feed and cool the tree. But it's an open wound, as capable of getting infected as an open wound on a human. For that reason, too, pruners of heavy branches are advised to make bottom cuts halfway through the branch closer to the trunk than the top cut, so that bark won't tear, leaving the tree open to infection.

We don't usually think of bark as living tissue, and some of it isn't, but there's young, still living tissue closer to the cambium layer of the tree.

The cambium layer is just a few cells thick, but it's the most important organ of the tree. It supplies new cells to the phloem, the part of the circulatory system just under the bark that conducts food to the roots. The phloem itself is just a few cells thick, too.

Cambium also supplies new cells to the xylem, further into the tree, that conducts water to the leaves. The xylem may be quite thick, looking in cross-section like a bundle of straws. It's what we usually think of as wood.

In any case, when the bark is punctured, smashed or torn, the tree compartmentalizes that damage to prevent spread of decay. It also has to work around the wound to transport water upwards and food down to the roots. That part of the tree is forever removed from the circulatory system. It may just be some nails you've hammered into the tree, but the phloem and cambium there have been destroyed, and part of the xylem as well.

The tree's ability to close off this damaged section and go on with its life is directly related to the health of the tree. If it's weak from drought or poor soil, it will have difficulty producing callus tissue to close the exterior wound and releasing protective chemical compounds. If it doesn't do this quickly enough, disease and decay can set in, killing the tree.

Note, too, there are many different types of bark, some tougher than others. Trees such as mature elms have ridges of tough, corky bark, but elm saplings have immature ridges that can be punctured with a thumbnail. Those ridges look like a disease on a sapling, rather than the immature ridges they are.

Pruning damages bark, of course, but proper pruning, just outside the "collar" of a branch, enables the tree to quickly summon chemicals to prevent infection and to begin callusing over the wound. A limb collar is a slightly raised area next to a larger limb or the trunk, sometimes appearing as pushed-up sleeve folds.

In time, a healthy tree will completely close the wound. If your tree has newly damaged bark, trim the edges into a smooth cut, and do whatever is necessary to prevent water from standing in the damaged area.

To prune trees, deal first with the three D's: dead, decayed or diseased, then with crossing branches that could rub against one another, damaging bark. Then prune to shape, being careful never to remove more than 30 percent of the tree's canopy. If the tree has grown too tall, "drop the crotch" (remove the leader down to another branch that is at least one-third of the diameter of the limb or leader being removed).

Also keep in mind that pruning stimulates vegetative growth, even if the pruning is done when the tree is dormant. When leaves start erupting, so too will "watersprouts," those useless twigs and branches that grow straight up from a horizontal branch.

In some cases you can use a dead tree as an ornament in your landscape; in other cases you must have the tree removed.

If you have the stump ground out, there will be a tempting spot to plant something else. Do not be tempted. Until that sawdust completely decays, it will use nitrogen for the decay process, nitrogen that other plants would need for growth. And think of the nutrients your late tree has already taken.

Winter preparation for evergreen trees may include spraying foliage with an anti-transpirant such as Wilt-Pruf. Follow label directions. They may require that you wait until the water in the foliage has descended to the roots, and that means we've had cold weather for a while. Follow label directions and spray when you have a few hours of daylight for the product to dry in above freezing temperatures. If you water deeply before winter, you shouldn't have any worries about the tree's transpiring all of its water resources. Don't set up a bog situation, though, for the tree roots also need oxygen they can't get if they're standing in water.

If your tree is a young tree or looks like it has tender bark, paint the south side of the trunk with white latex paint to reflect strong sun rays. In winter, our sun rises and sets low in the south. Alternatively, you could wrap the trunk with one of the coiled plastic wraps available through tree companies or garden stores. That should also deter rodents and/or deer from chewing on the trunk.

Some varieties of trees such as redbuds, for instance, are susceptible to Verticillium fungus. If you lose a tree to this disease, select a replacement that is resistant to that soil-borne fungus.

VIBURNUMS

If you're looking for different shrubs for your yard, consider Viburnums, woody ornamentals that are hugely varied from one species to another in growth habit, flowering, scent, leaf color and shape, size and shape, as well as in winter interest. And they flourish here. Some are native to America.

Some are evergreen, others deciduous. Viburnums are so numerous and varied in appearance, it takes an expert with a microscope to identify new varieties. About the only things Viburnums have in common, according to woody plant expert Michael Dirr, is that they have small flattish "drupe" fruits, each containing a single seed and leaves opposite one another on twigs.

Most varieties grow best in full sun, but some grow in shade. There are even some with variegated leaves in this large group of shrubs and trees.

When we bought our home in 1971, it had been landscaped with several different Viburnums, including a snowball bush, a leather leaf, a cranberry bush and a wonderfully fragrant broadleaf evergreen. Some were overgrown and have since been removed, but the snowball bush has been cut near the ground and rejuvenated.

Most Viburnums are hardy here and tolerant of our alkaline soil. They like some water, but most are far from being water hogs. Some are grown for their foliage, others for their blossoms, some such as the V. burkwoodii for their fragrance. One Viburnum, the nannyberry, or V. lentago, even produces fruit edible for humans. Edible does not mean choice or even tolerable. It just means it won't poison you.

My nannyberry Viburnum grew to about 20 feet tall, loaded each spring with clusters of white blossoms, followed by nary a fruit. I finally learned the shrub is self-sterile (most Viburnums are), so I planted a second nannyberry. It grew large before both shrubs set fruit. One taste was quite sufficient to finally satisfy my curiosity. Our larger dog thought she was getting away with something, stripping fruit into her mouth, but a few bunches of those berries satisfied her curiosity, too.

Prior to remodeling our house, the Viburnum next to our patio told me the temperature outdoors. If the leaves were curled into pipes, it was very cold, the temperature in the low teens or colder, but if they were just slightly curled, just a little cold, in the 20s. I thought it was a V. carlesii, but now, looking at Michael Dirr's book on Viburnums, I'm sure it was a V. burkwoodii, loaded in early spring with deliciously fragrant blossoms.

V. plicatum tomentosum is an especially beautiful shrub, branching horizontally, with horizontal tiers of white lacecap flowers. The popular name for this viburnum is doublefile. It grows large, about 15 by 15 feet when mature, a wonderful backdrop to smaller vertical shrubs or plants. Leaves are larger than some, being 2 to 5 inches long, and not as furry as its name implies.

Viburnums are attractive in hedges or as specimen plants.

I've found Viburnums are aphid magnets, especially in late spring or early summer, before beneficial insects are sufficiently numerous to exert control. Just blast aphids off with an occasional jet of water until the beneficials arrive to feast, but start these water jets before the leaves are so deformed by feeding aphids that water can't reach them.

Some of these shrubs, including the nannyberry, have gorgeous blazing red leaves in fall that hang on for days before they drop. The showy nannyberry has been used in gardens since the 16th century.

The Viburnum family of shrubs has a lot of variance, several cultivars more newly developed from V. carlesii parentage, and it's easy to grow in this area.

I don't believe they're friendly to wildlife in terms of providing food, however. I've never seen birds eating the black berries of V. burkwoodii, and never saw wildlife dining on the V. trilobum or American cranberry bush that we removed.

For landscaping purposes, the leatherleaf Viburnum (V. rhytidophyllum) is very unusual and could be attractive in the right circumstances.

VIRGINIA CREEPER

This wild vine is regarded as a weed by many, but its fall color ameliorates disfavor. Often we don't even know the vine has crawled up a tree until it blazes forth in autumn, red leaves in a Colorado blue spruce, for instance. It's very hardy, often bird-planted and not particular about sun exposure or water. It grows quickly, covering a fence in a season. If it's growing next to shingle siding or anything that must be painted, pull it out. It will worm under shingles and the sucker disks it uses for climbing are difficult to remove.

Virginia creeper has five leaflets, each about 6 inches long, with sawtooth edges. Do not confuse it with poison ivy, that has "leaves of three, let it be." Poison ivy has white berries in winter; Virginia creeper has blue berries usually consumed by birds before the leaves drop for winter.

WATER GARDENS

People starting water gardens dig and fill their ponds, then start looking for plants and fish to inhabit them. Fish in ponds are fun and relaxing to watch, and they are beneficial. There's more than one reason to buy your home pond or water garden fish locally: Idaho Fish and Game authorities don't want you to stock trouble fish even in your own yard, and local dealers know what is safe. It also bolsters the local economy.

Virgil Moore, director of the Idaho Fish and Game Department, says home pond and aquarium fish do show up in hot springs pools and local park ponds, such as ParkCenter Pond, even though they're not supposed to be there. Some say water birds such as ducks get water garden fish eggs on their feet and transport them to other waters, and others think fish-eating birds accidentally drop them from their beaks when over other waters.

Moore said herons usually eat fish where they catch them. He thinks people just get tired of the fish and illegally release them in ponds and thermal pools. He says there isn't a hot springs pool in the state that doesn't have tropical fish inhabiting it, even some pools a "stocker" would have to hike to get to.

People have released goldfish in park ponds, and some grow to 9 or 10 inches before they're caught by an angler, Moore said. It is illegal in Idaho to release live fish or eggs into any public water source without a permit.

Goldfish and koi are relatives of carp. Goldfish lose most, but not all, of their color as they grow. Both compete with native and game fish for food and space.

We've read about the Asian "snakehead" fish in Virginia and New Jersey that were found in sport fishing waters in Maryland and other Eastern states. The U.S. Fish & Wildlife Service has banned importation of those fish and their eggs.

They prey on other fish, including sport fish, and can move across land to invade other waters. They can live out of water for two days or more. People who have live snakehead fish at home are warned against releasing them or transporting them across state lines.

In addition to snakehead fish, others banned in Idaho are green and white sturgeon (they may carry disease that threatens native sturgeon), walking catfish, bowfin, gar, piranhas, rudd, ide and grass carp.

Well, then, should you stock your water garden with native species? Not unless you have a permit to do so. You must apply for a permit, have an inspection and receive a permit to stock native fish or game fish in a pond, Moore said. The inspection is to check whether conditions are right for the kind of fish you want to stock.

Authorities are concerned about stagnant water where mosquitoes may breed, because they may carry West Nile virus, which came to Idaho in force.

Water gardeners usually rely on their pond fish to eat mosquito larvae. Old tires and junk pose problems because rain may leave just enough standing water in them for mosquitoes to lay eggs. One way to avoid mosquitoes breeding in stagnant water is to drop in a "mosquito dunk," which should be available at garden centers and aquarium or water garden supply stores.

Clean leaves out of the pond after they fall, move tender plants indoors and check the pond filter so it's ready for spring activation. Set up a de-icer to let toxic gases escape and use a pond air pump if you have koi or fish in your pond. They don't need food in winter but do need oxygen. Hiding places for koi and other fish should be in place to protect from marauding raccoons and/or fish-eating birds.

WILLOWS

If you have a perpetual wet spot in your landscape, a tree such as a weeping willow will dry it out and keep it dry for you, but in its quest for water, it may invade sewer lines or septic tanks. Some say don't plant a weeping willow within 75 feet of any in-ground plumbing lines.

Weeping willows are huge trees, growing to 40 feet tall by 40 feet in diameter.

They look beautiful and graceful to the observer, but represent a lot of work for the homeowner, who must pick up the twigs and branches that drop every day.

They're easily started from cuttings, too easily started. You can cut up twigs of willow and soak them in water, then use that water to jump start cuttings of other plants, too. Willows are not particular about the time of year cuttings are taken and set into soil to root, but many other woody plants are particular about that.

Willows do have another beneficial aspect, too. They're the original source of salicylic acid (aspirin). Native Americans used willow bark tea for many ailments including the headaches that plagued so many Caucasian settlers.

WISTERIA

Most commonly grown varieties are the Chinese, whose vines twist counterclockwise and have racemes (clusters) of flowers that extend to about 1 foot, and the Japanese Wisteria, whose vines twist clockwise with racemes of flowers 18 inches to 4 feet long, depending on the cultivar.

These vines need a sturdy support. Prune lightly to keep the vine covering the area you want it to cover. Wisteria blooms on second-year wood, so heavy pruning would cut out future flowers. Pruning is recommended right after blooming is over.

Wisteria vines are available locally with Edwards Greenhouse selling grafted vines, and Five Mile Farm selling plants from cuttings, some of the plants a year older than the others. Other nurseries in this area have wisteria for sale, too.

Especially for out-of-the-ordinary plants such as this, you're a lot better off dealing with a local nursery that has knowledgeable people who can help you. You'll get post-planting advice, too, from the nursery people you bought your plant from if you run into problems.

If you're thinking of planting a Wisteria in this area, locate it so it gets at least six hours of strong sunshine each day. Some people plant two Wisterias side by side, and braid the trunks together to form a stronger trunk. Some growers claim the trunk must be 1 inch thick before flowering; others say the vine grown from seed or a cutting must be 7 years old before flowering. I have heard of one person whose vine flowered after only three years after a cutting was planted.

Wisteria is notorious for being reluctant to flower. You can always have The Talk with the vine: Tell it unless it flowers this year it's going to the landfill. A more reliable "cure" is root pruning. Use the longest-blade spade you have (best if the blade is 12 inches long), and cut straight down about 2 feet from the trunk, completely encircling the trunk. But give the vine four or five years to become established first.

Go light on the nitrogen fertilizer, heavier on the phosphate and potassium.

YARROW

Yarrow isn't used in cooking, but it's loved in Europe and America as an ornamental and aromatic herb. Many still prize its usefulness, too, as a healing herb. Its Latin name is Achillea, some say because Achilles used yarrow to stanch blood flowing from warriors' wounds during the battle of Troy.

Yarrow is a native of Europe, now naturalized on this continent. That it quickly became naturalized is indicated by the many medicinal uses Native Americans found for the herb. It has been used for many centuries for a variety of medical and magical purposes, as well as for skin lotions, fabric dyes, or even to predict the future.

In this country, it is most prized as an ornamental herb. Lens-shaped clusters of tiny daisy-like flowers stand above the fern-like foliage of yarrow, holding shape, color and aroma for a rather long time. Flower clusters are fine for cutting and arranging in bouquets, and cutting stimulates a second flowering.

Yarrow flowers dry easily, lending their beauty to craft projects such as dried wreaths and other arrangements. The flowers are borne on stalks rising up to about 3 feet above the ground, for some types. As long as the ground is not too wet or marshy, yarrow is easy to grow in full sun. The blooming period is June through September, depending on the variety.

Yarrow does spread, but it's not obnoxiously invasive. Plants can be divided in spring or fall, or can start from seed. There are over 60 varieties of yarrow, but flower colors are limited to shades of white, yellow, pink or red. Unlike many other flowers and herbs, close inspection of yarrow stimulates appreciation for the intricate beauty of its tiny individual blossoms.

YUCCA

Yuccas grow all over the West, especially on dry ground. Are they only native to the American West? I thought so, until I saw plans for 19th century Pennsylvania Dutch gardens.

Their kitchen gardens were laid out in a square, paths leading in from the corners, and in the center ... a Yucca. Pennsylvania Dutch folks were known for using everything on a pig except its squeal, but did they use the Yucca? I haven't found mention that they did, and William Woys Weaver, a food historian and author, expert on Pennsylvania Dutch customs, said he hadn't heard of their using the plant.

Native Americans dug Yucca roots to use for washing their hair, and the leaves or blades were woven for baskets and footwear by the earliest natives. Julian Martinez, husband of the famed potter Maria Martinez and a noted potter in his own right, decorated her pots using a portion of a Yucca blade as a paintbrush.

A map from the U.S. Department of Agriculture shows Yucca is native to Ontario and Alberta, Canada, Puerto Rico and the Virgin Islands, and all U.S. states except Minnesota, Alaska, Hawaii, Washington, Oregon and Idaho. What? It's not native or even introduced in Idaho? There goes my trust in USDA.

"Weeds of the West" indicates it's found "throughout the West, mainly on dry sandy plains and prairies." We usually see the tall spikes of blossoms as we drive through rural areas of the West, failing to notice the too-common spiky plants during non-blooming time.

Planted singly in a suburban yard, a Yucca attracts interest because of the shape of the plant and its leaves, even during non-blooming times. In my experience, Yucca takes years to get to a blooming stage. I think mine were originally offsets from a neighbor's Yuccas, and they took a very long time to get established, too. I have two, one larger and healthier because it's exposed to more sun than the other.

Yuccas reproduce by seeds and underground stems, producing offsets. They are drought-tolerant once established.

CHAPTER 7

Fruit trees

Fruit trees basics

We have the necessary chill hours for nontropical fruits in our area, but we do have a few specific problems growing fruit. For one thing, our pH (alkalinity) is so high that many fruit trees cannot absorb the iron in our soil, so the trees exhibit iron deficiency in the form of yellowing leaves, yellow between green veins, and in some cases, new leaves that are completely yellow.

This is most easily corrected with foliar applications of chelated iron. Dr. Esmaeil Fallahi, fruit tree specialist with the University of Idaho Agricultural Experiment Station in Parma, said orchard owners in southwestern Idaho spray chelated iron on new leaves after blossom drop, again within 10 days, and a third time in May to June 15. Spraying this early means there is less wax buildup on the leaves, allowing the leaves to absorb the treatment.

This supplement must be applied each year. In order to make it a sustainable garden, one would have to lower the alkalinity substantially so the plant or tree could take up the iron. Altering the pH is much more difficult, and since our water is about 7.0 alkalinity, it would tend to raise the pH if the soil alkalinity were lowered.

Another annual task is pruning. Many prune when the tree is dormant, preferably mid to late February, when we should be past the possibility of severely cold temperatures. When the tree resumes growing, though, it will grow vigorously, compensating for limb loss, sending up water sprouts (vertical branches) that are not fruit-productive. It's harder to see what you're doing in mid-summer, but pruning at that time does not stimulate vigorous vegetative growth.

Generally stone fruit trees are not long-lived in our area, principally due to peach tree borers. Some neighbors had a Siberian apricot tree that was an old tree, neither invaded by peach tree borers nor frequented by squirrels. Some folks don't think they're the best apricots, but I did like them, so I've planted a couple of those trees, hoping to get some to eat. We had special apricot trees for 14 years but never ate a one, because squirrels moved in, destroyed the fruit in their quest for the nut inside, and even ate the one I'd wrapped inside a net bag. The trees started showing signs of Coryneum blight, so we had them removed.

Boise is home to a very large number of squirrels who long for your fruit and nut harvest, and in some areas of the city, deer and other hoofed animals hunger for them as well as birds.

ALMONDS

I've been told they grow here, but I have no experience with them at all. In view of squirrel depredations on my apricots, I'm not planning on planting almonds.

APPLES

If you plant a new apple tree, of standard size, it may be nearly 10 years before you harvest a crop. Apple trees can be very long-lived, 60 to 140 years, but you may want a slightly shorter tree, bearing earlier. Semi-dwarf apple trees are 10 to 15 feet in height, and usually bear fruit years earlier than the standard (18 to 25 foot) trees. Mature dwarf trees are 8 to 10 feet in height, yet all bear the same size fruit.

Codling moth larvae have been the main source of fruit damage in our apples. Many growers are using a wettable powder called Surround, which is a kaolin clay for control. It must be re-applied after rains. (See chapter on insects.)

Apple trees are available in a columnar shape for folks with little room for trees. Pay heed to pruning recommendations by the vendor of those trees. Apple trees may be affected by fire blight, but I haven't had that problem in more than 40 years. See Pears.

APRICOTS

Apricot, peach, nectarine, cherry and plum trees may be damaged and ultimately killed by peach tree borers. Adults are clear-winged moths (slender black bodies with a red girdle) that lay eggs at the soil line of stone fruit tree trunks. When borers hatch, they enter the bark, and feed on tender tissues just under the bark. This is the circulatory system of the tree, and if they feed all around the trunk, they can kill it. Stir up the soil at the base of your tree trunks, and if you find a dark red jelly-like substance, it's the excretion of peach tree borers in your tree.

To prevent them, plant chives at the base of the tree or spread tobacco dust (snuff) or apply sticky tape around the base of the tree. If your tree has been invaded, you should look for the entry hole and squirt nematodes into the hole. I wouldn't use a systemic poison because it would affect the edibility of the fruit. Apricot, peach and nectarine trees are also susceptible to Coryneum blight or shothole fungus. (See the chapter on diseases.)

CHERRIES

An attractive food source for birds, squirrels and children. When his cherries were nearly ripe, the late Ross Hadfield sprayed them with wetted baking soda, so when children asked if they could have his cherries, he always said, "Oh, I just sprayed..." Some folks say birds won't bother yellow sweet cherries.

Rainier and Royal Anne cherries have a lot of red on them, and they do attract birds. You can try the hanging owl, balloon eye, fake snake or flashing foil to deter birds. Old wigs in the tree are no deterrent. In our area, cherries are also sources of food for the cherry fruit fly, that lays one egg in each cherry just as it's coloring. (See the chapter on insects.)

FIGS

These may be grown here in containers, prevented from freezing in winter, or otherwise heavily protected from coldest temperatures.

GRAPES

Table grapes, seeded and seedless, and wine grapes grow very well in our area. Fertilize lightly in June, prune in February.

Grapes are easily tucked into a fairly small space and can be trained against a fence or wall, or partnered with a gazebo, arch or pergola for beauty and good taste.

The late Ross Hadfield was the Valley's expert on seedless table grapes. Hadfield grew 19 varieties of table grapes on about a third of a city lot in Meridian. After he got hooked on growing seedless table grapes in 1963, he branched out from his original Himrod variety to test-grow grapes for an organization in New York. He vegetatively propagated some varieties, and one of his Himrods turned out to be a mutation, ripening to red rather than to "white."

Plan where you'll plant your vines, getting a good water supply at first (they need less later on) and good sun exposure, at least six hours per day. They prefer slightly acid soil, of ordinary fertility. Too fertile soil results in lush vegetative growth rather than fruit production. The European grapes (Vitis vinifera) are vulnerable to mildew and are not very cold-tolerant;

American grapes tend to be hardy and less subject to mildew and other diseases. This type of table grape, once established, prefers to grow downward, toward the ground, so it will have to be grown to a high point at which it can be left to cascade downward.

Hadfield found Glenora and Venus (both blue grapes), Canadice, Einset, Saturn, Suffolk, Reliance and Vanessa (all red grapes), and Remaily, Romulus and Lakemont (all white grapes), hardy in our climate. "White" grapes have green skins.

Grapevines are very long-lived, and a vine which appears to be played out can be revitalized with proper pruning in February as recommended by Hatfield. By that time, the possibility of Zone 4 temperatures (below minus 20 degrees) has diminished, and the grapevines have not yet started their spring growing surge.

Freezing usually damages only extremities of plants (if the rootstock is hardy) and that dead wood can be cut out in February. If you trim back a plant's branches too early, they may freeze and die back farther than you'd like. You want to be able to cut out the frozen portion and still have plenty of good tissue left to grow. So you wait until winter is nearly gone.

We prune grapes because the vines are so vigorous they'll produce more fruit than they can amply supply sugar for. If not pruned, the grapes are apt to be small, inferior and numerous. Pruning out old non-productive wood also can reinvigorate an old vine and make it produce a bountiful harvest.

Pruning grape vines also gives good opportunity to increase the number of vines. Grape vines are most often multiplied by vegetative propagation — that is, by cuttings or layerings from the parent vine instead of sexual propagation via blossoms and seed.

When pruning, select cuttings that are pencil thick, and have nodes less than 7 inches apart. Cut cuttings square at the base (closest to the trunk) about 1/4 inch below a bud, then make a slanting cut about 1 inch above the top bud, the cutting being about 12 inches to 16 inches long and including three nodes (growth bumps). The difference in cutting angles will help you tell top from bottom, otherwise it's no easy trick once the vine is cut loose.

Be sure you keep a record or some sort of identification so you don't mix up varieties. When you're finished pruning, bundle the cuttings by variety and dig pits deep enough to cover the vertically-placed cuttings with 2 inches of soil. Place the bundles upside down in the pits, and cover with soil, marking the locations.

By placing cuttings upside down, the growth hormones will concentrate in the upper portions of the cuttings. In three or four months, they should have callused over across the square cuts. Then turn the cuttings right side up (slanted side up, callused side down) and plant them with only the top bud about 1 inch above the surface. Be sure the holes are moist so that emerging roots can reach water. Plant the cuttings upright, not at an angle, or you'll get shallow-rooted vines.

Thus you fool growth hormones into stimulating fast and ample rooting of the cuttings. Hadfield had single wires holding up the "arms" or cordons of his grape vines that were set 5 feet off the ground, one cordon extending east, the other west from the trunk. Thus the pruned vines are really T-shaped. Eighteen inches higher, he had three wires to hold the fruiting spurs that grow from the cordons.

Because this type of grape "wants" to grow downward, this system holds the fruit well off the ground.

Grapes bear on 1-year-old wood, so your object in pruning is to cut out old wood, leave enough of last year's wood to grow "X" bunches of grapes this year (count the fruiting buds, leaving only 10 to 20 fruiting buds the first few years while the vine is in training). When vines are more mature you may leave 40 to 60 fruiting buds per vine. Growers usually leave half of the buds on one cordon, half on the other.

The Extension Office has modestly priced pamphlets with illustrations of steps to be taken with table-grape pruning. Grape vines planted for wine production are pruned differently than for table-grape production.

JUJUBES

They're hardy here, but use of the fruit is limited. Branches bear thorns, too.

KIWIS

The vines are hardy, but they tend to bloom too early for us to see it through to fruiting in this area.

MULBERRIES

These are hardy here and will thrive. You and your neighbors will appreciate the nonstaining white-fruiting variety after the birds discover your crop.

NECTARINES

See Apricots.

PAWPAWS

These are hardy here and are tap-rooted so prefer to be planted where caliche has been broken up. They do best as an understory tree, but don't expect Midwest-size fruits. Here they're 2 to 4 inches long.

PEACHES

See Apricots. Also subject to peach leaf curl. (See the chapter on diseases.)

PEARS

Use codling moth control. They also may suffer from fire blight. (See chapters on insects and diseases.)

PLUMS

Plum trees are vulnerable to peach tree borers. Unlike many other fruits, you can harvest plums and they'll ripen off the tree, but tree-ripened Italian Prune plums are a memorable treat. Small birds feed on some of the blossoms, but not enough to diminish my harvest.

QUINCE

Quince trees are hardy here, and the shrubby flowering quince brightens yards all over the Valley in spring. These shrubs sometimes set fruits that are edible, mainly used in jellies. Quince trees are a different species, but both tree and shrub fruits are edible, best after cooking.

WALNUTS

The devastating walnut tree disease called "thousand cankers" has come to our Valley, borne by walnut twig beetles native to the American Southwest who have moved north. If you can keep your black walnut or English walnut healthy, you may escape the disease. Imidacloprid systemic chemicals will kill the insects, but may render the nuts inedible, too.

Soaking nuts overnight in water makes it easier to extract large portions of meat, and don't forgo harvesting the nuts because the husks are black and unattractive. That's caused by the walnut husk fly, which lays eggs in the husks. The larvae can be controlled with Sevin, but many growers don't bother because the larvae don't penetrate the nutmeat. Sevin kills bees, so I wouldn't recommend spraying.

Some people scrape walnuts in husks over a homemade husker, made of nails protruding from a hardwood board. Most people husk black walnuts by running over them with the car in their driveway. Those husks will stain hands, so wear gloves when handling them.

Walnut trees, both black and English (Carpathian), emit a substance called juglone from their roots and leaves that has an allelopathic effect, impeding growth of many (but not all) other plants. To be sure you find the right neighbors; search on the Internet for "plants to grow with walnut trees."

CHAPTER 8

Weeds

As an arid, rural state, Idaho has an abundance and wide variety of weeds, ranging from weedy trees to grasses. Invasive species have been brought to this country in sheep coats and cattle tails, or brought intentionally as ornamentals (that went wild).

Some render landscapes hazardous, such as mature cheat grass with oily barbed seeds that feed range fires or cause jaw infections on grazing animals. For gardeners, some weeds are nuisances, while others, such as purslane, lambs-quarters and dandelions, are edible.

The following are among the weeds most likely to invade home gardens.

CANADA THISTLE

Introduced to Canada in the late 18th century, a contaminant of large animal feed. Grows 30 to 40 inches tall in our climate from extensive underground stems. Flowers on some plants are males, on other plants are females. Males survive and multiply via the underground stems, even if pollination doesn't take place. Control is difficult unless you resort to one of the herbicides such as Picloram, Clopyralid or Aminopyralid that can toxify your garden.

CHEATGRASS (Downy brome)

Accidentally introduced via packing material, and spread from the Denver area throughout the West. The grassy portion grows most over winter and very early spring, at which times it serves as forage for large animals (although it competes with native grasses for moisture), but when it sets its oily barbed seeds, it creates problems for cattle (lumpjaw) and firefighters (range fires).

CHICORY

One of the prettiest and most flamboyant wildflowers in this area is another chicory, escaped from cultivation, that graces roadsides with dramatic wands of blue flowers that close up in late afternoon. Settlers planted it for salad greens, using the roasted roots as coffee substitutes. By the time the stems stretch out to flower, leaves are few and tough.

CLEAVERS

Cleavers, or catchweed bedstraw, are botanically known as Galium apa-rine. In the past I've found a single specimen here, another there the next year. Then there were several plants in one area of my yard, and a friend who uses them for poultices pulled them out. They changed their growth habit from vining along the ground to upright. They look so different that way that even my herbalist friend didn't recognize them, and I had a thick stand of that weed. My garden helper pulled and dug enough of them to fill three garbage bags, bound for the landfill. I wouldn't try to compost them, lest I accumulate a yard full of them.

They have 2-inch wide whorls of six to eight narrow straplike leaves, square stems, and back-pointing bristles that catch on everything. The plants feel drily sticky, the bristles too soft and small to be painful, yet they'll attach to pets, clothing and other plants. In fields they foul harvest machinery. They are native to this area, so watch out for these dark green invaders.

CLOVERS

I've occasionally found red clover volunteering in my garden, and whenever possible, I let it alone. It is a legume, converting atmospheric nitrogen to soil nitrogen that plants can use. If it's blocking my plantings, I remove clover. It is quite easily controlled by pulling.

CRABGRASS

First appears as a pair of grass blades, one longer than the other.

Before it gets much larger and more complex, it's easily scraped out of a garden bed.

Seed germinates when forsythia blooms (takes the same number of heat hours for both events), so if you're going to use a pre-emergent crabgrass treatment, that's the time to do it. Corn gluten meal works very well against crabgrass, but not against tap-rooted plants or weeds.

DANDELION

Among the first things to bloom in Boise are the dandelions. It's a good thing, because the bees were waiting when dandelions began to bloom, and there wasn't much else for bees to feed on. Bees get up to 60 percent of their food from dandelions, according to some sources. Other beneficial insects join in on the dandelion feast.

Dandelions don't need to produce pollen for their own reproduction, but they do anyway. Because it's a favorite food of beneficial insects, pull off any blooming heads if you're about to spray pesticides above them.

Peter Gail, founder of The Defenders of Dandelions and the National Dandelion Cookoff in Dover, Ohio, says that although we may spend $20 to kill the dandelions in our lawn, we go to the health food store and pay more than that to buy weight-loss additives or tea or herbal potassium supplements, and don't notice their main ingredient is dandelions.

These are not native weeds. They were brought over on the Mayflower for food and as a healing herb. They're one of nature's richest sources of vitamin A, lecithin, calcium, B vitamins, potassium, phosphorus and other vitamins needed for human health. They first were planted in Plymouth, Mass., and then quickly spread westward. By the time of contact between white men and Native Americans, the natives already had figured out ways to use this beneficial plant.

Many people eat the leafy greens in salads, cook them as spinach, saute buds for vegetables, use flowers for waffles, muffins, fritters, pancakes, jelly and syrup, and drink coffee made of roasted and ground dandelion roots.

Why is it called "dandelion"? That's a corruption of "dent (tooth)-de (of)-lion." The leaves are said to be shaped like lion teeth.

Some use the blossoms to make wine, and that's when most of us think, "Oh, hey, I can eat these greens for food." That's the wrong time to harvest dandelion greens. They are least bitter and tastiest before blooming or after, but not during blossom time. Of course, never eat or use dandelion parts if they've been sprayed with pesticide.

As a medicine, the dandelion is an excellent diuretic, not robbing potassium as it works. It alleviates high blood pressure, aids digestion, treats PMS symptoms, improves circulation, relieves constipation and treats kidney and liver problems.

So why are people spending so much money to eliminate them from their lawns? It's a cultural fashion to have dandelion-free lawns. We go out and spray them with broadleaf weed control (2,4-D) and are surprised that they go to seed. That pesticide is a growth accelerator, sending the plant to seed more quickly than it would without the chemical.

You can dig them, but get all of the root, or you'll have three in place of one.

I think all of us, at some time, have picked up a full seed head to blow it clean of seeds, scattering them to the wind. And who hasn't picked a yellow bouquet for Mom? Made a whistle from the stem?

Dandelions are commercially grown, and you can buy seeds through Richter's, Cook's Garden, Territorial or Johnny's Selected Seeds. But you may not want your neighbors to tour your garden.

DODDER

Even the sight of dodder will make you shudder. I had seen photos of this weird relative of field bindweed, but seeing a fresh handful brought into the Extension Office was an unpleasant experience. The fast-growing weed has no chlorophyll and has only tiny stem-colored scales for leaves, all orange-yellow. The plant looks like a bunch of strings, resembling packing or filter material called excelsior. Seeds germinate on the soil, and a small root system is established, then tendrils reach out and attach to a plant. Once attached, the dodder gets its nutrition from the other plant, and its own root system withers and dies.

It thrives and multiplies so rapidly control is nearly impossible. If you ever see any of this stuff in your garden, get it out without delay. The sample brought into the office was probably bird-planted, so beware. The weed is usually associated with clover or alfalfa, but in this case, it was in a flower bed.

EQUISETUM

If you're seeing something different in your landscape, your eye may be picking up on Equisetum. These plants are a link to 400 million years ago, when their ancestors towered 40 feet or more into the air; today's much smaller versions are still very striking in their appearance.

Popular names are horsetail, scouring rush, shavegrass, horse pipes, snake grass, mare's tail, pewterwort and bottlebrush. It grows wild in Idaho, primarily in moist locations and is native in most parts of the world.

Twenty-five species of this genus live today, all herbaceous (tender tissue) and growing to 2 or 3 feet tall, although their ancestors in the Coal Age were woody trees. Equisetums have jointed bamboo-like stems that are vertically ridged. They do not flower, but reproduce from spores released from a cone atop each stalk. They also spread by rhizomes.

Horsetails die back in fall, but scouring rushes do not, according to a paper by Advanced Master Gardener Gene Gray. Horsetails have tan stalks with modified leaves like whorls of soft needles. Scouring rushes have scale-like leaves and the stalks are green with black bands at the joints. Stalks of both are jointed and hollow.

Both contain a significant amount of silica, and some people break off a handful to use to clean cooking utensils when camping. The silica in horsetails makes a very effective scouring agent, but the same constituent makes it perilous when used for forest toilet paper. Some species are poisonous to livestock, but bears consume Equisetum without suffering problems.

Native Americans and herbalists use horsetail to stanch bleeding and as a poultice for other medical problems. Some people use it internally for various medical problems, but these plants can rob one of thiamine, a deficiency that shows up dramatically in horses and may result in their death.

Gardeners in many parts of the world use common horsetail as a fungicide in their gardens, although it hasn't been specifically tested as such. You can buy dried horsetail from organic garden suppliers and mix a tea for use as a fungicide.

If you're going to grow it at your home, I'd strongly advise you grow it in a container and watch out for new plants arising from spores. The container will stop the rhizomatous spreading.

I've heard for years that most chemicals are ineffective against horsetail or scouring rush infestations, although the Pacific Northwest Weed Control Handbook suggests using Amitrol-T, Casoron or Norosac, MCPA, or Telar. Read label instructions for eradication in specific locations. A friend in southern Indiana, at his wit's end to eliminate horsetail from his nursery, finally found a solution to the problem. It's labor-intensive, but he said it worked.

He cut off each stem just below a joint, used an eyedropper and dropped a few drops of Enforcer Brush Killer into the standing tube. He said you have to treat each stalk individually, and advised treating one at a time, waiting until after treating one stalk before cutting the next. He had tried digging them, but that only encouraged further growth.

FIELD BINDWEED

I've had some queries about how to kill field bindweed, also known as wild morning glory or Convolvulus arvensis. I certainly wish I knew. It's in my front yard, a "gift" from a now defunct lawn service company. I'd sacrifice flowers for a season if herbicide killed it in the flower beds. The reason it's so very hard to kill is that you have to spray it when it blossoms for maximum effectiveness, and this plant grows so that a tiny fraction of the plant is in blossom at any given time.

It spreads by roots that extend down to lateral roots that in some areas run underground at a depth of 10 feet. They're not that deep in my yard. I doubt they'd penetrate the caliche (calcium carbonate hardpan) that lies about 30 inches below soil surface in my yard. But they can run atop that caliche, poking up onto the surface wherever they want.

Some say bindweed won't grow without light, but it does. Look in your crawlspace, and look at those pale shoots standing up from the soil. I've even heard of a family who removed a living room carpet, uncovering a large coil of field bindweed that had entered via a crack in the subfloor.

It's a native of Europe, where I suppose something must keep it in check. A friend in Norway said, "Oh, yes, it grows by my garage, but what can I do? I am just the one person..." If there is a natural control, as a horticulture-educated fruit orchardist, she should know of it.

GOATHEADS

Folks in eastern Colorado called these ground-hugging plants with the bicycle tire-piercing woody burs Mexican sandburs. It's also known as puncturevine. Its tiny hairy leaflets are borne opposite one another on branches from 6 inches to 5 feet long. The plant begins putting forth tiny yellow blossoms in July that become woody burs that remain viable for up to five years. Hoe it out or use chemical or biological control.

HOARY CRESS (White top)

A drive through the western part of the county reveals stands of this weed everywhere. Debbie Cook, advanced master gardener, said the Extension

Office recommends 2,4-D applied with a spreader-sticker product to make it adhere to the leaves longer for control.

She advised applying it when the plant is in bud, if you can identify it, or as soon as you can.

This weed is a perennial, growing 2 feet tall from a ground-hugging rosette of leaves, and reproducing by seed and root fragment. This member of the mustard family has lance-shaped blue-green leaves, the two top leaves clasping the stem and a flower cluster of tiny white blossoms.

JAPANESE KNOTWEED

This terribly invasive weed infests yards and fields in Ada County, and it looks very much like bamboo. It's a large herbaceous (not woody) weed with segmented hollow stems, broad oval leaves and creamy white racemes of blossoms in late summer or early autumn. It may grow to 12 feet tall in one growing season!

This tough, persistent weed may intrude through a crack in pavement or establish itself in an open field and run. Botanically known as Polygonum cuspidatum or Fallopia japonica, it was imported to the United Kingdom, then to America, as an ornamental.

Now it's known as one of the 100 most invasive weeds in the world, and it is hard to eliminate. Old canes of this weed are woody and sharp, so remove those before trying to eliminate this thug. Once they're gone, spread a large tarp or old carpet over the patch to deprive it of light. New growth will raise the cover, but just walk on it to crush stems back to earth.

This will not entirely kill the infestation, just slow its growth. After a week or two, you should then lift the cover and cut the canes to the ground, inject the in-ground parts of the plants with glyphosate (Roundup or similar products), and after giving the chemical a week or so to work, dig up the roots. Be prepared for more fight, because if you leave any trace of roots in the soil, they may regrow. Bag all cuttings and roots of this weed and send them to the landfill, or else you'll end up growing and fighting more Japanese knotweed.

LAMBS-QUARTERS

Member of the goosefoot family (Chenopodiaceae) that invades disturbed soils of gardens, competing for water. Green leaves are slightly lobed, undersides silvery-grainy. This is edible by humans and a favored food for the beet leafhopper that transmits curly top virus to garden plants. Flowers and seeds are inconspicuous.

MALLOW

Emerges from seed as tiny back-to-back heart-shaped primary leaves, easily removed before this plant gets large, developing a long taproot. Leaves are round and lobed, seed pods shaped like buttons or wheels of cheese, giving rise to the common names buttonweed or cheeseweed. This is an annual or biennial with purplish-white flowers. I don't think there's an effective chemical control.

PIGWEED

An erect annual, with prominently veined lance-shaped leaves and stems that are root red or tending to red in color. Remove by pulling or hoeing.

POISON IVY

In our area this grows as a small woody shrub rather than a vine.

Birds feed on the white berries in fall, then the seeds (contained in the berries) pass through bird digestive systems and emerge with their own fertilizer to be planted in urban yards and gardens. Branches have leaves of three — let them be. Use disposable gloves to remove and if you accidentally touch it, wash with Tecnu to avoid severe skin rash.

PURPLE LOOSESTRIFE

Imported as an ornamental, this has moved into wetlands, crowding out native plants.

It's very difficult to eradicate this noxious weed because you have to be careful not to contaminate the wetland it prefers to grow in and because it develops extremely vigorous, spreading root systems.

Ada County Weed & Pest Control agency collected 100,000 Loosestrife-eating Galerucella beetles near Moses Lake, Wash., for release in this area to combat the plant. Purple loosestrife (Lythrum salicaria) is the target of these beetles, not the gooseneck loosestrife that, in bloom looks like a gaggle of geese. That loosestrife is Lysimachia clethroides, and, although it has its own invasive qualities, it's not the public enemy that purple loosestrife and some other Lythrums are.

The plant is native to Europe, where it's not the menace it is in the U.S. Why? Because in Europe there are pests and diseases that control it, and because there's some evidence L. salicaria has picked up strength and steam from crossing with L. alatum and L. virgatum, a garden version of purple loosestrife.

Both L. salicaria and L. virgatum are classified as noxious weeds in many parts of the country.

Seeds are borne prolifically and are tiny, blowing up to 50 miles or so and taking root in appropriately wet sloughs, ditch or canal banks, puddles or along permanent streams. L. salicaria also grows in dry ground, but is less offensive.

In wetlands, L. crowd out native vegetation that provide food and cover for native species of insects, birds, mammals and aquatic creatures. Massive tough roots of Lythrum also do not sieve and cleanse water as do native wet-lands plants such as cattails. One of the problems with eradication is that the plant is quite pretty, and blooms bright purple blossoms on tall stalks from June to fall. Of course the prolific blooming means prolific seed setting, too.

"Sterile" hybrid Lythrums have been sold for home gardens, but they've been discovered to be actually producing some pollen that, when blown to L. salicaria blossoms, invigorates those plants so that they can reproduce among themselves. Garden varieties are called Morden Rose, Morden Pink, Morden Gleam and Dropmore Purple.

Purple loosestrife seeds are included in some wildflower mixtures, unfortu-nately.

A few years ago, a local garden store had a rack of wildflower seeds that included purple loosestrife. I called this to the attention of the store manager, and he promptly removed them from the rack.

A woman in Ontario dug out her "small plant" of purple loosestrife, and was shocked to find it had a root ball a foot in diameter, and that it was as thick and hard as if it were a tree's root ball.

Gallurecella beetles won't completely eradicate the L. salicaria, but they can deal it a controlling blow. It may take a few years, but they can reduce the plant's numbers.

They may attack other Lythrums, but they've been screened for preferential tastes and deemed properly beneficial. So they shouldn't attack non-Lythrum plants.

PURSLANE

Purslane is one of the most maddening garden weeds we try to destroy, but we could be eating it instead of pulling or hoeing it. I don't care for the taste, but many people do. It's grown on purpose in England and Holland and used the same as cooked spinach (it shares a high iron content with that vegetable), or fresh to add zest to a salad. Purslane is a ground-hugging mat of succulent-like flesh, red stems radiating outward from the central root. You hoe it out, and two or three days later it looks as alive as when you first saw it. Examination reveals it has rerooted. Severed stems may also root themselves. Botanically it's Portulaca olearacea, similar to the succulent-like ornamental Portulaca.

The way I've found best to destroy purslane is to sever the central root then turn the plant upside down. It won't reroot in an upside down position, but as it dries it will drop seeds for next year, joining others that remain viable for years. The seeds are so ubiquitous it's futile to worry about adding more.

Many gardeners put pulled or hoed weeds in buckets, then put them in the trash. Many of these weeds, especially pigweed, have deep roots that collect trace minerals. I prefer to leave the pulled weeds in pathways (unless they're a weed such as crabgrass) in hopes the decaying roots will return trace minerals to the soil. Decayed leaves and stems will add humus to the soil, too.

Purslane has an acid-like taste made more lemony in flavor when tender stems are pickled in wine, salt, wine vinegar and a little sugar. William Woys Weaver, author of "Heirloom Vegetable Gardening," has prepared this dish, but prefers the golden purslane to the regular garden purslane. The golden variety is more upright, and has larger leaves than the garden purslane weed.

Seeds for golden purslane are available from some nurseries, but ordering weed seeds makes you feel either like a traitor to the human race or like a fool, or both, I can attest.

Plant historians surmise that the plant was introduced to Europe from India, via Persia. But some seeds for purslane discovered in Kentucky date to the last millennium, centuries before known European or Asiatic contacts. The origin seems to be a mystery.

QUACKGRASS

One of our worst invasive weeds, quackgrass spreads by seed and by sharp pointed rhizomes. In a potato bed, it will spear and grow on through every potato in its path, essentially ruining the potato for human food. Blades of this grass are fairly wide, up to 1/4 inch wide, with a twist in the blade partway up, and often with constrictions near the tips. Do not try to till this under, for every root fragment will grow. Glyphosate controls above-ground plant, but runners may still emerge a short distance away. Walnut or black walnut leaves in a heavy mulch kill quackgrass, but new plants will emerge in a few weeks.

SAGEBRUSH (Artemisia tridentata)

Years ago, a new landowner in the Treasure Valley promptly hired someone to pull out all of the sagebrush. One of the master gardeners working at the Extension Office remarked, "I hope it wasn't on a slope."

On the one hand, you can understand someone who has just driven through hundreds of miles of sagebrush wanting to get rid of it. On the other, our common native sagebrush, appearing alone in a landscape, can be an attractive feature. And if it's on a slope, it may be holding the soil.

If you plant a sagebrush, locate it so that it won't be watered by a sprinkling system. Sagebrush is drought-tolerant, and a good candidate for a xeriscape garden. Part of the reason sagebrush is drought-tolerant is that it has deep and rather extensive roots. That aspect also makes it a good candidate for fighting erosion. Too much water and tender loving care shorten its life expectancy and the life span of any plant native to our area.

SOWTHISTLE

When your garden soil is nicely moist and friable, you should be able to pull any weed out with ease. That works with just about any weed except brittle sowthistle.

Spiny sowthistle, or Sonchus asper, is next to the top of my most disliked weeds (tops is field bindweed). When anything else will give way, sowthistle breaks off just above ground level.

This is a nasty weed. It has seeds on fine white hairy parachutes, which blow to every nook in your yard. Stems are hollow, and bleed a milky latex when broken (true thistles do not have milky latex). Leaves are spined and toothed, clasping the stem. It's advisable to wear gloves when trying to extract this weed. It is an annual, whose flowers appear all summer long, like small dandelions held on high.

Imagine my surprise at a comment from a New Zealand friend that she finds S. asper sold at Maori farmers markets. She said she had not eaten it, but knew Maori people gathered it from the wild, and said as near as she could remember, they harvested it before it went to flower (like most wild edibles).

It's their original spinach, called puha or rauriki. They usually rub the stems and leaves together under running water and then steam like spinach, according to "200 Years of New Zealand Food and Cookery" by David Burton. Stems and leaves "need to be boiled up to 30 minutes for all traces of bitterness to disappear, but cooking time can be reduced to just a few minutes if several changes of water are used."

"Plants of the Pacific Northwest Coast," compiled by Jim Pojar and Andy MacKinnon, says, "The young leaves of sowthistle can be eaten raw in salads or cooked as a vegetable."

I hope I never get that hungry.

TREE OF HEAVEN (Ailanthus)

The most misnamed plant in the world probably is the Tree of Heaven. If you have them growing in your yard, add removal of them to your list of fall chores. We had three in our backyard, each about a yard tall. That's one growing season. Give them two years, and they'll take over.

Tree of Heaven is Ailanthus altissima, sometimes called Chinese sumac or stinking sumac, although it is not related to sumac. Some call it the "tree from hell." It spreads by samaras (winged seeds) and by suckers from the roots. These trees do stink, too. Male flowers stink, female flowers are odorless, but the trees in general stink.

In its favor, it's drought-resistant, hardy to zone 4 and withstands urban pollution. It was imported to this country in 1784, a time when urban smoke

216 • Gardening in the Treasure Valley

and air pollution were minor compared to today. Left unchecked, the tree will grow to a height of about 60 feet, with a spread of about 40 feet. Limbs are chubby and coarse, emitting foul odors when crushed. Leaves are somewhat similar to sumac.

The wood is soft and breaks easily, so it's useless as a timber tree. It produces copious numbers of seeds that travel some distance in winds, spreading the "joy." Some say the new saplings will transmit their unpleasant odors to your hands when you try to remove them. They have a fuzzy appearance when quite small.

A Tree of Heaven stars in the novel, "A Tree Grows in Brooklyn." The trees take root in sidewalk cracks or retaining walls, and prying roots create further damage. Such a tree also survived several dynamite charges at the old Territorial Penitentiary in Boise.

VIRGINIA CREEPER

See Virginia creeper in the chapter on ornamentals.

VIOLETS (Viola odorata)

Some folks who want nothing but grass in their lawns complain about violets volunteering even in lawns. They spread by seed and runner, so they're difficult to control. The flowers are pretty and aromatic, so most of us just enjoy them. They'll even bloom in the dead of winter.

CHAPTER 9

Insects

Beneficial and
destructive

WHAT TO LOOK FOR

Most insects are beneficial, so until you know what a critter is, you're better off if you don't kill it. Beneficial insects or their larvae may kill and eat other insects or lay eggs on or in destructive insects or pests, and when the eggs hatch, they kill the pest-host.

Look at flowers such as carrots, mint, parsley or onion, and pay special attention to the tiny flying wasps repeatedly visiting those flowers. Most, if not all, of the wasps are beneficial. They love those shallow reservoirs of nectar that sustain them until they do their duty controlling destructive insects. Keep in mind that the bad guys show up first, and the beneficials don't show up until the feast is ready for them.

Lacewings and lady beetles (lady bugs) are well-known beneficial insects. Their larvae bear no resemblance to their parents; both look like tiny 1/4-inch dull alligators. The larvae of lady beetles have orange dots on their body, Lacewing larvae don't. Those larvae, not their parents, are the main consumers of aphids.

Less well known is a tiny (less than ¼-inch long) black-and-white minute pirate bug, equipped with a sharp long snout, through which it sucks the life juices from target insects.

Entomologists often count earwigs among the beneficial insects because they consume quantities of aphids. Since they also consume plant material in proportion to their numbers, I don't include them as beneficial insects.

Since they can capture and consume honeybees, entomologists usually count praying mantises as destructive insects. I have the large Chinese praying mantises naturalized in my gardens now, and I've seen them eat many insects, perhaps one honeybee in 40 years. When I first got them established, my earwig population dropped dramatically, so I include them among the beneficial insects.

An often overlooked beneficial insect is the mud dauber or paper nest-building wasp or hornet. Unless they're building a nest in a doorway where they'll be stinging you every time you pass through, let them alone and learn to co-exist. They patrol my garden beds before, with and after me, snatching up newly hatched larvae to use to provision their egg cells.

Early in summer and late spring, those hornets or wasps consume a lot of aphids, licking them into their mouths. By late summer, they're about to die and they've lost their appetite and have done all of the egg cell providing they're going to do.

I am not talking about yellow jackets, those avid meat-eaters that hassle fairgoers and can sting time and again. Yellow jacket traps don't trap other wasps, but they do trap yellow jackets. Some build paper nests, but many of them have in-ground nests. If you spot an in-ground nest, you can control them by putting a clear glass bowl over the opening.

Whenever considering any insect or pest damage in the garden, evaluate how much damage it is really causing. If they're causing more damage than you can tolerate, find the least toxic way to control them. That's often pitting insect against insect, or beneficial nematodes against in-ground larvae.

Beneficial vertebrates in your garden may include snakes, toads, frogs, chickens and ducks. You may have to restrict ducks or chickens, because they'll also eat plants and fruits. Most gardeners who use ducks and/or chickens for pest and weed control keep their feathered friends in "chicken tractors," floorless movable coops that allow the gardener to control where they forage.

Considering the thriving population of chicken-attacking dogs, cats and raccoons in this Valley, you'll have to have sturdy, lockable cages.

Some of the "forgotten pollinators" include butterflies, bumblebees and house flies. Spiders, especially the web builders, help control many insects in the yard and garden.

Destructive insects vary in numbers around the Valley. More cutworm parent moths appear in the North End than in South Boise, for example. When we first moved to Boise in 1971, night air was alive with sphinx moths battering against lights. They're parents of tomato hornworms, and are the size of hummingbirds. Over the past 10 years I've only seen one sphinx moth, and very little tomato hornworm damage. The late Boise State entomologist Dr. Charles Baker blamed widespread use of Bt for their demise.

Give some garden helpers a hand

One of our native American pollinators is a gentle, industrious Osmia lignaria, or orchard mason bee. Once they hatch in early spring they work and work and work, eventually working themselves to death.

Orchardists in the Pacific Northwest have been buying colonies of these bees to pollinate fruit trees since their period of activity coincides with fruit tree blossoming. These little black bees, about two-thirds the size of a honeybee, pollinate more blossoms more efficiently than honeybees. Their sting, about like a mosquito bite, is only evoked if a bee is pinched between the fingers or caught in clothing.

They are not hive dwellers, but live in holes they find (they cannot make their own holes), which is where we come in.

Get a 12- to 16-inch long block of 4-by-4 untreated wood, preferably fir or pine. Saw one end at an angle of 30 degrees or more, and mark out ¾-inch squares on the face of the block. Drill 5/16-inch holes in the middle of each ¾-inch square to within ½-inch of the back. Be sure the insides of the holes are smooth.

Tack a shingle over the angled end, and hang this nesting block under an eave or somewhere that the block won't be knocked down or disturbed.

When the wild bees hatch, they immediately mate and start preparations for their offspring. They gather pollen and nectar, and the female lays an egg in one of the holes, providing ample pollen and nectar to get the larva to pupa-hood.

What they're also doing is pollinating flowers, producing fruit.

Females will "stack" cells with eggs, pollen and nectar within each hole, then seal the end with mud that will harden. That's why they are called mason bees. The first year you may not get many, but they'll multiply over years, given this secure home.

Without this sort of nesting block, they nest in beetle holes in the ground, where the larvae and pupae are subject to predation by beetles and wasps. They, like honeybees, are subject to mite infestations, but these bees seem to be able to shrug off the mites within days of hatching.

A quick look at the bugs in your garden

What's eating your vegetable plants and fruits? I've heard of a store employee's incorrect identification of pest damage on plants, so keep this information for reference, and if your plant is not included, ask the Extension Office.

If you have tiny holes on Asian greens, eggplant, turnip, potato or tomato leaves, they're made by black pinhead-sized flea beetles or small grasshoppers.

When plants grow more mature, flea beetles cease to feed on all but Asian greens, but grasshoppers feed on everything all of their lives.

If you have irregular holes with smooth edges in leaves, clipped plant parts, leaves half eaten or fruit such as tomatoes or strawberries chewed into, that's snail or slug damage. Silvery mucus trails are also a giveaway that one or the other of those mollusks has been feeding there.

Cutworms cut seedlings off at the soil line, and I think it was some of their close relatives (army worms) that cut off two of my tomato seedlings 2 inches above soil line a year ago.

Cabbage loopers or larvae of imported cabbage moths eat holes (and leave black fecal matter) on cabbages, broccoli, brussels sprouts, collards and leaves of cauliflower.

If leaves of beets, spinach, Swiss chard or lambs-quarters have light-colored rambling trails on them, that's damage caused by larvae of leaf miners.

The adult is a small fly that lays eggs in tiny white narrow parallel lines on the backs of those leaves. When the eggs hatch, larvae tunnel into the leaf, feeding on matter between the top and the bottom cell layers of the leaf, ruining those leaves for human consumption. The trails do not penetrate completely through the leaf, and both upper and lower parts of the leaf are intact. Spray eggs with Neem.

If you're growing corn, and the silk is missing from the ears, earwigs have eaten the silk, but chances are good that the silks were pollinated before their destruction, so you'll have full ears of corn. Corn earworms may be inside the husk unless you're growing a variety with extra-tight husks or you've dusted with Bt (Dipel) or have dropped a few drops of mineral oil into the tops of the ears just after the silks have turned brown and started to dry.

Those worms also attack tomatoes, chewing off the skins in tiny curls.

If a leaf on an otherwise healthy squash plant suddenly wilts, look for squash bugs, whose bite is toxic to squash plants. Adults are about a 1/2 to 3/4 inch long, matte gray, and often are seen mating tail to tail. They lay red-orange eggs on petioles and between veins of squash leaves. Spray egg clusters or nymphs with Neem. Handpick adults and drop into bucket of hot soapy water or smash them.

Stalks and twigs lacking leaves on a tomato, tomatillo or eggplant? Tomato hornworms cause that damage. Look for droppings, then upward to find the caterpillar. Handpicking is best. Drop them into hot soapy water or step on them, keeping your mouth closed against a fast squirt of green hornworm juice.

Dark pinpricks on green fruit that turn yellow as fruit ripens are damage by stink bugs. There may be white spongy tissue underneath, where the skin adheres to the fruit in that spot, making peeling difficult.

Tomatoes with large chunks bitten from ripening fruit may be damage from squirrels or vermin. Squirrels often bite into tomatoes in search of moisture, and will quit if a water source is provided.

Potato plants may be defoliated by the feeding of Colorado potato bug nymphs. They're red with black spots on their sides, and look and feel wet (lady beetle larvae have hard dry shells covering their bodies). Watch for clusters of orange eggs. Adults are yellow-tan with black stripes running toward the tail.

Holes in turnips or other root crops or a sudden decline of cole crops are usually due to cabbage maggots feeding on roots. To prevent maggot damage, slide a square of slitted tarpaper over the bottom of seedling stalk so flies can't drop eggs next to roots.

Shallow holes may be excavated by feeding of the slugs.

Holes and brown debris in your carrots? Blame the carrot rust fly. Either cover the row when planting or erect a barrier to prevent low-flying adults from dropping eggs on seedlings. I've had no such damage since converting to raised beds. Some folks plant tea leaves (not used) with carrot seeds, and claim it works as a repellent.

Damage to plums? Plum curculios cause a little damage, but in a home orchard, it's not enough to worry about.

Codling moth larvae attack apple and pear fruits. Control them and plum curculios with a spray of kaolin clay, called Surround. Codling moths are a major problem here. I think many of them avoid sprays by feeding on ornamental crab apples.

If onion leaves look silvery, they're infested with thrips.

Mexican bean beetles look like lady beetles, but bean beetles have yellow heads, while lady beetles have black heads.

Another yellow malefactor is the wireworm. They tunnel half-inch deep holes in potatoes.

Centipedes, millipedes and sowbugs (aka roly-polies, roll-up bugs, wood lice, potato bugs, Porcellio or Armadillidiidae) occasionally bite into living plants, but generally they're first responders to decay, helping to further that process.

FIGHTING BACK

NEMATODES

If your insect problems lie below the surface of the soil, consider using beneficial nematodes. There are three different formulations available: one for lawns (sod webworms, billbugs, etc.), one for fleas and their larvae, and one for gardens.

The beneficial nematodes exist naturally in the soil, but application increases their number to give them a big advantage over their foes. Be sure to follow label instructions to get maximum length of operation from these helpers. Temperatures should be between 55 and 100 degrees, so don't wait until cold weather to use this control.

NEEM

Neem, derived from the Azidirachta indica tree, is not a knock-out instant killer, but instead it works on chewing and sucking insects, disrupting their hormones so they forget to eat, mate, lay eggs or even fly. It kills insect eggs and nymphs, especially valuable with regard to squash bugs. It also has a repellent effect that apparently doesn't deter pollinators. It only affects insects that chew or suck on leaves, so bees are not affected.

THE BLENDER METHOD

Some gardeners control insects by gathering a handful of pesky insects they want to control. They put them in an old blender with a little water and buzz them to liquid. Then they strain the liquid into a spray bottle, thin it with more water and spray it on plants that insect has infested. It's a deterrent to insects of the variety blended, but I doubt it would work with cannibalistic creatures such as slugs.

Don't use the good blender, or you'll be in trouble with the head of the kitchen.

HOMEMADE INSECTICIDE

Only after you have considered whether you can handpick your garden invaders, researched nontoxic controls and potential traps, should you consider kill-on-contact insecticide. And if you're at that point, you can make it yourself.

You can make an effective contact insecticide by boiling about eight habanero chiles with three cloves of garlic in two cups of water in a pot with a tight-fitting lid. Boil for 10 to 15 minutes, then remove from heat.

It's important to let the pot cool before lifting the lid. Pour it all carefully into a blender and blend it on high for two to three minutes. Don't inhale over the blender after the top is removed. Strain out solids, then add four cups of water and two tablespoons of Dr. Bronner's Eucalyptus or Peppermint liquid soap (found at health food stores or the Boise Co-Op). Spray on destructive insects when and where you see them, and never stand downwind of where you're spraying.

KNOW YOUR BUGS, AN ALPHABETICAL GUIDE

APHIDS

The ability of creatures to reproduce without partners is called parthenogenesis. The aphid reproduces parthenogenetically at times. At other times aphids have sexual partners.

Overwintered eggs hatch in spring, producing females. Spring and summer, aphids are mostly or only females, producing other females seconds after they themselves are born. When an aphid emerges it may be carrying an aphid carrying another aphid. They damage plants by sucking sap, and they must suck a lot of it to extract the nutrients they need, excreting the excess sap as sweet honeydew.

Ants love the honeydew, so often "farm" aphids as their own dairy herds. They take autumn-laid aphid eggs into their hills for winter, carrying eggs outdoors in spring where hatching eggs can feed under ant supervision. Ants stroke the sides of the aphids, causing more honeydew flow.

When aphids become crowded or the plant they're dining on begins to fail, some of the progeny emerge as winged aphids that can fly to new plants. Aphids love sowthistle weeds, and congregate on rather mature sowthistles in huge numbers. I let them go until I see a black-winged one among the hordes, and pull out the weed, putting it quickly into the trash barrel.

In spring and early summer, paper and mud dauber wasps lick up aphids for their own sustenance, one of the reasons I co-exist with wasps. If aphids become a nuisance, they can usually be blasted off plants with a stream of water. Most aphids can't fly, so they die on the ground. You can also kill them with a soap spray.

Once aphids appear in numbers, beneficial insects come to feed. Soap sprays will kill beneficials too, so beware. Lady beetle and lacewing larvae feed heavily on aphids. I like to let them do it.

ARGIOPE SPIDERS

The yellow-and-black Argiope (pronounced ARGH-ee-opee) aurantia spiders weave beautiful large webs in the garden designed to trap flying insect prey such as mosquitoes, moths, wasps or grasshoppers. They've even been known to trap birds as large as barn swallows.

They're also known as zipper or writing spiders because in each of their orb-shaped webs there is a white vertical column some say resembles a zipper, others say a column of Xs. I've seen small webs woven by very small (young) Argiope spiders in my garden, and I know that as they grow, their webs will grow, too.

The web maker is present, holding on to strands that will tell it when something is caught in the web. It immediately rushes to the site of the capture, biting and injecting a paralyzing venom, then wrapping up the prey in strong strands of silk. It will consume the captured one at its leisure.

A mature A. aurantia web may be up to 2 feet in diameter, elaborately beautiful when made visible by clinging dew. If the spider is threatened, it will bite a human, the bite no more painful or toxic as a bee sting on a mature human (not allergic to bee stings), but perhaps more dangerous to a toddler.

Their webs are difficult to see apart from the white "zipper," and it's easy to walk into one or put your hand into one while reaching for a ripe tomato.

The tending spider usually tries to escape notice and may even drop to the ground when the web is largely disturbed.

A mature female A. aurantia body may be about an inch long, with long legs extending farther. Males are about one-quarter the size of females. After mating, the female produces brown papery egg sacs containing up to 1,400 eggs. She attaches them to one side of her web to protect the eggs from ants. Other insects may lay eggs in those sacs, too.

ASH-LILAC BORERS

Ash-lilac borers have been attacking ash trees around the Valley, as well as lilacs and privets. Adults are Podosesia syringae, clear-winged moths that take flight about the time that lilacs bloom. They attack crotches of low branches in ash trees and attack privet and lilac shrubs just above the soil line. Once their eggs hatch, the larvae bore into the tree or shrub and feed on the tissue that transports water from the roots to the leaves.

ASIAN LADY BUG

A fall home-invading insect is the Asian lady bug (Harmonia axyridis). Our common lady bugs (Hippodamia convergens) usually just find a sheltered spot in the Foothills for the winter. The Asian lady bugs, imported because they tend to feed on insects higher in trees, look for warmer homes.

When one finds the right spot, it releases pheromones that summon swarms of others. There they occasionally drop into food, climb into beds and bite occupants (they are carnivorous, after all), and stain with excrement. They don't smell very good, either.

These are good guys, though, so if they look like lady bugs (orange with black spots, O-shaped and shiny), vacuum them up using a clean bag and pour them out outdoors or put in a container with honey-soaked cotton or a container with damp sawdust, in a cool but sheltered place.

ASPEN LEAF BEETLE

Smell something burning? Check first to see if the smell is coming from a home, but then check your trees. It might be the unspotted aspen leaf beetle, laying eggs and chewing on leaves of aspen, poplar and willow trees. Advanced Master Gardener Ben Grant said the larvae, which look a lot like lady bug larvae, smell like burning electric wires.

Grant said you can often smell them before you see signs of their damage.

They can produce more than one generation in a summer, and if left unchecked, can defoliate a tree, effectively starving it. You can control them with Malathion. Follow label techniques for timing and spray technique.

BEET LEAFHOPPERS

The Treasure Valley, like the rest of the Intermountain West from Canada into Mexico, is subject to a virus that occurs in the arid Middle East and in this area. It has been extensively studied by Texas A & M and New Mexico State University because it wreaks havoc with crops in their areas.

Some years it devastates the chile harvest in New Mexico, and when the winds are blowing northeastward, they may blow the leafhoppers with the virus into southeastern Colorado. It also occurs in the area around Fresno, Calif., and parts of the East Bay.

Beet leafhoppers, the tiny insects that bring devastating curly top virus to your garden, pick up the disease from sugar beets or other crops that have that disease, then they can ride the winds up to 200 miles before they land on a juicy tidbit, bite into it, and transmit that virus. It's useless to spray for these leafhoppers because they're transient, in and out.

How can you protect your garden from them? They dislike shade, so if you can manage a bit of shade that won't interfere with your plants' need for six hours of full sun, you could ward them off. They're attracted to the color yellow, so yellow sticky traps may work (but it may not catch all of the leafhoppers coming your way).

They winter over alive on host weeds such as wild mustards, Russian thistles and peppergrass. Once they bite into a plant, it's doomed and should be removed. Symptoms on squash and pumpkin plants are new leaves that are stunted and curled, older leaves yellowed; on bean plants, the leaves pucker and turn downward; and, in tomato plants, upper leaves curl upward, revealing purple veins on the backs of leaves that feel leathery.

Strong-smelling herbs, such as thickly-planted dill, may divert them to others' gardens. Lavender and fennel sometimes work as well.

Plant curly top resistant plants around your garden bed. The only ones I know of are some determinate tomatoes bred and tested by a University of

Idaho researcher. Those varieties include RowPac, Owyhee, Columbia, Payette, Roza and Saladmaster.

Sand Hill Preservation Center (www.sandhillpreservation.com) is the only commercial source I know of for these varieties. Your county Extension Office may also have seeds. They're all small red salad varieties with undistinguished flavor. (See also curly top virus in the disease section.)

BLACK VINE WEEVIL

Notched leaves on lilacs, roses, grapes, Rhododendrons, Azaleas and Primulas, or sections of yew leaves chewed off, indicate the presence of the black vine weevil adults. The adults themselves don't do much damage, but the adults (all females, no males) may lay 1,000 eggs during our growing season, and their larvae are deadly to these plants. The insect gained its name in Europe because of its color and its habit of attacking grape vines.

As few as eight larvae are capable of killing a large yew. Some master gardeners in this Valley reported losing several Rhododendrons to the voracious larvae. Prevention of larvae is easier than trying to destroy them once they've hatched underground.

Spraying with Sevin controls the adults, and if you can control them in May and June, you can prevent the egg-laying and larvae hatching. Carefully follow label directions to protect honeybees. Black vine weevils remain close to the area in which they hatched, within about a 30-foot radius, since they cannot fly.

Do not spray the soil if you have injected nematodes, however.

These weevils move only by walking, but if you have a single-trunked shrub attractive to them, you may stop their shrub invasion with a wrap of cardboard surfaced with Tree Tanglefoot. Do not put Tanglefoot directly on the bark.

Of course you don't know if the adults have already laid eggs in the soil, but don't take chances. If you have shrubs you treasure, apply nematodes to the soil around the shrub, and follow label directions about keeping the area moist.

Nematodes are unsegmented worms, some species beneficial and some, such as root knot nematodes, destructive.

Nematodes such as Steinernema carpocapsae and Heterorhabditis heliothidis can help combat adult weevils hiding in the soil as well as larvae, and both worms are commercially available from insectaries.

Local garden centers may carry beneficial nematodes. Pay heed to the expiration date on the container. Nematodes usually last about three months in soil, under favorable conditions. Since weevil larvae mature in greater numbers in late autumn, you should have active nematodes in place at that time, so you may need to apply twice in one season. They may seem costly, but consider the cost of replacing special shrubs.

BOXELDER BUGS

As summer dwindles to a close, shortened daylight hours or cooler temperatures send signals to insects to "fort up" against the coming winter. One of those insects is the boxelder bug that is more annoying than destructive. Boxelder bugs, or Boisea trivittatus, are the cause of a lot of calls to the Extension Offices. They are nuisances and unwelcome house guests. They cannot chew on anything, since their mouths only have sucking parts, so they don't eat holes in fabric or houseplants.

But they congregate in large groups, and their excrement stains. These social gatherings of boxelder bugs occur in spring, when overwintered adults emerge from warm hiding places and in fall, when they're seeking warmth and shelter.

You're most apt to find them on the south sides of houses, crawling out from under siding, to sun themselves on concrete foundations. Warm winter days entice them out of hiding, too. A smack with a trowel or shoe dispatches them, but they release a stench when smashed. That's one of the main reasons few predators feed on them.

One of the easiest means of control is to vacuum them up with a shop vacuum. Another means of control is to spray them with an insecticidal soap spray or a spray containing detergent and a little rubbing alcohol. If they're congregated on a nongrowing surface, you don't have to worry about plant safety. Remember, these sprays do not have a residual effect, so the spray must actually hit the insect.

You can also kill them by splashing them with boiling water. After they overwinter, these adults lay eggs and die. Those that show up in fall are the summer's hatch. Only the adults will survive the winter. The nymphs accompanying them will not.

This is usually one of the first insects people learn to recognize, but if you are unsure about it, the adult insect is about 3/8 inch long, a 1/4 inch wide, basically black long, flat ovals with red lines on it.

They feed on leaves and seeds of female boxelder trees and some maples and ashes. Some even invade fruit trees. You can keep them out of your home by caulking well around windows and doors, using a sweep strip on the bottom of doors to the outside and repairing screens.

BRONZE BIRCH BORER

The sight of a damaged white-barked birch tree just breaks your heart. Those leafless or sparsely-leaved treetops often herald the end of life for these lovely trees. The culprits are bronze birch borer larvae, offspring of a slender coppery beetle less than 1/2 inch long. These beetles are seldom seen, and since they attack the upper reaches of birch trees first, the damage from their larvae is not quickly noticed.

When leaves look sparse near the top of the tree, it often indicates where larvae of a bronze birch borer have been feeding on cambium and phloem tissues, just under the outer bark of the tree. The tree tries to protect itself by repairing that damage by forming callous tissue. This new tissue raises ridges in the bark, called "gouting." Leaves are then deprived of sustenance so they die and drop. You may be able to confirm this is the problem by using binoculars.

New eggs and new larvae, working lower on the tree in subsequent seasons, continue to consume the cambium and phloem tissue. When larvae have girdled the tree, destroying cambium all the way around the trunk, the tree above that girdling dies. Eventually, the pests kill the entire tree.

The cambium layer is the growth and repair layer of the tree, growing laterally and creating phloem cells outside the cambium (beneath the bark), and xylem tissue between the cambium and sapwood. Phloem tissue just beneath the bark conducts food down to the roots. Xylem tissue carries water up to the leaves where, in the presence of sunlight and carbon dioxide, it converts those items to food for the tree.

When you plant a tree, it grows outward. The branches will always be at the height they were when they sprouted. Upward growth comes from new cells at the tips of the leader and other branches and twigs. Xylem tissue dies and becomes sapwood then heartwood, as the cambium layer forms new xylem tissue inside itself (hence growth rings). Phloem tissue is constantly renewed, the old tissue becoming bark.

Birch trees have a tender, flexible bark that worked well for early natives building canoes. However, it is easily penetrated by tough insects (and weed whackers). Under that bark, insect larvae are shielded from pesticide sprays.

When bronze birch borer beetles emerge, they leave a hole in the bark that looks like a perfect capital D. Adults emerge in late spring and feed on leaves for several days before they begin to lay eggs on the sunny side of birch trees. They preferentially hit birches planted in unsuitable locations, such as sunny, dry city lawns. White barked birch trees' preferred habitat is in shady, cool, moist wooded areas. If planted in such areas, they're far less likely to be attacked by bronze birch borers.

River birch (Betula nigra) is quite resistant to attack by the bronze birch borer, but this tree doesn't have the soft white bark, either. The gray birch (B. populifolia) is moderately resistant to this borer's attack, but it is very susceptible to leaf miners and aphids. The Monarch birch, B. maximowicziana, is somewhat resistant to the Borers but also only moderately susceptible to aphids and leaf miners. Its hardiness is questionable, having been reported killed at minus 20 degrees.

Once a birch has been infested with these borers, there's not much you can do. Keep it as healthy as possible, with adequate water and fertilizer in winter or early spring, if needed.

Late the next spring, when adults are active, treat the trunk and lower limbs with Carbaryl, according to the Extension Office. Or, if the tree hasn't sustained heavy damage, try using Ace Caps (a systemic insecticide) in late May or early June.

CARROT RUST FLY

If you've started digging your carrots and are finding rust-colored tunnels in them, you're not alone. People bring maggot-mined carrots into the Extension Office wondering what to do.

The "rust" in the carrots is the excrement from the carrot rust fly maggots. You can cut off damaged sections and eat the carrot, but be sure you've cut out the stiff whitish-yellow maggots, about 1/3-inch long.

The fly itself is a black fly, 1/5-inch long, with yellow hair, legs and head. It lays its eggs on the crown of the carrot, and when they hatch, the maggots tunnel into the carrot. The tunnels then turn dark orange.

About three generations per year come around to lay eggs.

Do not leave any carrots in the ground in your garden, or you'll be providing the pest with winter housing and food. Because these flies will emerge from the earth in spring, it is important that you grow your carrots in another location in your garden next year. Don't make it easy for them.

Incidentally, this fly will attack other plants in the same family, too, such as parsley, celery, dill and fennel, so plant them in different locations as well.

Organic gardening sources suggest planting unused tea leaves with carrot seeds. Other sources suggest waiting until mid-May to plant because the first hatch of flies would have been unable to lay eggs in suitable hosts.

Harvest by early September, because another hatch can attack.

Onions, leeks, salsify and herbs such as sage, rosemary and wormwood are also said to repel the fly. The surest prevention is to cover the carrot row with some kind of floating row cover such as agricultural fleece, netting or Reemay, and leave it throughout the growing season. If the flies can't lay eggs on the crowns, the maggots won't damage the carrots. Raising the planting bed can exceed the carrot rust fly's flight ability, too.

CHERRY FRUIT FLY

We used to grow sweet cherries, fighting off birds and squirrels for them, only to find fat white maggots inside each fruit. They were maggots of the cherry fruit fly, a pest that pupates in the ground under the cherry tree over winter, then emerges in late spring as a fly that mates and lays an egg in a cherry five to eight days later. There is only one generation per year, but these fruit flies emerge at such different times during late spring-early summer, that you must spray several times to control them. The recommended spray schedule is with a product based on Spinosad or Malathion once a week or every 10 days until harvest. Spinosad is a naturally occurring substance, considered organic. Whatever you do, read labels carefully, and select only the substance that will control cherry fruit fly, and spray the correct amount at the recommended frequency. Pay attention to how close to harvest you may spray the substance you've chosen. Reckoning the cherries will be ready for harvest in seven days is very difficult, I think, and I wish the pesticide manufacturers would come up with a better way to time your last application.

If you do spray, start when the cherries in the top of your tree turn salmon-colored, on their way to red.

Because cherry fruit fly pupae overwinter in the soil, some nematodes may be effective in controlling them. The Arbico-Organics catalog claims Heterorhabditis nematodes are effective against these pupae, but they are costly. Even if you were able to destroy all of the pupae, the cherry fruit flies could fly in from another location. It's probably better to pit the cherries manually, discarding maggots with the pits. The little hole you see in the fruit is not where the egg was laid, but where the maggot created an air hole for itself.

An article by Tony McCammon of the University of Idaho said grasses and "other plants with extensive, dense root systems that physically impede fruit-fly larvae" can be used as ground cover around the base of trees. Lawn grasses apparently don't have sufficiently dense rooting systems, but clover does. Or landscape fabric.

CODLING MOTH

Worms that infest apples in this part of the country are mostly larvae of codling moths. There are some things that can be done to minimize this kind of damage, the most promising coming from Washington orchards. Normally, apple and pear growers spray about six times per growing season for codling moth, but by using an Integrated Pest Management strategy to disrupt mating, they've been able to drastically reduce insect damage on fruit with significantly less spraying (and cost).

This Codling Moth Areawide Suppression Program was set up by USDA in 1994, intended to confuse moths with sex attractants or pheromones so they cannot find a mate. This strategy is supplemented by monitoring and limited spraying of insecticide.

With more orchards joining in the program, the cost of pheromones and control is now less than using the old pesticides. They're now estimating damage at less than one percent of the crop using these techniques.

The Extension pamphlet entitled, "Quality Apples From Your Backyard Tree," advises spraying apples starting three weeks after full bloom, then every three weeks until mid-August. This is costly and labor intensive. Moreover, home spraying equipment doesn't do as thorough a job as needed.

I don't expect the pheromone solution will be of much benefit to home orchard growers in urban areas for the simple reason that ornamental crab apple trees harbor zillions of codling moths.

Pheromone-baited traps will tell the orchardist (or tree owner) when the codling moths are flying, however, so they can spray effectively.

What is this codling moth? It's a small moth, with a half-inch to three-quarter-inch wingspan. It's brownish-gray, nondescript, with a copper-tinged, dark brown band at the tip of each forewing. Females lay single eggs on leaves and later on fruit. Eggs are white, disk-shaped and smaller than a pinhead.

Just before hatching, the black head of the larva is visible. Larva heads change color to pink or brown as they mature and emerge from the fruit. Then they lower themselves to the ground or crawl down the trunk, to pupate on the tree's bark or in the soil.

This habit leads to one method of control: dormant oil spraying of the trunk, presumably suffocating pupae, or wrapping the trunk with corrugated cardboard so larvae will pupate in the vertical folds. That requires almost daily monitoring and destruction of the cardboard-harboring pupae.

A smooth trunk also can be wrapped with Tree Tanglefoot-treated cardboard, to trap those critters heading for a nap. Note that there'll be two generations each year.

As a public service, you could also wrap trunks of ornamental crab apples. Do not apply Tanglefoot directly on the bark.

Other methods of control are used about the time the apples are about the size of a nickel. Advanced Master Gardener Hilda Packard uses the Japanese method, covering each fruit with a paper sack and stapling it shut. She removes the sacks at the end of August to let the apples fully color up.

The late Advanced Master Gardener Ross Hadfield bagged his apples in pantyhose, the hose stretching to accommodate the growing apple. He's had no difficulty with this, but when I tried it, the apple colored in a fabric pattern, not very appetizing. Either method is very labor intensive. Some spray with Surround, a kaolin clay product.

You can also set out traps of molasses and vinegar, in gallon milk jugs with the sides cut out. They, too, must be monitored carefully.

Or just count on buying your apples.

COLORADO POTATO BEETLES

Watch for the pea-sized hard-shelled adults, tan or yellow with black stripes on their backs, heads orange with black spots. Adults feed on leaves and more importantly, lay eggs on undersides of leaves. Orange eggs are laid in clusters of about 25.

Larvae are reddish orange, with black dots on their sides, very rounded (larger than their parents), and they feel wet to the ungloved hand. They feed greedily on leaves unless stopped with Bt tenenbrionis (that has no effect on adults), traps around the edge of your potato patch (they don't fly in, they walk), Pyola, Neem or just hand crushing. Wear gloves.

Lady beetles, lacewings, spiders and predatory stink bugs also feed on eggs.

These are called Colorado potato beetles because eastern Colorado was their original native range, where they fed on weedy buffalo bur. Once they got a bite of potato foliage, they fanned out across the country.

CUTWORMS

When you're digging holes for transplanting, keep your eyes peeled for dull-gray cutworms, curled in a C shape. Adults are about the diameter of a pencil, and are 1 to 1 1/2 inches long when straightened out. If you kill them immediately, you shouldn't have to install cutworm controls to save your seedlings.

You might lose one or two, but cutworms don't usually range far from where they hatched. They're offspring of gray moths and are more numerous in the North End than in other parts of the Valley, perhaps responding to porch lights.

EARWIGS

What do we do about the earwigs? Well, first of all, they are considered beneficial insects because they eat eggs, young and adults of insects such as mites, aphids and destructive nematodes. They obviously damage plants in the garden, too. They're elusive, but you can roll up sheets of newspaper and place them next to plants especially attacked by earwigs. They crawl into the rolls at night, then in the morning, you shake them out into a bucket of hot, soapy water.

Bamboo or short sections of old garden hose work, too, but you must empty the traps daily. Sluggo Plus claims earwig control.

ELM SEED BUGS

Our invasion of stinky bugs, elm seed bugs, is nationally known, if you search on the Internet. The larvae of these bugs do eat some elm seeds, but those of us who constantly battle unwelcome elm seedlings think they don't eat enough.

The adults winter over in the warmest places they can find, but try to escape from extreme heat in summer by invading our homes. Those warm winter resorts may be on a south-facing fence, a building or a house. They mate in early spring and lay eggs, larvae hatch in late spring-early summer, then develop into new adults.

They cause no real damage, but killing them releases a noxious odor from their scent glands. They're red and black, resemble boxelder bugs (in shape, conformation and size), and may be controlled the same way you control boxelder bugs, according to Mike Cooper, entomologist with the Idaho Department of Agriculture.

To keep them out of your house, caulk around all doors and windows, and make sure your weatherstripping around doors is in good condition, no cracks or tears, and the threshold weatherstripping is intact.

If the bugs do get inside, they foul the air and leave mashed spots on walls and cupboards if you swat them, so vacuum them up instead, or spray them with soap. You can use two tablespoons of Dawn dishwashing detergent per gallon of water, distributed by a spray bottle. This mixture was discovered by Boisean Christopher Ward, a master gardener intern, in 1994. Some people add a teaspoon or so of rubbing alcohol to augment the killing power of the mix.

This spray must touch the insects, for it has no residual effect, but since the bugs tend to appear in swarms on structures, it's very effective. I would not use it when part of the spray will fall on valued plants, however.

If you vacuum the bugs into a clean bag or small vacuum, watch out they don't just crawl out. You may have to empty them into a bucket of soapy hot water.

FALSE CHINCH BUGS

One year the Valley's infestation with false chinch bugs was so bad a woman in Meridian said it looked like the ground was moving. In my garden, they covered a grain amaranth seed-head, making it sparkle with life. I cut the seed-head off, then dropped it into the mulcher/grinder. That took care of the bugs in an "organic" way.

Bob Stoltz, then entomologist with the Extension Office in Twin Falls, advised letting them alone for a couple of days. They often disperse and move on. If you do see they're causing damage to your plants, you can brush them into a pail of soapy water or spray them with a soap spray. If they get into your house, vacuum them up.

The gray-brown insects are true bugs, having the X on their backs, but they're quite tiny, less than 1/10-inch long. They'll suck sap juices from a lot of different plants, feeding on lawns, grapevines, small grains, corn, milo, sorghum, soybeans, cotton, potatoes, beets and trees.

FLEA BEETLES

If you see tiny round holes on your plants and can't find an insect, the culprit is the flea beetle — a tiny shiny black insect that jumps when you disturb it. Control by covering the crop with a row cover or diatomaceous earth (DE) or any insecticidal dust rated to kill flea beetles. Do not use the DE sold for swimming pool use — it has been heat-treated and rendered ineffective against insects.

FUNGUS GNATS

Seeing spots before your eyes? Maybe they're gnats.

Even when there's snow outdoors, indoor gardeners are battling insects. The most common indoor plant pest is the fungus gnat, a tiny black frowzy pest whose wings often are out of alignment. They fly, but one wonders how.

The adults don't damage plants, but they lay eggs in the soil, which hatch into larvae, which begin eating organic matter in the soil and even small roots. They do some damage, although seldom enough to show.

Fungus gnats are annoying, however, and are elusive to swat. Bt is available to control them in the larval stage, but that can add up to huge expenses for commercial greenhouses.

Some, such as Edwards Greenhouse, top pots with a layer of sand, foiling egg-laying intentions of fungus gnats. Some think the sand misleads gnats into thinking there's no organic matter there for the babies to eat.

GERANIUM BUDWORMS

Geranium (or tobacco) budworms devastate ornamental flowers of petunias, Geraniums, Nicotiana, Ageratum, chrysanthemums, snapdragons, strawflowers, roses and other flowering plants. They resemble the "worms" one occasionally finds in ears of corn, but they have microspines on some segments of their abdomens. Their color is largely determined by what they've been eating. Many are black to pale brown, but some are green or red or whatever color of flower they're feeding on. Some may be banded, others not.

Handpicking is best, and though they're difficult to see, studying your plants with care will train your eye to spot them or their eggs. They may grow up to 1 1/2 inches long. They feed after hatch for about three weeks, then drop to the soil and pupate, leaving devastation behind. In northern areas, two generations are common in a season. They'll be even more numerous in August and September.

Here's where it really pays to know the life cycle of this pest. Eggs are laid by light green moths that have wavy cream lines across their wings that spread to about 1 1/2 inches wide. Wings also have some brown and tan flecks.

They lay single eggs on leaves or buds of plants their offspring will feed on. After eggs hatch, the larvae burrow into nearby flower buds in search of reproductive parts, their most favored food. In doing so, they eat through parts of blossoms, so if the plant blooms, the flowers are ragged and misshapen. Often, damaged buds don't open at all.

Being the color of the flower they feed on makes them doubly difficult to see and handpick. They are vulnerable to Bt but they must ingest it for it to be effective. Use the Bt identified as "kurstaki" or "Berliner." A brand name is Dipel, which may come in dust or liquid form. After you treat the plants, give them a boost with a super-bloom fertilizer high in phosphorus to help them recover quickly.

Many caterpillars pupate in soil, and they are usually made of brown shiny material, in case you discover one or more in your garden bed. Budworm pupae lie between 2 and 6 inches below soil's surface. Although they appear to have no means of locomotion, they can re-bury themselves quickly if they're brought to the surface.

If you've put your potted Geraniums in the garage for the winter, your potting soil may contain some of these pupae. To avoid perpetuating this pest, pull Geraniums out of the soil and hang them upside down in the garage or replace the potting soil.

Another solution is to screen the potting soil before re-use. I'd screen using 1/4-inch hardware cloth (coarse screen), available by the foot at building supply stores.

Temperatures below minus 20 degrees would kill pupae unless they're in a sheltered location such as near a building foundation.

GRASSHOPPERS

There is an organic bait available from insectaries such as Arbico that contains a single-celled protozoan that, when eaten, creates a disease specific to grasshoppers and Mormon and black field crickets. But it kills only immature 'hoppers and crickets. It's called Nosema locustae.

Grasshoppers are cold-blooded creatures, apparently, and late sleepers. I go out in the garden early in the morning and see 'hoppers slowly climbing up stems into the sun. They're too slow-moving to escape beheading by pruners or scissors.

When they have grown too large for Nosema locustae control, smash all you can, for they'll lay eggs and "gift" us with hordes the next year.

IMPORTED CABBAGE BUTTERFLY

The white-winged imported cabbage butterfly flits about to mate and lay eggs on cabbage, broccoli, brussels sprouts, collards, planted and wild mustards, turnips, kale and similar plants. The larva is blue-green with a faint yellow line down the middle of its back. It looks velvety, with the body tapering at both ends, no discernible head. The adults often lay eggs on inappropriate plants, so you may find larvae on tomato plants or even herbs.

In broccoli, incidentally, the larvae seem to go for the buds, where they're most difficult to spot and reach with Bt, to which they are vulnerable.

They may have several generations each summer. They overwinter as a chrysalis, equivalent to an above-ground pupa.

The white butterflies (black spots on wings) are more difficult to catch than you'd think, so don't even try to control them. Their caterpillars are easier to control.

JAPANESE BEETLES

Japanese beetles were late to invade our region; they probably came in on some potted plants from another part of the country. They are about 1/2-inch-long, oval, metallic green with bronze wings obscuring their backs, and white "brushes" or dots around the margins of their bodies. They feed voraciously on leaves of many ornamental and fruiting plants such as roses, dahlias, shrubs and stone fruit trees.

They lay eggs 2 to 4 inches deep in soil in late summer, and when those hatch, the grubs feed on grass roots. They pupate in late spring and emerge as adults in late June, when they skeletonize leaves and flowers, feeding in large numbers on each plant or tree.

LEAFCUTTER BEES

Many of the large leaves in our yard look like they've been hit by the mad scallop cutter each summer. These special effects are caused by leafcutter bees or Megachile rotundata, and they do no real damage to plants unless there are zillions of holes cut on one plant. Leafcutter bees are the "Gentle Bens" of the insect world, capable of stinging but stinging only when provoked by rough handling. Their stings are only a fraction as painful as the stings of their cousins, the honeybees. They cut smooth-edged, dime-sized holes in the edges of leaves for their egg cases.

We have a large number of leafcutter bees in the Treasure Valley because they're valued for their ability to fertilize alfalfa blossoms, a feat that not all bees can perform efficiently. Once fertilized, of course, the alfalfa blossoms produce seeds. A recommended number of bees per acre is about 20,000.

Seed growing is big business in this Valley, and alfalfa seeds are part of this industry.

Small neat outbuildings set in fields puzzle newcomers because they're too shallow to be outhouses, and it's unlikely that a farmer would store tools in them. They actually house the boards full of leafcutter bees, out there waiting for the crop to flower.

Leafcutter bees are slightly smaller than honeybees but are a little darker in color and have light-colored bands on their abdomens.

They usually nest in soft, rotted wood. They excavate their own tunnels or use old holes dug by wasps, beetles or other insects, or they may use man-made "beeboards." One cause of concern is that they sometimes excavate pith in large rose canes for their nests — one reason why rose fanciers use glue or a thumbtack on large pruned canes. Whether this causes real damage is questionable. They seldom damage the cambium, the rose bush's lifeline.

The bee constructs a thimble-shaped nest in the hole, using the piece of leaf it has cut. If it proves unworkable the bee discards it and goes to get another. The bee provides each of these thimbles with nectar, pollen and an egg and stacks the thimble-nests.

These are considered "solitary" bees, but they're highly gregarious, a fact permitting many nests together on one bee board. Each hole will have several stacked "nests." Females return to their nests at night and spend the night faced inward. They don't emerge until the temperatures rise above 68 degrees.

How do they tell which nest is theirs? If they've created their own nest, they select locations near recognizable markers, such as knotholes. Patterns painted on nesting boards help bees locate their own nests.

These hard-working bees have also been found to be effective pollinators of blueberries, canola, forage legumes and carrots, raised in an enclosure for breeding purposes. Estimations are that 150 leafcutter bees can be as effective as 3,000 honeybees in screened enclosures.

LEAF MINERS

A master gardener from another county told me that Neem, applied weekly, deters leaf miners from spinach and Swiss chard leaves. I tried that without success. I know Neem kills eggs, because it works on squash bug eggs, but leaf miner flies hit very small spinach leaves, laying eggs that hatch within three to five days. A weekly spray is going to miss some that will hatch.

The adult is a tiny gray fly that lays eggs on leaves of spinach, Swiss chard and beets in the vegetable garden (and on Aquilegia and other flower leaves in the ornamental garden) in tiny white stripes about 1/8 inch long, clustered together. They appear as white spots until you look closely.

Once the eggs hatch, a tiny white maggot burrows into the leaf, and begins feeding inside the tissues of the leaf, between the upper and lower layers of cells. The maggot meanders, its route marked by pale green then brown tissue on the leaf exterior. When they think it's time, they emerge from the leaf, drop to the ground and pupate. In the same season, they emerge as a fly to re-start the cycle. There may be two or more generations per season.

Since you can see where the maggot is (or where it's been), you can tear off that part of the leaf and eat the remainder.

I used a "picnic table" net tent over Swiss chard in my garden, but it wasn't effective because it wasn't fastened down on all sides. Some chard grew larger than expected and raised the tent, but this chard wasn't attacked by leaf miners until very late in the season. Seedlings of this variety sitting on the deck were not attacked either.

That variety, paler green than most chards, is called Bieta Bionda di Lione, and seeds are available from Seeds from Italy (www.growitalian.com). Usually the paler the green, the fewer nutrients, but the milder the flavor. Earwigs have eaten holes in the leaves, but they're easier to wash off than leaf miners.

MAMMALS
(Not insects, granted, but garden pests nonetheless)

Cats: Cats and kittens can be a lot of fun to watch and good company, but most of us draw the line at letting them use our potted plants for litter boxes. They dig, exposing the roots, then deposit their feces, barely covering it. It's quite a nuisance and could be dangerous, since some cat feces can transmit disease to humans.

There's no need to get rid of the cats, just outwit them. One way is to keep the soil wet, but that encourages fungus gnats that are annoying in their own right. Some innovative ideas I've recently seen involve using toothpicks and/or pine cones.

Pine cones in pots have some sharp places on them when fully opened, unpleasant to cats. If your pine cones aren't fully opened, try putting them in a warm place for a few days, such as atop the refrigerator.

Put them rim-to-rim in your plant pots and if the precious cat insists on scooting them aside, you can peg them down with bamboo skewers or push toothpicks into the soil and "impale" the pine cones on the toothpicks.

Some people just push toothpicks partway into the soil every square inch or so. The cat is not even tempted to try to dig there. It looks odd, but it works.

Or take advantage of cats' famous dislike of citrus aromas, and drench felt squares or cotton balls in citronella oil, and leave those on the soil.

Advanced Master Gardener Lindarose Curtis-Bruce says using natural products such as wool and cotton hold the aroma much longer than synthetic materials. She discouraged her cats from using potted plants by scolding, then providing them with a covered kitty litter box. The cover seems to have made a major difference.

Deer: If your garden beds are subject to predation by deer, there are commercial repellents available in garden centers. But deer eventually get used to them and quit being repelled. One thing they don't get accustomed to is a strong-smelling herb such as lavender, lemon balm, mints, chives, summer savory, oregano, dill and quillquina (or papalo). They may taste one of these herbs, but they rarely "chow down." Water scarecrows work, if strategically placed.

Gophers: If you have gophers and live in Ada County, outside of the city, you may get help from the Ada County Weed and Gopher control unit, at 577-4646. If for some reason they can't help you, traps are available at Zamzows or D&B Supply, at least.

If you have pets, you don't want to risk secondary poisoning of your pets, so don't use poisoned bait, and be cautious about the trap. One of the most effective is one that stabs and instantly kills its target. We've found one of the large box rat traps (similar to the common mousetrap, but upside down) quite effective. You have to place it in a recently used run. Gophers sometimes will bury the trap in excavated soil, but place it again and be patient.

Squirrels: Boise city dwellers also must cope with squirrels. They may bite into tomatoes in search of moisture and cease if a water supply is available. They will take all of your fruit such as apricots, spoiling the fruit to get at the nut inside. They have also been seen pulling up plant tags and dropping them a short distance away.

Voles: Very damaging in the garden, voles are larger than a mouse but smaller than a rat and have a short tail. Cats kill them when they emerge into view, but terriers will dig them out and kill them.

The rest: If your garden is being ravaged by some unknown animal, lightly powder the area they've frequented so you can see footprints and identify the culprit. A cyber friend in California sat up in a lawn chair with a flashlight, waiting to see what was biting into her tomatoes at night. She was quite shocked to see it was a rat. We also have skunks and raccoons in and around Boise, both of which are also difficult to control. Look in the telephone book under "Pest control."

MORMON CRICKETS

In June 1971, shortly after we moved to Boise, we took a drive up Rocky Canyon. There I saw Mormon crickets for the first time, creeping across the road, their bodies popping when our tires ran over them.

They're the size of mice or voles, and startling, although harmless to humans. I called the state entomologist (Idaho had one listed under the state pages then), and was told they knew about the Mormon crickets in the Foothills. They were keeping an eye on them.

Technically, these are not crickets, nor are the Mormons responsible for them. They're ground-dwelling katydids (Anabrus simplex Haldeman), which got their common name in 1848, when they ravaged the fields belonging to Mormon settlers in Utah. Mormons' prayers for help were apparently answered by the timely arrival of flocks of seagulls that fed on the insects.

They're part of the natural ecosystem of the West, having been here for at least two millenia that we know of. Our area may be their camping and feeding spot for years to come, since outbreaks may last from five to 21 years.

Their numbers began increasing in the late 1990s, according to Mike Cooper, entomologist with the Idaho Department of Agriculture. They've ravaged millions of acres of sagebrush and other desert plants in northern Nevada. U.S. Department of Agriculture Animal Plant and Health Inspection Service employees spread carbaryl bait on federal lands to halt infestations when appropriate (subsequent invaders will feed on the corpses of the dead katydids, presumably also ingesting poison).

State workers have similarly treated state-owned lands, especially near residential areas. This bait is said to not be harmful to bees and other beneficial insects.

Mormon crickets cannot fly, but they walk, climb and hop. They hatch when soil temperatures reach 40 degrees. The first few weeks of their life, they move randomly about in search of food, molting their skins when they grow too large for their present one. They go through seven of these "instars," or stages, before they reach the adult stage.

At some time during their later stages (60 to 90 days after they've hatched) they join with others of their age and the adults to migrate en masse. They mainly move during daylight hours, when temperatures are between 65 and 90 degrees.

When they're in a huge moving horde, they may travel a mile per day, eating as they move. About two weeks after reaching adulthood, they suspend eating and start mating and egg laying.

How can we protect our gardens? Cooper says contact poisons will kill them. The carbaryl bait put out by federal and state workers loses effectiveness when the katydids stop feeding. After egg laying, they resume eating.

Carbaryl, a contact poison, comes in different strengths and brand names, including Sevin, Bugmaster, Crunch and others. It's available as bait, dust, wettable powders, granules, dispersions and suspensions.

Spokesmen for Bayer say that the company's Advanced Multi Insect Killer also kills Mormon crickets.

Whatever you use, be sure to carefully read and follow label directions. An effective, but old-fashioned way of protecting your property is to erect a 2- or 3-foot high nonclimbable wall (roofing tin or aluminum flashing) around your property. Cooper said he had seen the crickets climb those concrete highway lane barriers, though. Walls would have to be smoother than concrete.

SCALE

Scale is so-called because the organisms erect body armor around themselves at maturity, at which time they're no longer vulnerable to sprayed pesticides. There are basically two types of scale, soft and armored. Once the coverings form, they don't look dangerous, but in numbers, they may suck the life juices out of a plant or tree. Armored scales look like bumps on a limb, as if they belong there.

Prior to maturity, they spend their life as crawlers, when they are vulnerable to sprayed pesticides, even soap sprays. The problem here is that the crawlers are nearly microscopic in size, so it's very difficult to tell when they're moving about.

Hold a white sheet of paper under a branch or twig and tap on it. If crawlers are present, you'll see tiny moving specks on the paper. If you suspect your scale is oyster scale, hold a dark sheet of paper under a twig, for those crawlers are light-colored.

Armored scales tend to congregate on orchard trees, soft scales on non-woody plants, but not always. Maple trees may be loaded with cotton scale, small puffs of cotton on the twigs and branches.

Soft scales build up waxy exteriors, and the females lay eggs under that cover. Once those hatch, the crawlers roam around the area when they are vulnerable. The adults may move a little, but the armored scales do not move.

Some scales look like small gray round targets, with a "bull's-eye" and a concentric ring around the bull's-eye. Scales are prey to many beneficial insects, so be very careful about using chemical controls lest you kill the insects intent on devouring or parasitizing them. Killing the enemies of your enemy will add to your problem.

If scale is within reach, moisten a cotton puff or Q-tip in rubbing alcohol and rub off the scale, even adult armored scale. Mealybugs, which resemble some soft scale, can be eliminated the same way.

If not within reach, find out the exact identity of the scale and look for control methods. Systemic insecticides applied as soil drenches seldom control armored scale, since the insecticides don't move to the cells where it usually feeds.

Some scales are vulnerable to light horticultural oils if applied at the right time in their development.

SLUGS

I've got to start carrying a bottle of anti-slug spray (about 50 percent household ammonia, 50 percent water). Ammonia doesn't hurt plants (another slug control, salt, does hurt plants), and ammonia is a fertilizer as well as a slug killer.

For slug control, go out after dark with a flashlight and a bottle of ammonia and water spray, and spray every glistening slimy body. Advanced Master

Gardener Stella Schneider, who lives in the North End, sprayed the ground around her garden beds, and said her flashlight illuminated many little dots on the ground that appeared when the spray hit them. The dots were baby slugs, and she saw far less slug damage in succeeding days.

SOWBUGS

There are two kinds of sowbugs that closely resemble each other. One rolls into a ball, leading some to call them "pillbugs." The other does not ball up. Both are called sowbugs. "Pillbug" should not be confused with "billbug," whose larvae are serious lawn pests.

Sowbugs are grayish-brown creatures with bodies of segmented plates and seven pairs of legs. They are slow and clumsy and harmless to humans. Children play with them, and psychology students use them as subjects in experiments. Technically, they are isopods, more closely related to crawdads than to insects.

They inhabit damp, dark places and feed on rotting vegetation. They are important in the decomposition of organic matter, but their presence at damage sites causes them to be unfairly blamed for a lot of garden destruction.

Rapid-moving insects come in, tatter leaves, and make their getaway. When the gardener comes in, the sowbugs are there, like bystanders caught in a policeman's spotlight.

They can cause plant harm, but usually their damage is limited to fruit that is lying on the ground, often first attacked by snails or slugs and beginning to decay before the sowbugs get there. Occasionally they chew on leaves touching the ground, or seedlings. Their overall destruction is slight, however.

There are insecticides labeled for killing sowbugs, but killing them probably won't stop the damage you intended to halt, since other creatures are more likely to have caused serious problems.

If they truly are causing problems, grow strawberries in barrels so the fruit is hanging, rather than lying on the ground. Elevate ripening melons and squashes by layers of pebbles and mesh, allowing light and air circulation beneath them. Water early in the day, and limit moisture-retentive areas near target crops.

SPIDER MITES

Some people in this area complain about the infestations of spider mites. They thrive in hot, dry, dusty conditions. One of the easiest ways to discourage their remaining and proliferating is to give them moist, humid conditions. If they're outside, knock them down with a blast from the hose and hose them down at frequent intervals.

STINK BUGS

One of the reasons I quit growing raspberries was the prevalence of shield-shaped stink bugs. They left their foul odor on everything they crawled over, including raspberries. A fellow in the East has devised a simple trap for them that is easy to make: Use two sheets of corrugated cardboard (size is not important, but I think it's best that their width be a little less than the diameter of a bucket). Install three pieces of lath, lying flat, parallel to one another, evenly spaced across one piece, either gluing or stapling it to the bottom piece of cardboard. Then glue or staple the top piece of cardboard to the laths.

Lay or prop your slotted trap in your garden, preferably near your raspberries or wherever you've found stink bugs. Early in the morning, take a bucket of hot soapy water out to the garden, pick up the cardboard trap, and tap it on the inside edge of the bucket so all critters taking refuge inside fall into the soapy water and die. You'll also get a lot of earwigs using this trap, since they also like to hang out in dark crevices.

Stink bugs also suck on tomatoes, their "bites" leaving a yellow spot. This is more than cosmetic damage, because the "bite" stitches the tomato's skin to the flesh of the fruit. Even after you douse these tomatoes in boiling water for a minute or two so you can remove the skin, you'll find it adhering to the flesh where the stink bug bites occurred.

SYRPHIDS (Hover flies)

You've all seen them. They look like slender bees stopped in midair, then zipping off in one direction or another. Syrphids are called "hover flies" for that distinctive behavior, their tiny wings moving so fast they're almost invisible. They feed on flower pollen and nectar, but most of their larvae (maggots), blind and seldom seen, eat their way through numbers of aphids, scales and thrips, earning the right to be called one of a gardener's best friends.

In our area, they're also valuable for gobbling leafhoppers that can spread curly top virus. Maggots of some species of hover fly eat decaying matter, furthering that process. This stage of their life lasts just a week, but in that week, a well-placed maggot can consume up to 400 aphids.

Hover flies (also known as flower flies) are common on every continent except Antarctica. There are about 6,000 species in 200 genera of hover fly, all similarly marked with black and gold or yellow stripes around their bodies. They're members of the insect family called Syrphidae. They're such active feeders in flowers it's no surprise that many also are pollinators. Although they look like stinging insects, they're quite harmless to humans.

Eggs are laid singly on leaves or shoots, near aphid colonies. The eggs are about 1 millimeter long and have a pebbly surface. Maggots (offspring of true flies such as these are maggots) are legless, wormlike critters. Their heads are at the narrow ends. They may be white, green or brown. They pupate on plants or in the soil, as tear-shaped blobs of green, tan or brown.

You can attract these beneficial flies to your garden by planting flowers such as yarrow, parsley, chamomile, buckwheat, statice and alyssum, all of which have shallow nectar reservoirs.

TOMATO HORNWORMS

One of the largest and most destructive of the garden insect pests, the tomato hornworm technically is the larva of a sphinx moth. This moth, nearly the size of a small bird, feeds on flowers as a hummingbird does, giving rise to the common name hummingbird moth.

Hornworms quickly grow up to the size of a man's finger, and can strip leaves and stems and damage the fruit of tomato plants. These worms are green, with camouflaging stripes, and they have a thorn-like horn at the rear end. Once they're longer than 1/2 inch, not even Bt is very effective against them.

It's easy to pick them by gloved hand, and not nearly as nasty, if you catch them when they're tiny.

Study your tomato plants carefully each day, turning over leaves to look at their undersides. When you find a bead about the size of a pinhead that's lighter colored than the leaf, it's probably a hornworm egg. Spotting and squashing the eggs is easier than it sounds, and discovery becomes surer with practice.

Also watch for a round hole in a tomato leaf. Turn the leaf over, and chances are good that there's a tiny worm on the other side, eating to grow into a giant hornworm. Small hornworms tend to chew from behind the leaf or branch, although when they're quite large, they feed from any position they like.

Another sign a hornworm is near is the trail of droppings. When the hornworm is less than an inch long, the droppings look like pepper. When it is large, they look like rectangular dark brown beads.

If you spot the pepper-like droppings, look at the leaves and branches above that location, turning over leaves until you find the culprit. Then shake the branches so the droppings fall off, or else you'll search for the perpetrator you killed another day, wasting your time.

They pupate in soil at maturity, looking like shiny cigar stubs that move and dig. If you find one, don't take your eye off it. It appears inert, but isn't. Hornworms occasionally also may be found feeding on eggplants, choke-cherry or plum trees.

WASPS

One of the main benefits of growing parsley lies in the flowers, held like an umbrella over the top of the plant (hence it's "umbelliferous"). The wee flowers making up the umbrella are attractive to and much loved by beneficial insects such as certain tiny wasps. From the parsley, it's a short flight for them to enter the garden in search of leaf miners. They lay an egg in a leaf miner maggot inside its leafy tunnel, and a mature wasp later emerges from the pupal case, not a leaf miner. Each wasp can thus parasitize up to 90 leaf miners, so as the wasp population grows, the leaf miner population diminishes. Wasps also parasitize other larvae and caterpillars as well. Attracting them is easier and much cheaper than using insecticides.

Their larger wasp cousins, the mud daubers and paper nest builders, gobble aphids from garden plants early in the growing season and patrol the garden ceaselessly in search of larvae with which to provision their egg cells. They can find tiny worms in broccoli more easily than I, as well as newly hatched tomato hornworms.

WHITEFLIES

Whiteflies suck plant juices and can seriously weaken plants. They also excrete a sticky honeydew that will nourish a sooty mold, which can either kill the plant or render it so unattractive you'll discard it.

I've used Safer's Insecticidal Soap and homemade soap sprays, plus Ortho insect bombs in my greenhouse at correct intervals, and still faced a small cloud of white tiny moth-like creatures when plants are brushed. Those are whiteflies.

Whiteflies are notorious for developing immunity to insecticides.

The best solution is prevention. One grower of unusual plants with an unwavering dedication to organic control closely inspected her indoor plants at least once a week, taking them outside and spraying them with a garlic concentrate spray. She found it an effective repellent.

If you have only a few whiteflies, get rid of them as quickly as possible. Make your own sticky traps out of yellow paper plates (they're drawn to the color) sprayed with Tree Tanglefoot, and place them within 10 inches of the infested plant.

When the plant is disturbed, whiteflies fly out of the plant, and if you're fortunate, they'll hit the sticky trap.

But if they are already on your plants en masse, one of the weapons I've heard can work is dousing smaller plants in a bucket of soapy water. Use Dr. Bronner's or Fels Naphtha soap, not a detergent.

Other possibilities: The plastic bag-cigarette treatment: You bag the plant and pot together, then have someone blow cigarette smoke into the bag, seal it tightly and leave it overnight. If the plant survives, the insects reportedly won't. (Note: I first suggested this in 1994, when it was a little easier to find a smoker!)

CHAPTER 10

Diseases

AFFLICTIONS OF ROSES AND OTHER FLOWERS

Wet springs can mean rose fungus, but you can fight it

We didn't used to get black spot on rose leaves in the Treasure Valley, but we certainly suffer from it now. Cool wet springs contribute to the transmission and nurturing of this debilitating fungus, Diplocarpon rosae, which literally puts black spots on rose leaves and reduces flowering and vigor of the entire shrub.

To help prevent an outbreak from resurfacing in the next spring, remove the afflicted leaves from roses and put them in the trash. If any are on the ground, carefully gather them. The fungus spores are on the leaves and can be spread to new rose leaves by splashing or blowing water.

Don't just yank off the leaves from the canes. That can damage the canes and provide an entry route for Pseudomonas syringae, another disease of roses common in the Valley. Instead, nip the leaves off with scissors or pruning shears and put them in the trash.

Then, early the next spring, install non-splashing mulch such as soil-aid, grass clippings, straw or bark around your roses.

Black spot may be controlled by a fungicide such as a Neem-based product. Some people have had success controlling black spot with a spray of skim milk and water, at least one-third milk to two-thirds water.

Cane blight can be devastating to Idaho rose gardens

There is more than one P. syringae pathovar that can attack our rose canes, but it was an undetermined pathovar that wrought destruction in private and public gardens in 2010 and 2011.

Popularly known as bacterial cane blight of roses (P. syringae, undetermined pathovar), the disease reached devastating levels here. Vivid damage showed up in the rose garden in Julia Davis Park, with the death of 500 rose shrubs, one quarter of the total in that display garden.

Rick Freitag, the Boise Parks Department crew chief in charge of that rose garden, said he walked through the garden in late February 2011 and saw about seven roses that apparently had been winter-killed. Two weeks later, they determined it was cane blight, now visible on dozens more.

Sandra Ford, a member of the Idaho Rose Society, said that society had donated $3,000 to the city for replacement of the roses. Freitag said they weren't able to get all of the varieties replaced, but they replaced most thanks to that donation.

Ford said she lost 10 rose bushes out of her own garden to that disease in 2011, and 14 the year before.

Freitag said Dr. Krishna Mohan, plant pathologist with the University of Idaho's Research and Extension Center in Parma, had identified the disease and advised spraying a copper-based fungicide such as Phyton 27 in fall, before rains begin; again when half of the rose leaves have fallen; and in early spring, before leaves begin to appear, as that's when the bacteria are most active.

Mohan's investigation indicates the bacteria first show at leaf scars, vegetative buds or wounds, as reddish brown areas on the bark. These blotches expand, later turning dark purple, then black or necrotic (dead). In the early stages, the cane under the bark is moist, but dries when it dies. These black areas may involve the entire cane and ultimately the death of the shrub.

If your roses have blackened canes, use your thumbnail to scrape through the black. If you get to dry wood, the cane suffered winterkill. If that's the cause, you may be able to prune below the black into green wood and save the shrub.

If you scrape through the black and find moist tissue, with red to chocolate brown cambium, it's probably bacterial cane blight. If possible, prune at least 10 inches below the last visible blight, then spray with the copper spray and put your pruning shears to soak for 10 minutes in a chlorine bleach solution of one part bleach to 10 parts water. This blight can kill a healthy rose shrub within days.

Mohan has been investigating and testing this bacterial infection since 1996, when he first found it. Some years the disease is more widespread than other years, depending on spring weather conditions.

No cultivar seems to be immune. He's found the disease on climbing, floribunda, grandiflora, hybrid tea, hybrid perpetual, miniature and shrub roses.

Bacterial cane blight may appear in summer and fall, too, from bacteria thought to have entered the cane through pruning wounds. Some protection against this blight can be afforded by mulch that prevents water splashing onto foliage, such as soil aid, composted bark, conifer needles or bark chips. Remember, though, the bacteria may also be carried by driving rain, bypassing mulch.

P. syringae also attacks lilacs, forsythia, hibiscus, pear, plum, peach and woody ornamentals. Some P. syringae subspecies attack such diverse plants as garden beans, wheat, crucifers, Canada thistle, sowthistles and dandelions.

It is spread by wind, rain, insects or unsterilized pruning tools and overwinters as disease cankers on stems or leaves, in plant debris, on perennial weeds or in the soil. Its presence is usually noticeable in early spring as water-soaked dark blotches on stems, flower clusters, buds or leaves.

Prevention includes keeping an open canopy on trees or shrubs to reduce humidity on plant tissue, correct pruning for the species, good spacing of woody plants, and sterilizing pruning tools with a 10 percent bleach solution.

It's best to be wary of "replant disease."

Incidentally, Freitag says he has not seen evidence of replant disease from replacing those roses in Julia Davis Park. This disease is anecdotal from individual growers anyway, and may or may not cause you trouble in replacing your roses.

Dead rose bushes should be promptly removed, but don't rush to replace them with other roses planted in the same place unless you remove a large chunk of the old rose soil and replace it with fresh soil. The soil condition, also called sick soil syndrome, affects many members of the huge Rosaceae family, especially apple trees. Not being able to immediately replant a lost rose is an annoyance to a gardener, but it is far more than annoying to an orchardist who's lost an apple tree.

It may take five or six years for the soil to recover unless you plant something like wheat for two or three years in that location or replace a large portion of soil. Any member of the rose family planted in that spot could struggle to survive and fail to thrive unless you remediate the soil condition.

If you're going to plant anything else, do your homework so you can avoid planting any other member of the rose family in that location. Perhaps since the disease doesn't consistently appear in rose beds, plant pathologists have not researched it in this context. The economic harm it causes orchardists, though, has been reason enough for pathologists to extensively study and find controls for the disease on apple trees.

Baking soda or skim milk may banish mildew

Powdery mildew occurs in plants that need better air circulation and sometimes sun exposure. Some plants are more prone to it than others.

Roses begin to show signs of mildew in June, when it appears as gray-white dusty-looking spots on leaves. It looks as if you could just brush it off, but this is a sucking fungus, and the sucking parts penetrate deep into twigs and leaves. It will spread unless you treat it, and it can cause the death of canes.

Remedies include improving air circulation and/or using a fungicide. Organic fungicides include Neem-based sprays and homemade sprays. Some folks see success with a spray of 50 percent skim milk (the amount varies, down to about 1/3 skim milk) to 50 percent water.

If you have a light infestation, affecting only a few leaves, spray it with a mixture of baking soda and water, about three teaspoons to a gallon of water. It's even better if you add two or three tablespoons of Sunspray Ultrafine Oil to the mix, although that's not essential.

The oil may be available through garden centers. It's also available through Gardens Alive and other mail-order companies.

Spray about every five or six days for a few weeks and whenever you see new "spots" before your eyes.

If your infestation is heavier, spray with a fungicide containing triforine, obtainable through garden centers.

Plants susceptible to powdery mildew include many trees, numerous flowers and even some vegetables — though the fungus is site-specific, so each is a little different. The baking soda probably won't work on trees, but should work on flowers and vegetables. Neem should also control the fungus.

This garden fungus can infect the gardener

If you work with thorny roses or shrubs or baled hay, beware of infections in small skin cuts or jabs. Be especially alert if you also handle sphagnum moss.

A fungus called Sporothrix schenckii may infect your skin through those skin wounds. The disease is also known as sporotrichosis or rose thorn disease. The infection looks like bumps caused by insect bites at first, one to 12 weeks after infection.

The bumps may be pink, red or even purple. The bumps later become open sores, and the fungus then may enter the lymphatic system and in rare cases eventually infect lungs, joints or even the central nervous system.

The open sores are very slow to heal, but they may be identified at this point. If you've had such bumps that developed into open sores, have your doctor take a swab or biopsy of the tissue and send it to a laboratory. Be sure to tell the doctor that the bumps appeared soon after working with thorny plants, sphagnum moss or hay. The fungus also resides in the soil.

Victims are usually gardeners or farm, forest or nursery workers working on topiaries.

Specific medication is available if sporotrichosis is the diagnosis. To prevent it, wear gloves when handling spiky materials, including conifer seedlings. Long sleeves help too, although most thorns will penetrate sleeves, and some penetrate gloves.

Daffodil leaves nourish next year's flowers, but watch for fungus

Prompt removal of faded daffodil flowers may result in a larger, healthier bulb if foliage is left intact to feed the bulb. Some say when the foliage has turned yellow, it's through feeding; others say leave foliage until it's brown and dry.

Watch bulb leaves for reddish-brown leaf spots indicating the presence of Botrytis.

This and other fungus diseases are common when the weather is damp and cool, or when one waters in the evening, splashing water drops on foliage.

Drip and soaker hose watering nourishes roots without getting foliage wet. If you're using sprinklers, water early in the morning so the heat of the day dries out foliage before the cool of evening.

INFECTIONS IN THE VEGETABLE GARDEN

When it comes to shallots in Idaho, take care when starting out

If you can't find shallot heads for planting at local garden stores, plant shallot seeds. Do not plant supermarket shallots in your garden because the spores of a fatal Allium disease may spread.

The disease is called white rot, and spores or starts of that disease may be distributed in irrigation water. Once it infests fields, the fields apparently carry the disease for many years.

Because Southwestern Idaho is an important commercial onion growing area, the state has an embargo on Allium bulbs such as onions, garlic, shallots and ornamental Alliums that were not produced in this area.

Mail-order companies know about the embargo, but often suppliers and employees of chain stores in this area do not. Allium bulbs do show up in those stores, unfortunately.

Locally owned garden centers and greenhouses carry disease-free Allium bulbs. (See more about Alliums in the vegetable chapter.)

A spot of tea helps seedlings fight fungus

In late January, when it's time to start onion, leek and shallot seeds, I plant them thickly in a pot whose surface is 4-by-4 inches.

All seedlings are vulnerable to fungus diseases such as damping off, where the plant pinches in at the soil line, collapses and dies. This is preventable by using a sterile planting medium, good air circulation and watering with lukewarm chamomile tea.

Two or three chamomile tea bags in a quart of water is an effective mixture.

Some people sprinkle cinnamon on the surface of the soil to control these diseases or buy a synthetic chemical mix.

When planting, I gently tease each Allium seedling apart from the rest, and use scissors to trim the end of the leaves and the roots for easier transplanting.

Carefully check basil for disease

If the leaves of well-watered basil plants are wilting or dropping, and especially if there are brown streaks on the stems, the plant probably has Fusarium wilt. Pull the plant and send it with the trash (do not compost it).

The disease can be transmitted to other plants by contact, so be careful to isolate the diseased plant, and scrub your hands with soap. I think I'd throw away gloves if you used them to pull out diseased plants.

Green basil is most susceptible to the disease, and the large-leaved or lettuce-leaved basil may drop its leaves without first wilting. Purple and lemon basil seem to be more resistant.

This Fusarium oxysporum of basil is seed-borne and remains resident in the soil for several years.

In the future, you'll have to buy tested seeds and plant them in soil where contaminated basil has not previously grown. Seed companies like Johnny's Selected Seeds and Richters are testing basil seeds, and other seed sources undoubtedly test as well.

Wet spring means uncommon garden diseases

When the Valley is hit with unusually cool and wet weather, our kitchen gardens are vulnerable to plant diseases that are uncommon in our area. I'm referring mainly to early blight (Alternaria solani) and late blight (Phytophthora infestans) — either or both of which may attack tomatoes, eggplants or potatoes at any time in the growing season, regardless of their names.

We usually call both diseases fungi, but late blight technically is a water mold, producing spores only in the presence of water. It makes its first appearance as pale green or olive green blotches that quickly enlarge to brown-black oily lesions on tomato and/or potato leaves. It may also etch dark brown lesions on stems. The blotches on leaves may also produce a whitish-gray fuzzy growth.

Late blight spores won't last through winter in the soil but can persist on infected plant material that's kept alive through the winter. There are new strains of late blight that have appeared in the past few years, intensifying concern of pathologists, farmers and gardeners. Late blight was the calamitous disease that destroyed potatoes and caused mass starvation in Ireland in the 1840s.

Treasure Valley commercial spud growers apply preventive fungicide at regular intervals to protect their fields against late blight. But University of Idaho Plant Pathologist Dr. Krishna Mohan says hot weather can spur such fast growth in plants that many new leaves become vulnerable to infection.

In warmer conditions, he urges growers to spray at least once a week to keep the new plant parts protected.

Early blight may not show its presence until foliage is fairly mature. First symptoms usually occur on older (lower) leaves — large dark brown spots with lighter "bull's-eye" margins around the spots between veins, and/or dark brown lesions on stems.

Either blight can completely destroy a crop, although if one plant shows symptoms, it doesn't mean your other plants are infected. You can pull out an infected plant and hope the others are not similarly diseased.

To protect your plants against blights, mulch around them with grass clippings (not laced with herbicide), soil aid, shredded leaves, pine needles, bark chips, etc., to prevent water from splashing onto foliage. Some remove lower leaves of plants such as tomatoes and roses to prevent fungus infection from splashing water.

Water carefully, either by irrigation or soaker hose, to avoid wetting foliage.

Don't panic at the first sight of discoloration. Some discoloration is normal, but if it begins to affect several leaves, either take a branch to the Extension Office for positive identification or look for photos of the blights online.

Copper-based sprays are usually recommended for control of late blight. Neem is an effective fungicide, useful on powdery mildew and perhaps early blight. Some use a milk spray on fungus infections such as these, claiming effectiveness. Most use a spray bottle containing half skim milk and half water or 1/3 milk, the rest water.

Battle tomato blossom end rot with water

We and several other gardeners in the Valley have had several tomatoes with blossom end rot some years, evidenced by a brown papery bottom on the tomatoes and premature pseudo-ripening. I avoid growing plum tomatoes because they're quite susceptible to that condition.

Blossom end rot, or BER, is a symptom of insufficient calcium. Our soil probably has enough calcium, but the plant can't use it if soil is too dry or too wet. Plants need moist soil for calcium uptake, so adjust your watering accordingly if you see this symptom on your tomatoes, peppers or squash. Varieties susceptible to BER are extra sensitive to moisture levels.

Using drip or soaker hose watering for tomatoes raises the question of how long to let water run. That depends on the flow in your system. Tomatoes should get 1 to 1 1/2 inches of water per week, preferably applied in the early morning and not splashing onto foliage. You could set clean tuna cans under your drip or soaker system to measure the amount your hose emits.

Never use an overhead sprinkler or hand water tomatoes planted in the ground. It's OK, of course, to water tomatoes growing in containers by hand, but under ideal outdoor circumstances tomato roots penetrate quite deeply. In our area, roots may be stopped or diverted by subsurface hardpan, so it also helps to know the depth at which your caliche or firm clay lies.

Curly top virus is spread by tiny beet leafhoppers

Curly top virus is present in the Treasure Valley some years, but whether or not your garden suffers from it is largely a matter of chance. There are a few things you can do to try to prevent damage.

This virus, fatal to garden plants such as tomatoes (even tall, vigorous plants), peppers, beans, beets and other plants, is carried by tiny beet leaf-hoppers. Once one bites an infected plant, the beet leafhopper carries and transfers this virus for the rest of its life. Even if you live in the middle of the city, you're not safe from it. Those 1/8 -inch-long gray-green insects can ride the winds for over 200 miles. They overwinter on weeds such as wild mustards and some thistles.

In summer they're just passing through, like any transient. There's no use spraying for them because chances are you'd kill a thousand beneficial insects and still miss this creature.

What can you do? Beet leafhoppers don't like shade, so if you can provide some light shade for your susceptible plants, that should help. Remember, though, most garden plants require full sun for at least six hours per day.

I'd try putting up shade panels directly over plants, so they still get morning and afternoon sun shafting in under the shade. I'm not positive this would be enough to deter the leafhopper but it would make you feel better.

You could cover crops with light row cover, but would need to hand-pollinate crops such as eggplants, squash, melons and pumpkins. Tomatoes and peppers are self-pollinating, but wind helps pollination.

Another option is to plant an abundance of strong-smelling herbs around your tomatoes. Years ago, when everyone else in Boise was losing mature tomato plants to curly top, one friend was not. Her tomato patch was surrounded by dill.

Another thing you can try is hanging yellow sticky traps around plants you want to protect. Beet leafhoppers are attracted to yellow and stick on the traps. Unfortunately, beneficial insects also will be trapped.

Most experts will tell you to plant varieties that are resistant to curly top. There are a few varieties of tomato that have been found to be resistant to the virus, but the only commercial source of seed is Sand Hill Preservation Center.

You can use an insect repellent such as Garlic Barrier, which is available in garden stores in the Treasure Valley, and it repels many insects, including bees. I don't think the label says anything about leafhoppers, but they're usually so insignificant, perhaps they weren't tested.

Cut a sponge into thin strips and soak them in Garlic Barrier, then hang them near your tomatoes. When this repellent is sprayed, I'm told the odor dissipates quickly, although the repellent capability persists. I don't know whether this is true of the sponges.

When tomatoes have been infected with curly top, leaves curl and turn yellow, exposing dark purple veins on the leaves. Those leaves feel leathery, too. The disease spreads quickly throughout the plant, and then it dies. Leaves may curl and yellow and develop purple veins for lesser reasons, too, so take a small branch to the Extension Office for diagnosis before you yank out your plant.

The disease also afflicts peppers, eggplants, beets, beans, muskmelons, pumpkins, watermelons, squash, zinnias, shasta daisies, alyssum, columbines, petunias, carnations, larkspur, coreopsis and cosmos.

Distorted leaves and stunted plants are symptoms of curly top virus.

(See also beet leafhoppers in the insects section.)

"Snowflakes" on your peppers? Could be a virus

My bad gardening news in 2008 was the first virus I've ever had in my pepper crop in the garden.

Krishna Mohan, the University of Idaho plant pathologist in Parma, said the symptoms on my peppers are consistent with pepper mild mottlevirus or PMMV.

It shows up most prominently when peppers have ripened to red, and looks like snowflakes under the waxy skin of the peppers.

The "snowflakes" are pithy, and detract from flavor, but the peppers are still edible, according to Mohan.

The virus is infectious and may be transmitted from one plant to another during routine maintenance unless hands and tools are washed between plants with milk or soap, according to the Asian Vegetable Research and Development Center.

Tools may be soaked for 10 minutes in a chlorine bleach solution (do NOT rinse) before using on another pepper plant.

The virus is seed-borne, and the virus may be "significantly reduced," at least, by soaking seeds in a 10 percent trisodium phosphate (TSP) solution for two and 1/2 hours while stirring seeds in the solution, and changing the TSP once during that time. Then rinse seeds thoroughly and spread them to dry.

The presence of this virus means that we should not grow peppers in the same spot for at least a year. I wouldn't grow any other Solanaceous plant there either. That includes eggplants, tomatoes and potatoes.

This virus does show subtle mottling on the leaves, but not in my garden, where plants are too close together to see which plants have the virus.

TREE MALADIES

Need help diagnosing problems in fruit trees?

If you are seeing unwelcome lesions, corky spots or disfigured fruits in your apple trees, take a fruit and a leaf, at least, to the Extension Office for positive identification.

Meanwhile, carefully pick up all fallen fruit and dropped leaves and put them in special bags bound for the landfill. Extraordinary garden cleanup is warranted when disease is involved.

Our dry climate is not attractive to many fungi, such as apple scab, but it could occur. Your best control for scab is to plant a scab-resistant tree.

If you have scab, though, you may be able to control it with a compost tea spray applied when leaves begin to emerge and a second application after petals fall.

An expert organic gardener in New Zealand, Moira Ryan, had success with that pair of sprayings, nearly eliminating the infection. She repeated the two sprays the next year and has not seen resurgence of the fungus for the past several years.

A boron deficiency also leaves corky spots on and inside apples, and may also cause cracks in the fruit.

It is important to get a correct diagnosis of the problem so you can get helpful ways to correct it.

Spring can leave an unwanted reminder on apples

An unusual wet, cool and prolonged spring in 1998 left undesirable relics that didn't show up until much later that year. Our Golden Delicious apples had russeting on nearly every apple, and so did apples of other varieties. Russeting is a coarse rough coating on apples, natural on some, not acceptable commercially. Scab is a coarser, more corky-looking disease that generally appears in rough circles on the fruit, sometimes deforming it. They're different conditions from different causes.

Some sources say that cool weather and wet fruit is all that's needed to produce russeting on Golden Delicious apples, but russeting on susceptible varieties also can be caused by powdery mildew. That's a hard disease to spot on apple trees, since the leaves tend to be white and powdery on the underside anyway.

Powdery mildew exists on the leaves but overwinters in the buds. Buds infested with powdery mildew spores will open later than healthy buds and are more prone to winterkill. If we have temperatures below minus 15 degrees, it may kill the powdery mildew and host buds. If not, we'd better spray with fungicide in the spring before buds begin to open.

What do we do with these powdery mildew-infested leaves? Compost them or send them to the city's compost, just as you would healthy leaves. The same is true for sycamore leaves from trees that have anthracnose, according to Dr. Mohan.

These diseases are widespread in this area, and it's futile to try to restrict the spread.

But if you have a tree that has been identified as having Fusarium or Verticillium wilts, do not send any parts or leaves to the compost or try to compost them yourself. They should be sent to the landfill.

These wilts affect many types of plants, including tomatoes. They are grown from soil-borne fungi and are fatal to plants. Once either disease is identified on a plant in your yard, you will need to sterilize the soil by solarizing, fumigating or using fungicides. Dispose of all parts of the plant immediately and then plant varieties resistant to that disease.

Watch for fungus on apricots and other stone fruit

We certainly wouldn't make the grade as commercial orchardists.

Our apricots were dotted and smudged with red dots, indicating the tree was afflicted with Coryneum blight. This is also known as shothole fungus because it spots leaf tissue that then dies and drops out, leaving holes in the leaves.

I knew the trees were afflicted, but we did not get them sprayed in a timely fashion. After the leaves dropped in the fall we should have sprayed with Ziram 76 WP or fixed copper and sprayed again the next spring.

Those are the sprays recommended by the Extension Office. Ortho recommends spraying with a fungicide containing Chlorothalonil after leaves drop and again one to two weeks after petals drop. The dormant spray could be lime sulfur instead, according to "Ortho Home Gardener's Problem Solver."

This fungus is common in our area and also appears on peaches, nectarines, cherries, plums and flowering almonds. On cherries and plum fruits the symptoms are roughened surfaces.

July is a good time to examine your trees for the disease. Look for small reddish spots on the fruit, small holes on the leaves, and leaves looking as if they got blasted by a shotgun. On peaches, the red spots have prominent whitish centers. The fruit would not be commercially valuable, but it is edible. Some prefer to peel the blotchy skins before eating or canning the fruit.

The Extension bulletin recommends controlling the disease by pruning off branches and twigs infected with cankers and applying fungicide sprays during the dormant period in late fall and early spring.

One possible cause of rough-looking apricot leaves

If your apricot tree has ragged-looking leaves around its periphery, look carefully at some of the leaves.

They may be green peach aphids, light green, almost chartreuse, but they're definitely aphids. Blast them off with jets of water and keep after them daily until they're gone.

If you can hit them early in the day, the foliage can dry off before dampness of evening, averting problems with mildew.

Damp weather spreads peach leaf curl

Our peach and nectarine trees don't usually get peach leaf curl, since it's spread by cool rainy weather in the spring. Our weather usually is too dry, but damp years can bring on widespread infestations.

Areas of the country with higher humidity and more rain than we receive are affected by this kind of fungus disease more often than we are. It is moisture-borne, splashing water bounces fungus spores from tree bark to leaves. The defining symptom is puckered, thickened and curled leaves from the time they emerge from buds in the spring.

Treatment usually is reserved for the dormant season, after leaves have dropped and/or before the buds open in the early spring but after they've begun to swell. Then, spraying with lime sulfur or a fungicide containing Chlorothalonil should control the fungus.

Later in the season, the affected leaves will be covered with gray spores, and those spores will be blown onto the bark to await another wet spring. If you have just a few clumps of afflicted leaves, pinch them off and put them in the trash. It will reduce the available spores for next year, in my opinion.

Thin your peaches to about 6 to 8 inches apart. If your tree has a bad case of peach leaf curl you may get inferior fruit. Thinning will make fruiting easier on the tree, whether or not the tree is diseased.

Avoid fire blight with resistant plants — or hope

Fruit trees such as pear, apple, plum, serviceberry, quince and crabapple, as well as ornamentals such as roses, Bradford pears, mountain ash, hawthorn,

Spirea, Cotoneaster, Pyracantha, Photinia and others can be slammed by fire blight.

This bacterial disease strikes emerging blossoms first, but may also show up on bark as a watery, light tan ooze seeping out of cankers on limbs and trunks of trees and shrubs. Pear blossoms turn black and fall, apple blossoms turn brown and fall. If this is the first sign of the disease, you can sometimes keep it from entering the wood with a timely spray of Bordeaux mixture or other copper-based fungicide.

Infected trees or shrubs have new shoot tips that have dead brown leaves still attached, and often a peculiar shepherd's crook shape near the end of the twig. In short, infected branches look burned. Thus the name "fire blight."

If it's in the wood, on twigs or small branches, cut 8 to 12 inches below the infection (or that distance toward the trunk), then sterilize your pruning tools with a 1:10 mixture of chlorine bleach to water before cutting into another tree or shrub.

This disease pops up in this Valley with some frequency. The best way to avoid it is to plant resistant varieties or hope you escape it, as I do.

Watch your water to prevent root rot

Is it possible to over-water plants? Yes. Only bog-loving plants thrive without oxygen to their roots. Even though water contains oxygen, roots cannot use that oxygen.

Armillaria or Phytophthora root rots are responsible for many problems of ornamental plants. Armillaria root rot kills trees, young trees quickly, old trees more slowly. Watch for needle browning and mushrooms appearing near the tree. If you can gently pry the bark off a troubled tree near the soil line and if you see a white mycelium on the wood, the tree probably has Armillaria root rot. Mycelium is the threadlike part of a fungus, from which fruits (mushrooms) arise, somewhat analogous to the roots of a tree.

Phytophthora root rot is technically a water mold, similar to a fungus, that appears in the root zone or crown of heavily watered plants, rotting the roots. Mulch pulled tight against the stem or trunk also holds water, making the crown vulnerable to this rot. The crown is the juncture of stem (or trunk) with roots. Always keep mulch a few inches away from plant, shrub or tree bases.

When a plant dies, we usually dig or pull it up to look at the roots to learn the cause of death. When we see rotting brown or black roots, we often find many millipedes, pillbugs or sowbugs among those roots. They have tiny mouths and have waited until rot reduced the size of roots so they can begin to consume them. They're first in line in the decomposition process. They didn't cause the problem — they're just the suspects who were caught.

One problem of overwatering or over-fertilizing in our area is due to our subsurface hardpan, caliche on the south side of the Valley, heavy clay on the north side. Liquids penetrate the soil, hit the hardpan, and run along its surface, even into a neighbor's yard. Your water plus your neighbor's may saturate your soil.

Slime flux stinks, but isn't terminal

Slime flux is characterized by watery sap flowing out onto the bark and down the tree. It's unsightly and appears alarming, but it's not going to kill the tree, says Debbie Cook, arborist with the Community Forestry division of Boise's Parks and Recreation Department.

This sour-smelling condition may persist for years. It's caused by bacteria that infest the heartwood, fermenting the sap and causing abnormally high sap pressure, forcing it out of cracks and crotches. If the tree also is under stress from lack of water, leaves may droop and wilt.

Anthracnose can make many of Boise's sycamore trees look pitiful

Wet, cool springs tend to worsen sycamore blight (anthracnose) infestations, so after the trees leaf out in such years, they then drop most of their leaves. Leaves remain in the upper canopy, but they're sparse below.

The trees will re-leaf during the summer and may defoliate again before winter. This is a tough disease and tough to treat, partly because the trees grow so tall.

A vigorously healthy tree can withstand this, but the disease races through the Valley occasionally, and siege after siege weakens any tree. Even huge trees may die.

Spraying should be done before the disease appears in the spring, or control won't be completely effective. If your sycamore is suffering, make arrangements to spray or have it sprayed next spring when the buds begin to swell. It will take at least two successive sprays to get a handle on the disease.

You can also give it a good dose of fertilizer in the fall, and clean up and destroy fallen branches and leaves, where the mycelium of the fungus can overwinter.

The Extension Office has an information sheet on sycamore blight.

Water well to fight deadly walnut disease

A disease they're calling "thousand cankers" has been detected in walnut trees in Boise, according to Cook, arborist in Boise's Community Forestry Department. The disease is a circulation-blocking fungus spread by walnut twig beetles native to the American Southwest. No effective cure has been found.

This disease can kill a mature tree in a year or less. It has wiped out walnut trees on the eastern slope of the Rocky Mountains in communities such as Boulder, Colo. It mainly affects black walnut trees, but English walnut trees also are vulnerable.

Symptoms of the disease are yellowing, wilting and browning foliage, as if the tree were drought-stressed. These symptoms usually show up first at the top of the tree and progress downward rapidly. Leaves that turn brown often remain attached to the twig or branch after it dies. Trees that showed symptoms in fall may leaf out in spring, and then quickly exhibit symptoms of the fungus infection and die, or they may not leaf out at all in spring.

Walnut twig beetles could have spread northward naturally, or they may have been transported in firewood. If you intend to use walnut wood for woodworking, at least remove the bark to prevent the beetles from emerging to attack other trees.

If your tree is healthy, make sure it remains so by adequate watering, such as deep watering every two or three weeks through the heat of the summer, and avoid damaging the bark with swings, by nailing up signs or tree houses, or by banging it with a lawnmower. Occasional watering on warm winter days will help maintain tree health, too.

Some experts say Imidacloprid, applied systemically, can help prevent the disease by killing the walnut twig beetles, but it must be applied before the tree is infected. The nuts may not be safe to eat after that pesticide is applied.

The domino effect of this will be more nuisance visits to gardens by hungry squirrels for a year or so until their population diminishes.

Verticillium wilt may attack maples

This vascular-clogging fungus affects many different types of plants. In this area it's attacking maple trees, primarily Norway, sugar, red, silver, Japanese, big-leaf, boxelder, hedge and sycamore maples.

It can invade through wounds at the top of the tree, but it usually invades through the roots, spreading upward. It will be most evident in mid- to late-summer, when leaves dry and wilt without apparent cause, some falling prematurely.

Small trees may be killed in a year, but large trees survive, slowly declining, for a longer time.

Not all wilting leaves signal Verticillium. If you see leaves appear to wilt, water the tree well and examine the leaves the following day.

If they're still wilting, make a slanting cut and examine the area under the bark (the vascular tissue). Verticillium wilt would show up in maple trees as olive green streaks, but in other species the tissue may be streaked tan, brown or black.

Symptoms of Verticillium wilt on trees may include leaf discoloring, curling or drying, partial defoliation, stunted growth and heavy seed crop, but these also may be symptoms of other tree health problems. Adequate watering and appropriate fertilizer when necessary can prolong the life of a tree infected with Verticillium.

Factors other than Verticillium wilt may cause wilting and poor vitality, including drought, improper planting, compacted soil, circling roots, root or crown rot, or even trunk injury.

What can you do? USDA's Home and Garden Bulletin 81 advises pruning dead and dying twigs, sterilizing pruning tools between cuts, giving the tree abundant water, and fertilizing with ammonium sulfate.

Protect trees from crown rot

All over the Valley, you see raised flower beds built around the bases of trees. It's a good location for shade-loving flowers, but is it a good idea for the trees? No.

A young tree may adjust, but a mature tree may begin declining and ultimately die from crown rot.

We're talking about the root collar area, where the roots join the trunk. This area, where the trunk begins to flare with extended roots, must have air to survive. If the crown is covered with soil, the area can stay moist and airless, inviting damage from damp-loving insects and/or disease organisms associated with dampness.

It may take quite a long time for a large tree to show it's stressed by crown rot, a condition most often associated with construction conditions. Costruction often piles soil around a tree trunk and compacts soil over roots.

That stress will begin showing up in early leaf discoloring and drop and dieback in the upper canopy of the tree. It's best to act before these symptoms appear, so if you have a tree with soil built up around the trunk, above the root juncture, you can carefully pull the soil away from the trunk, exposing the collar to air. Leave an exposed area about 6 inches wide around the trunk. Or if there's a lot of activity in that area, such as construction, or the nearby grade has been raised, you probably should build a low brick wall around the tree, so that soil doesn't wash back against the trunk.

You could fill in the area with gravel, but soil will wash back into the zone, and renew the problem unless a barrier is placed.

Redbuds are susceptible to many diseases

Redbud (Cercis) trees are pretty trees, blossoming pink or white (not red as you'd expect from the name) in spring. These trees, members of the Leguminosae family, are small, with pretty heart-shaped leaves much loved by leaf cutter bees. Those bees cut dime-sized circles from leaf margins inward, to line their nest cells.

Redbud trees may live to 90 years, but they're susceptible to canker and Verticillium wilt. Redbuds die a limb at a time, of one or the other disease.

If you see dead limbs in your redbud, remove them. With care, redbuds can live for years even with Verticillium wilt, but if you eventually lose a tree, replace it with something that's not vulnerable to Verticillium or canker disease.

Resistant trees include Arborvitae, fir, spruce, pine, juniper, beech, birch, ginkgo, honeylocust, sycamore, sweetgum, pear, mulberry, apple, hawthorn, willow, white oak and hophornbeam. Dogwood and linden are resistant to some strains of Verticillium wilt, but not to all.

Gardening calendar

A SEASONAL TO-DO LIST
TO KEEP YOU ON TRACK

JANUARY

- Read catalogs and dream. Order seeds early, taking care not to order if you still have viable seeds from last year.
- Check stored vegetables frequently, removing those that have rot or other spoilage indicators.
- If you haven't already, cover compost pile with tarp to prevent rain and snow from leaching nutrients out of the pile.
- Plant onion, shallot and leek seeds indoors.

FEBRUARY

- Inventory holdings in freezer and pantry so you can plan what to include and how much to plant in your veggie garden this year.
- Inspect garden tools. Remove any rust. Sharpen spades.
- Check the "bones" of your landscaping for visual appeal, and make plans to improve it with added shrubs or hardscaping.
- Plant seeds of broccoli, cabbage and other cole crops indoors.
- Prune trees/shrubs (except for spring bloomers such as forsythia and lilacs), trees and grapevines.
- Late in the month, begin removing winter mulch.

March

- If you haven't already, begin seeding tender plants such as eggplants and sweet peppers indoors. Plant tomatoes indoors at the end of the month.
- Outdoors, plant potatoes, peas, spinach, lettuce, beets, onions and Asian greens.
- Transplant or direct-seed cole crops such as broccoli, cabbage, cauliflower and Brussels sprouts.
- Start adding compost to your soil. Compost should be in place before planting anything outdoors.
- Remove remaining protective winter mulch from perennial beds, trim out old foliage and apply mulch for summer as soon as true leaves develop. Mulch will conserve moisture and help prevent weeds.

- Cover seedlings and transplants with agricultural fleece to protect from birds.
- Expect roller-coaster temperatures. Don't get impatient and plant outside too early.
- Plant bare-root roses and trees.

APRIL
- Shear back groundcovers and wake up your flower beds with a general fertilizer.
- Prune roses when forsythia blooms. Fertilize.
- Protect tender plants from frost.
- When the forsythia blooms, use crabgrass pre-emergent chemical or a corn-gluten meal treatment to control crabgrass.
- Plant conifers and shrubs. Also plant summer bulbs: Alliums, cannas, Hostas and daylilies.
- Prune buddleias, shrub dogwoods and caryopteris.
- Prune lavender to shape as it shows signs of new growth.
- Begin hardening off indoor seedlings to acclimate them to outdoor life. Shelter tender seedlings from wind.
- Watch for aphids and knock them from plants with a blast of water. Beneficial insects will take over soon.
- Set up supports for peonies, Delphiniums and other "floppers."

MAY
- Deadhead (remove spent blossoms from) tulips, daffodils and crocuses. Don't remove foliage until it's yellow or brown.
- Continue pruning spring-flowering shrubs immediately after they have bloomed.
- Local lore says that when the snow is melted off Shafer Butte north of Boise, it's safe to plant most annuals outside. May 10 is the average last date of frost in the Treasure Valley.
- If you haven't fed your roses, do it now.
- In mid-May, direct seed corn; in late May, cucumbers, beans, squash, other warm-weather vegetables and melons.
- Feed your lawn with 1/4 of its annual fertilizer allotment, unless you're

using a mulching mower.

- Plant annuals to fill in perennial beds and conceal yellowing foliage of spring-flowering bulbs.

JUNE

- Plant out seedlings of peppers, tomatoes, eggplants and basil. Watch for late frosts.
- Stop feeding trees by June 15, to allow them to progress toward winter dormancy.
- Tackle weeds regularly and frequently so you keep a handle on the situation. Remember, mulch also keeps weed seeds from germinating.
- Feed roses.
- Monitor lawn. When it gets a bluish cast and footprints don't bounce back readily, water deeply.
- Keep your eye out for destructive insects; if necessary, use the least toxic controls first.

JULY

- Plant short-season beans, beets, carrots, collards, radishes, cabbage, broccoli and similar plants for second harvest in fall. Plant spinach later.
- Make sure you are watering trees deeply.
- Thin fruit and do summer pruning to correct shape of shrubs and trees. Pruning now will encourage the least unwanted growth.
- Watch for destructive insects, and hand-pick or blast off with water, if possible.
- If tomatoes get brown papery bottoms or peppers get brown papery sections on the side, it's usually because of a calcium deficiency caused by uneven watering. As long as temperatures are predominantly under 100 degrees, deeply water in-ground tomatoes once a week. Higher daytime temperatures mean you need to water every four or five days. Container plants need more frequent — even daily or twice-daily — watering in very hot weather.
- Harvest shallots and onions when tops die back. Harvest garlic.

AUGUST

- Fertilize roses for last time this season. Most gardeners stop fertilizing roses by Aug. 15.
- Prune maple and birch trees, removing crossing and weak branches.
- Harvest peppers to stimulate further production. Harvest and dry or freeze herbs.
- Divide crowded and nonblooming bearded iris. If you're going to divide Oriental poppies, do it during summer dormancy.
- Collect, dry and label seeds from nonhybrid plants.
- When corn silks turn brown and dry, start checking for ripeness (ear ends inside husks should be rounded instead of pointed).

SEPTEMBER

- Plant fast-growing lettuce and Asian vegetables early in the month for harvest before winter.
- Plant spinach and mache for early spring crops.
- Pot up frost-tender herbs and peppers for wintering indoors.
- Divide peonies, if you feel you must. They can grow for many years without being divided.
- Feed lawn 1/4 of its annual fertilizer requirement.
- Harvest winter squash when a thumbnail won't penetrate the skin; cantaloupe when it dislodges easily from the vine, when ants appear, or when your cat/dog takes a bite; and watermelon when the belly is yellow and the vine tendril nearest the melon is brown and dry.
- Harvest basil if temperatures are predicted to fall below 38 degrees.

OCTOBER

- Average killing frost is about Oct. 10.
- Plant wildflower seeds that need stratification (freezing and thawing).
- Later in the month, plant garlic and shallot cloves.
- Remove long canes of roses that could damage other canes by wind whipping. Give trees deep drinks of water.
- Start cleaning garden. Disconnect hoses. Have sprinkler system blown out in early October.

NOVEMBER

- Spread last half of lawn's annual fertilizer allotment in two sessions, a week or two apart.
- Use power mower to vacuum and shred leaves for use as winter mulch or as additions to compost.
- Plant spring flowering bulbs after soil temperature drops below 60 degrees. (Buy your bulbs earlier in the season if you want a better selection. Keep in a cool, dry place or refrigerate.) For winter cheer, buy bulbs for forcing indoors.

DECEMBER

- Harvest parsnips, kale, beets, turnips, leeks and carrots after a moderate frost or light snow. Flavor will be sweeter then.
- Check trees and shrubs for weak or broken branches that may be felled by snow later. You can remove these now, sparing your tree or shrub damage that might admit disease.
- Once the ground freezes, mulch perennials, taking care not to pull mulch tightly around the main stem or trunk. Leave an inch or two ring open around stem or trunk, lest you create ideal conditions for crown rot.
- Rake leaves from flower beds to keep them from matting and directing moisture away from plants.
- Cover strawberries with pine needle straw or other straw not contaminated by herbicides.
- Make holiday wreaths or holiday decorations of conifers or other evergreens.

ABOUT THE AUTHOR

As the Idaho Statesman's weekly gardening columnist for 20 years, author Margaret Lauterbach has advised Treasure Valley gardeners on everything from sowing to composting to coping with the Valley's soils, pests, diseases and unique climate.

Lauterbach, who has gardened in Boise for more than 40 years, has been a master gardener and an advanced master gardener in Ada County, under the tutelage of Susan Bell, horticulture agent at the University of Idaho Extension.

Lauterbach was raised in Colorado, where the scarcity and value of water were ingrained along with an appreciation for farmers. Her first gardening experiences were working with her grandmothers, one in a town garden and the other on a farm near Fort Morgan, Colo. When she and her husband, Dr. Charles Lauterbach, moved to Boise, they bought a home on a large lot so she could have an abundant garden. Dr. Lauterbach taught theater arts at Boise State University until his retirement.

Margaret Lauterbach has a bachelor's degree in journalism from the University of Colorado-Boulder and a master's degree in psychology from Central Washington State University.

Made in the USA
San Bernardino, CA
28 February 2014